JOHN OWEN

John Owen is considered one of the sharpest theological minds of the seventeenth century and a significant theologian in his own right, particularly in terms of his contributions to pneumatology, christology, and ecclesiology.

Carl Trueman presents a major study of the key elements of John Owen's writings and his theology. Presenting his theology in its historical context, Trueman explores the significance of Owen's work in ongoing debates on seventeenth century theology, and examines the contexts within which Owen's theology was formulated and the shape of his mind in relation to the intellectual culture of his day - particularly in contemporary philosophy, literature and theology. Examining Owen's theology from pneumatological, political and eschatological perspectives, Trueman highlights the trinitarian structure of his theology and how his theological work informed his understanding of practical Christianity.

With the current resurgence of interest in seventeenth century Reformed theology amongst intellectual historians, and the burgeoning research in systematic theology, this book presents an invaluable study of a leading mind in the Reformation and the historical underpinnings for new systematic theology.

Great Theologians Series

Series Editors:
Revd Professor John Webster, University of Aberdeen, UK
Professor Trevor Hart, St Mary's College, University of St Andrews, UK
Professor Douglas B. Farrow, McGill University, Canada

The Ashgate series, *Great Theologians*, presents a cluster of high profile titles focusing on individual theologians from the ancients through to the contemporary. The series includes a balance between important new perspectives on major figures who have already received much research attention in the past, and lesser-known theologians or those on whom there has been little published to date. Offering a fresh approach to in-depth theological studies, each book presents an accessible, stimulating new study and comprehensive overview of the theologian and their writing, whilst providing a detailed survey of the historic and contemporary international research already undertaken from a range of different perspectives, and analysing important trends of interpretation and research. This series is intended to provide an invaluable and lasting resource at the upper level of study and academic research.

Other titles in the series:

Thomas G. Weinandy
Athanasius
A Theological Introduction

Nicholas M. Healy
Thomas Aquinas
Theologian of the Christian Life

Joseph L. Mangina
Karl Barth
Theologian of Christian Witness

David S. Hogg
Anselm of Canterbury
The Beauty of Theology

John Owen
Reformed Catholic, Renaissance Man

CARL R. TRUEMAN
Westminster Theological Seminary, Philadelphia, USA

ASHGATE

Published by
Ashgate Publishing Limited
Gower House
Croft Road
Aldershot
Hampshire GU11 3HR
England

Ashgate Publishing Company
Suite 420
101 Cherry Street
Burlington, VT 05401-4405
USA

Ashgate website: http://www.ashgate.com

British Library Cataloguing in Publication Data
Trueman, Carl R.
  John Owen: Reformed Catholic, Renaissance Man. – (The Great Theologians)
  1. Owen, John, 1616–1683. 2. Puritans - England – Biography. 3. Theologians
  – England – Biography. 4. Theology, Doctrinal – England - History – 17th century.
  5. England – Church history – 17th century.
  I. Title
  230.5'9'092

Library of Congress Cataloging-in-Publication Data
Trueman, Carl R.
  John Owen: Reformed Catholic, Renaissance Man / Carl R. Trueman.
     p.   cm. – (Great Theologians Series)
  Includes bibliographical references and index.
  1. Owen, John, 1616–1683. 2. Puritans – Doctrines. 3. Reformed Churches – Doctrines.
  4. Theology, Doctrinal – History – 17th century. I.Title.
  BX9339.O9T78 2007
  230'.59092–dc22   2006029282

ISBN 978-0-7546-1469-2 (hbk)
ISBN 978-0-7546-1470-8 (pbk)

This volume has been printed on acid-free paper

Printed and bound in Great Britain by MPG Books Ltd, Bodmin, Cornwall.

Contents

Preface

As always, the most pleasurable aspect of finishing a book is the opportunity to thank all those involved in the project. I am particularly grateful to Professor John Webster whose own interest in Owen was instrumental in commissioning this volume. John was, by nice historical coincidence, a Fellow of Owen's old college, Christ Church, Oxford, at the time. Thanks are also due to Professor Trevor Hart of St Andrew's University, to Professor Douglas Farrow of McGill University, and to Sarah Lloyd and the editorial staff at Ashgate for inviting me to join their series and for agreeing to publish a volume on Owen, a neglected theologian who deserves more scholarly attention than he has received. That they exhibited the patience of Job as deadline after deadline was missed by their delinquent author is a source for me both of wonderment and of gratitude.

I would also like to thank colleagues at Westminster Theological Seminary, PA, for help and encouragement: the Board of Trustees for the generous allowance of a semester of study leave in 2005 when much of the text was written; Mr Sandy Finlayson, the Librarian, for helping to set up site access to Early English Books Online, the result of the generous gift of a much-appreciated anonymous donor; my colleague in Church History, Jeff Jue, for stimulating conversation about all things seventeenth-century; Scott Oliphint, Dick Gaffin, Bill Edgar, and Lane Tipton for more general friendship and encouragement; and Peter Lillback, president of WTS and member of the Church History Department, whose decision to appoint me to an administrative position precipitated my need to complete the book before my research time completely disappeared. Someone once wrote that "nothing so focuses a man's mind as the thought that he is to be executed tomorrow;" much the same can be said about the confirmed academic who is faced with a move into administration. In this context, I should probably also mention Justin Taylor's constant badgering of me by email about 'when the Owen book will be finished,' badgering which finally made me feel guilty enough to sit down and write the final chapter.

I cannot adequately express the significance of my debt, personal and intellectual, to my good friends Willem Van Asselt of the University of Utrecht and Richard Muller of Calvin Theological Seminary. Their advice and encouragement has been invaluable; and their friendship, encouragement, and conversation (not to mention the countless hours we have over the years spent together outside cafes in Utrecht) are most precious to me.

Finally, thanks to my family. To Catriona for all of her love. To John and Peter for helping keep my work in perspective. To mum and dad for their encouragement and support.

The book is dedicated to the memory of my grandparents.

In memory of my beloved grandparents

Sidney Robins and Elsie Florence Robins

Chapter 1

John Owen: Reformed Catholic, Renaissance Man

Introduction

The name of John Owen (1616–1683) is little known today even in theological circles outside of very conservative evangelical churches and the narrow and highly specialized field of early modern intellectual history.[1] This is unfortunate, for Owen was without doubt the most significant theological intellect in England in the third quarter of the seventeenth century, and one of the two or three most impressive Protestant theologians in Europe at the time. It was his misfortune, however, to be on the losing side: for Owen was a Puritan and allied to the Independent party in the struggles which tore England apart in the 1640s and 1650s; as such, he was one of history's losers; and, as history is generally written by those who win, Owen was swiftly and decisively written out of the intellectual history of England in the aftermath of the Great Ejection of 1662 when non-conformists were not simply expelled from the Church of England, but excluded from the establishment, political, cultural, and intellectual, with all of the later impotence with regard to influence and the writing of history which that implies. At the same time, and as if to add insult to injury, the whole of western European university culture was undergoing

---

1   The literature on Owen is small but growing. His works, in 24 volumes, were reprinted in the nineteenth century by Johnstone and Hunter in London (1850–55), the edition which will generally be cited in this work. The reprint of this edition by Banner of Truth omits the Latin section of vol 16 and the whole of vol 17 (all in Latin). For his life, see Andrew Thomson, 'Life of Dr Owen' in *Works* 1, xxi–cxxii; Peter Toon, *God's Statesman: The Life and Work of John Owen* (Exeter: Paternoster, 1971). On his theology, see the following books: Sinclair B Ferguson, *John Owen on the Christian Life* (Edinburgh: Banner of Truth, 1987); Carl R Trueman, *The Claims of Truth: John Owen's Trinitarian Theology* (Carlisle: Paternoster, 1998); P DeVries, *"Die mij heft liefgehad" De betekenis van de gemeenschap met Christus in de theologie van John Owen (1616–1683)* (Heerenveen: Groen, 1999); Sebastian Rehnman, *Divine Discourse: The Theological Methodology of John Owen* (Grand Rapids: Baker, 2002). Two dissertations worth consulting are Alan Spence, 'Incarnation and Inspiration: John Owen and the Coherence of Christology,' PhD thesis (University of London, 1989); and Kelly Kapic, 'Communion with God: Relations between the Divine and the Human in the Theology of John Owen,' PhD thesis (University of London, 2001). Alan C Clifford's book, *Atonement and Justification: English Evangelical Theology 1640–1790* (Oxford: Oxford University Press, 1990) contains some very brief treatment of Owen, alongside Baxter, Tillotson, and Wesley. My disagreements with his analysis are laid out in considerable detail in *The Claims of Truth* and thus I will not burden the reader with a detailed recapitulation of the issues in this current monograph.

cataclysmic change as the curriculum and basic patterns of thought which had stood pretty much since the twelfth century were being reshaped and revised in light of new ways of thinking about the world. Again, Owen was on the losing side: as a champion of Reformed Orthodoxy, his thinking was in large part shaped by the traditional curriculum and patterns of thought it embodied; and as this world passed away, so did the contribution of the great John Owen.

That Owen was on the losing side should not however be taken as indicative of any intrinsic mediocrity in his own thinking. By the standards of his age he was profoundly learned, at ease with both the wider theological tradition of Western catholic thought (in the broadest sense), the trajectories of classical philosophy as mediated through the medieval schools and the Renaissance, and contemporary theological literature, Protestant, Catholic and heretical. Indeed, if one wishes to understand either the nature of Reformed Orthodoxy in the seventeenth century or the kind of theological thought which helped to shape aspects of the Cromwellian project and the identity of non-conformity in Restoration England, then there are few if any better candidates for study than John Owen.

His Life

John Owen was born in Stadhampton, near Oxford, in 1616, the son of local vicar, Henry Owen, a man of Puritan sympathies.[2] After education at a local grammar school, he matriculated at Queen's College, Oxford, in 1631, graduating BA in 1632. His time at Oxford was apparently marked by extreme acts of self-discipline, survival on only four hours of sleep a night to allow more time for study, and a growing reputation as a flautist, a long jumper, and a javelin thrower.

Following his BA, he graduated MA in 1635, was ordained deacon and then proceeded to study the seven-year course for a BD.[3] During this time, his tutor was a man named Thomas Barlow who was both a vigorous opponent of Arminian theology and an acute metaphysician. His influence on Owen, both theological and metaphysical, was profound; and by all accounts they became good friends, despite significant differences on the matter of conformity. Indeed, Owen helped Barlow at

---

2   The literature on Puritanism is vast and contains no real consensus on what exactly is the defining feature of a Puritan. For the sake of argument, in this work I will use the term Puritan and its cognates to refer to those who wished to see a further reformation of worship in the Established Church in a direction which emphasized liturgical simplicity and the centrality of preaching and which thus wanted to see the church move beyond the basic settlement established by Elizabeth I and focused on the Book of Common Prayer. Such Puritans were not separatists, however, as by and large, they remained within the church until expelled in 1662.

3   For the Oxford theology curriculum in the seventeenth century, particularly as it connects to the controversial contexts, see Nicholas Tyacke, 'Religious Controversy' in idem (ed), *The History of the University of Oxford IV: Seventeenth-Century Oxford* (Oxford: Clarendon Press, 1997), 569–619.

Oxford during the 1650s, when he was Vice-Chancellor, and Barlow himself later interceded for Owen when he was in trouble for preaching in his own home.[4]

With the increasing power of the Laudian party in the Church of England, Owen felt it necessary to leave Oxford and stay at the home of John, Lord Lovelace, in Berkshire, though, with the outbreak of war in 1642, Owen moved to London, his patron's Royalism no doubt making further stay somewhat impractical.

It was around this time that Owen went to Aldermanbury Chapel to hear the famous Puritan divine, Edmund Calamy, preach. On the day in question, however, Calamy was absent and a substitute preacher, whose name Owen was later unable to recall, preached a sermon Mt. 8:26. Owen's disappointment at the absence of Calamy soon gave way to elation when he experienced some form of conversion as a result of the unknown preacher's message. It would appear that it was at this point that Owen's commitment to anti-Laudian church policies was combined with the not-untypical experiential piety which marked out many Puritans.

In 1642, Owen published his first work, *A Display of Arminianism*. It would appear that he had already privately circulated a Latin text on the priesthood of Christ in opposition to the teaching of papists, Arminians and Socinians, but *A Display* was his first published (and, indeed, his earliest extant) piece of work. We will examine many of its themes and arguments in more detail in subsequent chapters, but it is worth noting at this point that the work was marked by a clear grasp of the philosophical and metaphysical issues at stake in the debate with Arminianism, and by the positive use of medieval and contemporary Catholic sources to establish many of his points, indicating the broad and eclectic nature of theology which he is formulating.

The book, while in retrospect clearly the work of a theologian at the start of his career, brought him instant fame, and the Parliamentary Committee on Religion conferred upon him the living of Fordham in Essex, the parish where he met and married his first wife, one Mary Rooke, who was to bear him 11 children, all of whom predeceased him with only one living to adulthood. Owen was to stay in Fordham until 1646, when the right to appoint the minister reverted to the local patron and he was forced to move on. However, in the same year Owen received his first invitation to preach before Parliament and thus began a new and highly influential stage in his career.

Having obtained a new living at St Peter's in Coggeshall, Owen read a little book by the Puritan emigrant to the New World, John Cotton: *The Keys of the Kingdom*. He was to credit this book with altering his opinion of church governement from a broadly Presbyterian ecclesiology, where ultimate power in the church lay in the higher courts and assemblies which operated at a supra-congregational level, to that of Independency, where power was restricted to the individual congregation, albeit one with a strong eldership and not an egalitarian democracy. The shift in Owen's thinking was to be highly significant. In the short term, he decided to gather a congregational church at one and the same time as being the local Anglican minister.

---

4   For further discussion of the relationship of Barlow and Owen, see Chapter 2. For details of Barlow's life, see the new edition of *Dictionary of National Biography* (DNB) article by John Spurr.

This decision clearly indicates that Owen was no separatist and that his commitment to Independency was not the equivalent of a narrow sectarianism. Then, in the medium term, it was to facilitate an alliance between the young clergyman and the rising political cause of Independency, particularly as that cause found its champion in Oliver Cromwell, the political leader of the Independents *par excellence*. Finally, in the long term, it was almost certainly a factor in his formulation of notions of religious tolerance both under Cromwell and, more significantly, in the world of non-conformity after 1662.

Owen's greatest moment in the political drama of 1640s England came on 31 January 1649, the day after Charles had been executed. On this day, it was Owen who was chosen to preach the sermon to parliament, a sermon which proved so popular that he returned to the capital on 19 April to preach before the House of Commons. On that occasion, he was heard by Oliver Cromwell who subsequently met him while they were both waiting to pay their respects to General Fairfax. The results of this meeting for Owen were spectacular: he first acted as Cromwell's chaplain on the latter's infamous expedition to Ireland, and was then appointed Dean of Christ Church and Vice-Chancellor of the University of Oxford, a post he held from 1651 to 1657.

During all of this time, Owen had gained an increasingly impressive reputation as a theologian and controversialist. For example, in 1647 he published one of the most thorough defences of the classic understanding of particular redemption, *The Death of Death in the Death of Christ*, as a result of which he found himself engaged in controversy with another rising theological star, Richard Baxter, particularly on the issue of the relationship of atonement to justification. Then, in 1654 he was commissioned by the government to write a major critique of Socinianism which he published in 1655 as *Vindiciae Evangelicae*, a work which was essentially a blow-by-blow refutation of the two catechisms of John Biddle and the major Polish work, the Racovian Catechism. Both *The Death of Death* and the *Vindiciae Evangelicae* indicate that Owen's thinking was becoming more and more sophisticated both in terms of his biblical exegesis and also in terms of his grasp of the Christian tradition and the ease with which he was able to deploy sophisticated concepts in laying out his position.

With the publication of *Vindiciae Evangelicae*, Owen probably reached the high-water mark of his political career, for in 1657 his strong republican sympathies led to a serious breach with his former patron, Oliver Cromwell when the latter spent some time considering whether he should have himself crowned king or not. Owen resigned the Vice-Chancellorship and thus bowed out of public life: a year later, when Cromwell died, he was to have no role to play in the funeral of his once close friend. His activity on behalf of Independency, however, continued, and it was in this same year that he helped his colleagues, Thomas Goodwin and others, to draft the Savoy Declaration, essentially a mild modification of the Westminster Confession along more strictly Independent lines.

With the return of the king in 1660 and the brutal repression of Puritanism under the Clarendon Code of the 1660s, Owen found himself definitively excluded from the establishment. In 1662, with the passing of the Act of Uniformity, he was forced out of the Church of England once and for all and became, along with his old adversary,

Richard Baxter, one of the leading lights of English non-conformist church life and thought. Indeed, he and Baxter even put aside their differences for a very short while in an (ultimately unsuccessful) effort to produce a non-conformist consensus in the face of persecution. Yet, while he was excluded from Anglican orders, Owen himself did not suffer as others such as Baxter and John Bunyan did, and enjoyed a certain amount of favour at court – remarkable considering his previous connections to one of the major regicides. In addition, with time on his hands, he engaged in producing a series of massive theological tomes, including a major Latin work of covenant theology, *Theologoumena Pantodapa*, 1661, a series of treatises on the work of the Holy Spirit (1674–93, the latter treatises appearing posthumously) and a commentary on Hebrews (1667–84, final volume posthumous) which is quite possibly the most elaborate and important precritical commentary ever written on the book. He also spent time reflecting upon the nature of religious toleration and in a number of shorter works clearly pointed forward towards the kind of settlement embodied in the legislation of 1689. His own death in 1683, however, meant that he never saw the realization of this particular vision.

Owen: Puritan or Reformed?

Before addressing the shape of Owen's theology proper, some preliminary comments need to be made upon the heuristic categories appropriate for understanding his thinking. Perhaps the most obvious of such would be that of Puritanism. As a leader of the Independents, and one who clearly identified with the likes of Edmund Calamy and Thomas Goodwin, it would appear obvious that Owen is without doubt a Puritan theologian. While I do not wish to deny this, I remain unpersuaded that this is, in general, a helpful historical category for understanding Owen's theology.[5] First, as noted above, there is little consensus on exactly what constitutes a Puritan, let alone the reification of that elusive essence in the phenomenon known as Puritanism. Second, whatever else Puritanism is, it is fairly minimalist in terms of its theological content – if John Milton, the quasi-Arian counts as a Puritan, for example, we can scarcely include even that most basic of Christian distinctives, the doctrine of the Trinity, in our definition.[6] Third, Puritanism has, on the whole, far too parochial a range to allow us to see the full context of Owen's thinking. I have

---

5   Commenting on my earlier work on Owen, the Dutch scholar, P DeVries, makes the legitimate comment that I underemphasize the Puritan dimension of Owen's thinking, by which he seems to mean the experiential piety of his work. This is true, though in my defence I plead that my work was concerned with his exposition of God and atonement, not with his views of human religious experience; further, I myself do not think that an understanding of Puritanism which focuses on experiential piety is a particularly adequate or helpful way to approach the subject: see DeVries, 63, n. 121.

6   Much of Milton's theology must be inferred from his poetry, at best a hermeneutically tricky exercise which can only provide cautious and provisional conclusions. Nevertheless, *if* the disputed work, *De Doctrina Christiana* is the authentic production of Milton, then quasi-Arianism seems to be a legitimate way to characterize his theology: see Don M Wolfe et al (eds), *Complete Prose Works of John Milton*, 8 vols (New Haven: Yale University Press,

already argued elsewhere at some length that Owen needs to be understood in terms of the wider ongoing Western tradition of theological and philosophical thought, that even his contemporary intellectual context needs to be seen as European and not primarily English or even British. Thus, the use of a category like 'Puritanism,' which brings with it all manner of narrowly parochial connotations, really needs to be deployed very carefully and in very specific contexts if it is to be at all helpful in our understanding of his thought.[7]

In light of the above, the category which I will use as best facilitating the exploration of Owen's thought in context is that of Reformed Orthodoxy, on the grounds that this is at once both more easily defined and less limiting than the category of Puritanism. The term Reformed Orthodoxy refers to the tradition of Protestant thought which found its creedal expression on the continent in such documents as, among others, the *Belgic Confession*, the *Heidelberg Catechism* and the *Canons of Dordt*, and in Britain in the Westminster Assembly's *Confession of Faith and Larger and Shorter Catechisms*. Historically speaking, the immediate roots of this tradition are to be found in the work of Reformers such as Huldrych Zwingli, Johannes Oecolampadius, Martin Bucer and, a generation later, such men as John Calvin, Heinrich Bullinger, Peter Martyr and Pierre Viret.[8]

In analyzing the development of this tradition, Richard Muller has divided the history into four broad periods. Now, while such periodisation of time is inevitably somewhat anachronistic, when applied loosely to the development of Reformed Orthodoxy it can nevertheless fulfill a useful heuristic purpose and is therefore worth noting very briefly. The first period runs from 1523 to 1563 (from Zwingli's *Articles* to the *Heidelberg Catechism*) and is marked by the basic statement of the general Reformed position. The second period, that of early orthodoxy, from 1563 to c. 1640, represents the time during which Reformed theology began to establish itself in the universities, work out and elaborate the basic positions established by the earlier generations, and consequently to develop a methodological sophistication and self-awareness which led to the more obvious appropriation of the traditional language and methods of medieval scholasticism as well as more innovative approaches such as that offered by Peter Ramus. The increasingly complex polemical environment, with the arrival of highly sophisticated Catholic apologists such as the Jesuit, Robert Bellarmine, the rise of a parallel orthodoxy in Lutheranism, and the fracturing of Reformed Protestantism with the advent of Arminianism and Socinianism, called for theological work of growing complexity in order to defend and refine the Reformed theological heritage in the face of such novel threats. All of this provides the context

---

1953–82), vol 6, especially the introductory essay by Maurice Kelley; also the discussion in Barbara K Lewalski, *The Life of John Milton* (Oxford: Blackwell, 2000) 415–41.

7   See my comments in *The Claims of Truth*, 9–13.

8   On Reformed Orthodoxy, see Richard A Muller, *Post-Reformation Reformed Dogmatics*, 4 vols (Grand Rapids: Baker, 2003); also the essays in Carl R Trueman and R S Clark (eds), *Protestant Scholasticism: Essays in Reassessment* (Carlisle: Paternoster, 1998); and Willem J Van Asselt and Eef Dekker (eds), *Reformation and Scholasticism* (Grand Rapids: Baker, 2001).

for understanding why it was that Reformed theology written in say, 1640, did not look the same as Reformed theology written in 1540.

While Muller's fourth period, that of Late Orthodoxy (c. 1700–90) need not concern us here, his third period, that of High Orthodoxy (c. 1640–1700), contains the whole of Owen's active life as theologian and churchman. It is during this period that the Arminian and Socinian threat calls forth yet further integration of polemics into the development of theological systems. This is one the key factors in determining that this period marks the high point of systematic elaboration of Reformed theology immediately prior to the triumph of those new scientific and philosophical perspectives which were to lead the complete recasting of theological system in the eighteenth and nineteenth centuries. Given Owen's polemical preoccupation with both Arminians and Socinians throughout his career, he fits perfectly the theological type described by Muller.

While discussion of key areas of Owen's Reformed theology will be postponed to later chapters, it is worth noting at this point that Muller's taxonomy is historiographically useful for locating Owen within the broad methodological and theological developments of Reformed thinking in the sixteenth and seventeenth centuries; it also has the advantage over the term 'Puritan' of locating Owen within a wider European theological movement. Even a cursory glance at his library catalogue or the marginalia of any of his major works reveals the simple fact that Owen's theology was not developed in any narrow national context but was self-consciously constructed in dialogue and confrontation with theologians from all over Europe. The quest for clear, systematic articulation of Reformed theology, and for defence of the same in light of the attacks of opponents, was a European struggle, albeit subject to specific local manifestation.[9] Indeed, his theology exhibits many of the classic distinctives of the period of High Orthodoxy. In terms of his polemical counterpoints, Roman Catholics, Arminians and Socinians are without doubt the most significant targets, although, as an English writer, he also spends some time targeting more localized heretical groups such as the Quakers.

On a more positive note, Owen also articulates his theology in terms both of careful exegesis and of constructive dialogue with the exegetical and theological traditions of the church. There are numerous claims made about Reformed Orthodoxy which, on closer examination, can be demonstrated to be without foundation. For example, a previous tradition of scholarship argued that Reformed Orthodoxy exhibited an increasingly rationalistic bent which manifested itself, among other things, by a tendency to abstract doctrine from any exegetical context and produce systems of thought which were essentially deduced, or at least constructed around, one central dogma, predestination.[10] More recent scholarship has subjected this thesis to devastating criticism on methodological grounds (the older scholarship

---

9   Owen's library catalogue was published posthumously to allow for sale of his books: *Bibliotheca Oweniana* (London, 1684).

10   See Hans-Emil Weber, *Reformation, Orthodoxie, und Rationalismus* (Gutersloh: Bertelsmann, 1951); Ernst Bizer, *Frühorthodoxie und Rationalismus* (Zurich: EVZ, 1963); Basil Hall, 'Calvin against the Calvinists,' in G E Duffield (ed) *John Calvin* (Grand Rapids: Eerdmans, 1966), 19–37. For a thorough bibliography and critique of this approach, see

frequently used anachronistic theological criteria for making historical judgments), and on textual grounds (the texts show no evidence of the existence of a central dogma, nor on the whole, of the radical abstraction of doctrine from the practice of biblical exegesis).[11] In addition, the sheer lack of clarity in much of the older literature concerning what constitutes 'rationalism' was extremely misleading, and it has since been pointed out that to equate the use of syllogisms or Aristotelian language with either a commitment to Aristotle as an equal source of theological authority to scriptureor of an incipient rationalism of the kind which found its mature expression in the work of Descartes is entirely misleading and extremely unhelpful.[12]

It is not within the scope of this book either to go over the tired old territory of refuting the charges of systematic centraldogmas, crass Aristotelianism, and lack of any exegetical sensitivity that a previous generation routinely hurled at the heads of the Reformed Orthodox. Suffice it to say at this point that Owen's work gives no evidence of being organized around a single doctrine (whether predestination or any other); and that his use of the language associated with the language of Aristotelian commentary tradition is simply indicative of the fact that he was raised and educated in a system of education with roots in the Middle Ages and the pedagogical literature of the Renaissance – indeed, given the universal acceptance of this language in the realm of intellectual life at the time, and the fact that it was used by Protestants, Catholics, Remonstrants etc., one wonders what alternative vocabulary he might reasonably be expected to have used?[13] As to exegetical endeavours, much debunking

---

Richard A Muller, 'Calvin and the Calvinists: Assessing Continuities and Discontinuities between the Reformation and Orthodoxy', Parts 1 and 2 in Muller, *After Calvin*, 63–102.

11   See Muller, *Post-Reformation Reformed Dogmatics* (hereafter cited as *PRRD*) II, *passim*.

12   The problem of 'Aristotelianism' has proved particularly troubling to some scholars, particularly those apparently unfamiliar with the relevant works on the history of philosophy in the Middle Ages and the Renaissance: see, for example, the undifferentiated notion of Aristotelianism which underlies Alan Clifford's arguments in *Atonement and Justification*. In recent years, the work of Charles Schmitt has highlighted the absurdity of talking about 'Aristotelianism' with regard to the Renaissance and later as anything more than a very broad tradition of commentary upon certain texts. As regards stable, philosophical content, there was little or no consensus. In addition, the sheer scope of this commentary tradition, in terms of the areas of learning which it shaped, was so comprehensive that, until the advent of equally comprehensive paradigms in the late seventeenth century, all of Western thought could be classified in this rather meaningless sense as 'Aristotelian': see Charles B Schmitt, *Studies in Renaissance Philosophy and Science* (London: Variorum Reprints, 1981); *idem, John Case and Aristotelianism in Renaissance England* (Kingston: McGill-Queen's University Press, 1983); also Trueman, *The Claims of Truth*, 34–44; Richard A Muller, 'Reformation, Orthodoxy, "Christian Aristotelianism," and the Eclecticism of Early Modern Philosophy,' *Nederlands Archief voor Kerkgeschiedenis* (hereafter cited as *NAKG*) 81 (2001): 306–25. On the alleged 'rationalism' of Reformed Orthodoxy, see Trueman, *The Claims of Truth*, 90–92.

13   See Carl R Trueman, 'Puritan Theology as Historical Event: A Linguistic Approach to the Ecumenical Context,' in Van Asselt and Dekker (eds), *Reformation and Scholasticism*, 253–75. The importance of the study of language, and sensitivity to what is conventional, what is unconventional, what range of meaning, intention and action can be articulated or performed by linguistic agents at any given point in time is crucial to sound intellectual

has already been done with regard to the ignorance of the Reformed Orthodox regarding their sensitivity to the Bible as a book containing many genres and styles, and the old clichés about proof-texting, the Bible as a manual of systematic theology just there for the blunt systematising thereof, and so on, are dying a slow, painful, but nonetheless decisive death. In fact, the seventeenth century witnessed a remarkable flourishing of linguistic and exegetical studies, driven by both the positive and the polemical exigencies of Protestantism's commitment to scripture, in the original languages, as being the very Word – and words – of God.[14]

Some idea of the kind of bibliographical emphases to which an Oxford theology student of Owen's day would have been exposed is provided in the fascinating, and posthumously published, basic theological reading list of Thomas Barlow, Owen's tutor.[15] Barlow allows his convictions about the nature of theology and of human knowledge of God to shape the catalogue: there is a light of nature and a light of scripture which are the foundations for natural theology and revealed theology respectively. Of these, Barlow stresses Aquinas, and commentators on Aquinas, as of particular use, indicating his own strong Thomist instincts, many of which parallel concerns in Owen.[16] Barlow immediately proceeds, however, to list over six pages of editions of the Hebrew and Greek texts of the Old and New Testaments, of the Septuagint and the Vulgate, and various lexical and linguistic aids.[17] He then follows with sections devoted to biblical commentaries (from ancient to modern, and reflecting many theological perspectives, from orthodox to heretical),[18] works on ancient Jewish society,[19] a variety of books on the canon,[20] basic outlines of early church history,[21] and books on the apocrypha and non-canonical early writings.[22] Thus, the first 21 of the book's 70 pages are devoted specifically to books of direct relevance to understanding the text and the context of scripture. Then, a little later in the treatise, Barlow spends time listing useful books on biblical chronology and

---

history, as is made clear by the work of Quentin Skinner: see the essays in his *Visions of Politics I: Regarding Method* (Cambridge: Cambridge University Press, 2002).

14 See Muller, *PRRD* 2, *passim*; also Stephen G Burnett, *From Christian Hebraism to Jewish Studies: Johannes Buxtorf (1564–1629) and Hebrew Learning in the Seventeenth Century* (Leiden: Brill, 1996). Reformed divines frequently exhibit an astounding knowledge of Semitics and linguistics: in Britain, for example, Westminster divine Thomas Gataker, published a major linguistic study of the Greek of the New Testament in relation to the Hebrew language: *Thomae Gatakeri Londinatis de novi instrumenti stylo dissertatio qva viri doctissimi Sebastiani Pfochenii, de lingvae Graecae Novi Testamenti puritate* (London: 1648). Gataker was exceptionally talented, but not untypical of the culture of Reformed Orthodoxy in his concern for linguistic and exegetical studies.

15 *Autoschediasmata de Studio Theologiae; or, Directions for the Choice of Books in the Study of Divinity,* (Oxford, 1699).

16 *Autoschediasmata,* 2; for Owen's Thomism, see Trueman, *Claims of Truth, passim*.

17 *Autoschediasmata,* 3–9.

18 *Auotschediasmata,* 10–14.

19 *Autoschediasmata,* 14–15.

20 *Autoschediasmata,* 15–17.

21 *Autoschediasmata,* 17–18.

22 *Autoschediasmata,* 18–21.

geography, including maps, with which the Bible student should be familiar.[23] The biblical emphasis, even in this book list provided by the most philosophical of seventeenth-century Oxford's theologians, is clear and exemplary.

That Owen's library catalogue and his work is marked by a vast knowledge of the biblical commentary tradition, Rabbinic, medieval, Catholic and Protestant, should thus come as no surprise, given that he was reared in precisely the same pedagogical context as that reflected in his tutor's recommended bibliography; and that his remarkable commentary on Hebrews should exhibit his vast learning in textual matters, in exegesis, in the history of interpretation, and in the subtle and complex move from exegesis to theological synthesis, is surprising only to those who have never spent any time reading a typical seventeenth-century Reformed Orthodox text. As Henry Knapp has demonstrated in impressive detail, for example, Owen's commentary on Hebrews is a masterpiece of linguistics, textual exegesis, interaction with exegetical traditions, and theological synthesis.[24]

In addition, it is worth noting that the very controversial context within which Owen himself operated prevented just the kind of crass argumentation that allegations of 'proof-texting' seem to imply. Faced with Protestant errors and heresies, such as Arminianism and Socinianism, the pressure to engage in careful exegesis of scripture was intense, as these two groups also cited scripture as the authoritative basis for their theology. This meant that any mere blunt citation of biblical texts by Owen was doomed to be inadequate as a response. For example, in the *Vindiciae Evangelicae*, Owen was engaged in refuting Socinianism largely as it received expression in John Biddle's two catechisms, both of which proceeded to a large extent by slapping down one proof-text after another, as if the meaning of every scriptural passage was so self-evident that no exegesis, no attention to context, and no further argumentation was needed. Faced with this approach, for Owen simply to have offered his own proof-texts would have proved thoroughly inadequate for the task in hand.[25] Instead, Owen sought to place the various texts put forward by Biddle into their proper, biblical context, showing how they related to the whole scope of scripture and to the analogy of faith. The issue between Owen and the Socinians, one might say, was not so much one of the authority of scripture as of the interpretation of scripture, and this required Owen to deploy the various linguistic and theological skills which he had acquired as the basis for an accurate understanding of the Bible's teaching.[26]

---

23   *Autoschediasmata*, 25–27.

24   See Henry Knapp, 'Understanding the Mind of God: John Owen and Seventeenth-Century Exegetical Methodology' (unpublished PhD Dissertation, Calvin Theological Seminary, 2002).

25   Owen basically concedes this difficulty when, in the very first chapter, he acknowledges the apparent similarity between the Socinians and the Orthodox on the issue of *sola scriptura*: *Works* 13, 85.

26   In my earlier work on Owen, I made the statement that 'it would be inaccurate to interpret the Protestant notion of *sola scriptura* in such a way as to regard it as a sufficient safeguard in and of itself to safeguard the church against heresy in the seventeenth-century context. In fact, Owen's defence of orthodox Christology in the face of the radically biblicist attacks of the Socinians clearly depends upon setting the notion of *sola scriptura* and scriptural exegesis within the ongoing catholic theological tradition.' *The Claims of Truth,*

As to church tradition, the Reformed Orthodox in general, and Owen in particular, were well schooled in the history of theology, reading and citing a large number of patristic and medieval texts with approval, and engaging in dialogue with the same, in order to produce a thoughtful and articulate theology which was marked by historical integrity and, on the whole, respect, albeit critical respect, for the church's theological tradition. This is an important point to grasp, as the Reformation emphasis upon scripture as the sole authoritative source for theological truth never precluded a careful sifting of the great texts of the past for help in expressing this truth, and these texts were not restricted to any single artificially constructed period of church history but were drawn from the wider Christian tradition as it developed throughout the ages. Respect for the past was something which pre-modern Christianity assumed from the outset, and this was reinforced by the impact of humanism, with its cultural project of recovering and repristinating the world of classical antiquity. Indeed, to borrow a term from William Perkins, one might say that Owen and those like were *Reformed Catholics*, given their concern to interact with the ongoing catholic traditions of theology, albeit from a distinctively Reformed perspective.

Again, the reading list of Owen's tutor, Thomas Barlow, is clear on this cultural point: in addition to the extensive recommendations on the text of scripture and on the commentary tradition, he also recommends books on how to use patristic authors, and a large number of texts on church councils decrees, both Catholic and Protestant. The point is clear: while scripture has unique authority, the history of theology, especially as that history is embodied in the actions of the church, is to be taken very seriously. This represents neither a Catholic view of an authoritative church *magisterium* in matters of interpretation; nor a later, individualistic theological piety of the kind so often associated, rightly or wrongly, with later evangelicalism; rather, it is a typical Reformation approach to both history and the church, one which takes tradition seriously while yet striving to give final, decisive authority to scripture.[27]

Given this typical concern of Reformed Orthodoxy for tradition, albeit in a subordinate and critical relation to scripture, it is no surprise that in Owen's writings we encounter a wide variety of Christian authors from the past, and some even have appendices containing quotations from a variety of patristic authors, Greek and Latin, as a means of reinforcing the arguments of the main text.[28] In this context, it is worth noting that, above all, we find Owen interacting extensively with, and positively using at every opportunity, the writings of Augustine who is quoted by

---

164, n. 41. Taken out of context and slapped down as a proof-text, this statement is ambiguous and has been read as implying that Owen denied the principle of *sola scriptura* as classically understood. Were I to write it today, I would certainly have expressed myself in a different manner simply to avoid being misread by those who struggle with sentences expressing subtle arguments; all I meant to say (as any intelligent reading of the book as a whole clearly indicates) was that claiming scripture as authoritative is not the same as agreeing on what scripture says; that there is therefore need for interpretation; and that Owen used the church tradition as an aid in trying to discern what scripture itself authoritatively says, an approach which in no way places tradition on an equal or superior level to scripture.

27 *Autoschediasmata*, 27–35, 45–53.

28 For example, *The Death of Death in the Death of Christ* (1647), *Works* 10, 422–24; *The Reason of Faith* (1677), *Works*, 4, 111–15.

him more than any other single author.[29] This is not surprising, as the Reformation itself was, on one level, a struggle over how Augustine was to be interpreted, a battle over 'who owned Augustine'.[30]

Augustine is of theological use to Owen primarily in the areas of anti-Pelagianism and Christian experience. Thus he is cited extensively in conflict with the Arminians as demonstrating the priority of God's grace in salvation.[31] Further, we might add that his usefulness in this area of Owen's theology lies not so much in any uniqueness which his thinking possessed but in the fact that he is the archetypal representative or the fountainhead of the Western anti-Pelagian tradition which continues throughout the Middle Ages and which Owen's judicious use of medieval theologians, such as Thomas, traces out through church history.[32] As to religious experience, at the heart of his major work on the Holy Spirit, Owen devotes a long chapter to Augustine's conversion, as described in the *Confessions*, as representing the classic Christian experience of this phenomenon and as giving profound insight into the effect and experience of sin. Thus in Owen we find the controversial, the dogmatic, and the experiential Augustine, picked up and developed within the context of a distinctively Protestant, Reformed, and, if we wish to accent the piety, Puritan theology.[33]

Owen as Renaissance Man

It is, of course, always very tempting when writing about theologians to narrow the focus to specific theological influences at a very early stage. Indeed, one of the problems of the older literature on Reformed Orthodoxy was its tendency to search for the solution to doctrinal problems and issues raised in the texts exclusively in terms of doctrinal or, at best philosophical, issues. Literary productions such as theological texts are, of course, highly complex actions, with their content being shaped by historical context, synchronic and diachronic, by literary genre, by linguistic conventions, and by the general cultural background of the author and the issues at hand. To adopt narrowly doctrinal methodological criteria in the study of historic theological texts is thus profoundly wrong-headed, ignoring the basic fact that theologians never think or act in a vacuum or approach issues simply in terms of one category of discourse. A simple example of the need for this will suffice. If we take John Calvin's *Institutio* (1559) and Francis Turretin's *Institutio* (1679–85) and compare them, we see obvious differences. The ordering and division of topics

---

29   Rehnman, 41.

30   Cf. the famous quip of BB Warfield: '[T]he Reformation, inwardly considered, was just the ultimate triumph of Augustine's doctrine of grace over Augustine's doctrine of the church', *Studies in Tertullian and Augustine* (Oxford: Oxford University Press, 1930), 130; for a set of superlative essays on one Reformer's use of Augustine and other patristic sources, see A N S Lane, *John Calvin: Student of the Church Fathers* (Edinburgh: T&TClark, 1999).

31   In one particularly memorable, rhetorical passage, Owen casts Augustine as a mighty champion who repeatedly casts the heretical knight-errant, Pelagius, to the ground: see *Works* 10, 114–15.

32   Rehnman, 41–43.

33   *Works* 337,–66; De Vries, 294–95; Ferguson, 45–48.

is different; the form of argument is different; much of the language used is different. Does this allow us to see the two works as representing two entirely different theologies? Does such a blunt comparison allow us to judge the development of Reformed theology *tout court* between 1559 and 1679? Of course not. For a start, why should we expect theologies written 120 years apart to be the same in form and content? In addition, we clearly have two different genres of work: Calvin is explicitly writing book of doctrinal common places to aid exegesis; Turretin is producing a book of theology which deals with particular controversial topics as a means to aiding students in combating theological opponents. The purpose and function of the two books are significantly different in terms of their authors' original intentions. Two different genres; two different purposes; two different books – for the same reason, Wordsworth's poetic reflections on daffodils and the entry on the same flower in the average gardening manual look entirely different. Not that the gardening manual represents an ossification of the vitality of the daffodil under the rationalizing tendencies of contemporary scholastic or Aristotelian gardening theory. No. What we are faced with in these two different writings on daffodils is not intellectual hardening but two different genres, two different intentions, two different, but in their own context valid, approaches to daffodils. Given this basic point, to unlock the mind of a man like Owen, or to read the texts he wrote with any degree of competence, we need to establish as a foundation the kind of intellectual culture from which he emerged; and this culture is, of course, highly diverse.[34]

Perhaps the most important aspect of this intellectual background to Owen, particularly as it relates to his early intellectual and cultural formation, is the world of the University of Oxford, where he was both a student and, later, a key policy-making official. Thus, the university curriculum, and Owen's own actions relative to it, are important guides to tracing out some of his attitudes to wider intellectual culture. Now, the work of W T Costello on the seventeenth-century curriculum at Oxford's great rival institution, Cambridge, made significant claims about the essentially medieval nature of early modern university pedagogy, stressing the basic continuity of content and pedagogy between the early years of the University up

---

34   Rehnman, *Divine Discourse*, provides an excellent study of the various sources for Owen's thinking which give a clear indication both of the breadth of his reading and the eclectic nature of his intellectual background. In the context of question of method with regard to the study of seventeenth-century Reformed Orthodoxy, Richard Muller has issued the following pertinent challenge to exponents of the older scholarship: 'For the reappraisal [of Reformed Orthodoxy] to move forward, there is much to be done in the way of cross-disciplinary study and examination of writers whose work has been neglected, in some cases for centuries. The challenge is to return to the documents with renewed vigor and an ever-clearer sense of the historical context. For the proponents of the older paradigms, the challenge is to shed their twentieth-century dogmatic criteria, to recognize the failure of an emblematic, decontextualized use of documents such as Beza's *Tabula*, to avoid the excessive levels of generalization belonging to their standard claims about "Aristotelianism," "rationalism," "scholasticiscim," and the like, and to argue their thesis from actual documents, using the actual terms found in the documents, respecting the limits of meaning determined by historical context, and expanding their bibliography to include and respond to the collateral literature cited by exponents of the reappraisal.' *After Calvin*, 193.

until the impact of Enlightenment thinking in the later seventeenth century.[35] There is certainly a lot of truth in this. At the most basic, material level, the libraries of institutions such as Oxford and Cambridge were, of course, filled not only with recent books but also contained many of the books and manuscripts which formed the staple of the medieval curriculum. Not surprisingly, many of the same authors continued to be studied, particularly in the fields of logic and metaphysics. In addition, a central part of the student's education was the academic disputation, an approach to learning which both embodied a rigorous commitment to structured analysis and argument, and helped to develop and refine the body of accepted knowledge. Indeed, it is this practice of disputation which is one of the hallmarks of medieval pedagogy; it should also be noted, given the amount of nonsense written about scholasticism, Catholic and Protestant, which uses the term as a pejorative, that it is the practice of teaching by disputation which stands at the heart of proper definitions of scholasticism and its cognates. Thus, the old chestnut of an unavoidable opposition between scholasticism and humanism, as representing two mutually exclusive ways of thinking about the world, needs to be avoided at all costs when it comes to analyzing later medieval, Renaissance, and early modern texts: such a simplisitic, binary approach rests on a category mistake and serves only to distort historical analysis.[36] Scholasticism is a specific pedagogical method and should not, therefore, be confused with metaphysical content or philosophical commitments, as the practice of disputation, and the technical vocabulary associated with it, did not represent a single, unified system of thought, nor even a consensus position on the scope and competence of logic and human reason. Rather, they represented simply the pedagogical procedures of higher learning during a particular period of time, broadly speaking from the twelfth century to the end of the seventeenth.[37]

Nevertheless, more recent work has accented the impact of Renaissance patterns of thought on such medieval institutions in the sixteenth and seventeenth centuries; and this in a manner which, while not abolishing the medieval pattern, yet led to fairly substantial revision of that model in light of new insights and pedagogical concerns.[38] For instance, the teaching of logic came to occupy a much smaller place in the curriculum, being seen as essentially propaedeutic to proper study. This is evidenced

---

35 W T Costello, *The Scholastic Curriculum at Early Seventeenth-Century Cambridge* (Cambridge: Cambridge University Press, 1958).

36 While now somewhat dated, the work of Paul Oskar Kristeller is enlightening in this regard: see his *Renaissance Thought: The Classic, Scholastic, and Humanist Strains* (New York: Harper and Row, 1961). For a more recent approach which follows basically, though not entirely, in the same vein, see Erika Rummel, *The Humanist-Scholastic Debate in the Renaissance and the Reformation* (Cambridge: Harvard University Press, 1998).

37 See W J Van Asselt and E Dekker (eds), *De Scholastieke Voetius* (Zoetermeer: Boekencentrum, 1995), 14–16; P L Rouwendal, 'De Leerwijze van de Scholen' in W J van Asselt and P L Rouwendal (eds), *Inleiding in de Gereformeerde Scholastiek* (Zoetermeer: Boekencentrum, 1998), 54–66; A Kenny and J Pinborg, 'Medieval philosophical literature,' in Norman Kretzman, Anthony Kenny and Jan Pinborg, *Cambridge History of Later Medieval Philosophy* (Cambridge: Cambridge University Press, 1984).

38 See Mordechai Feingold, 'The Humanities,' in Tyacke , *The History of the University of Oxford IV*: 211–357.

by the rapid development in the seventeenth century of manuals and compendia of logic which replaced the older, more thorough tomes on the subject from the Middle Ages. In addition, the disputation itself underwent considerable transformation, if not exactly in form then at least in purpose, becoming an opportunity for displays of eloquence and polished public performance.

Two further developments which indicate clearly the impact of Renaissance thinking on Oxford education were the cultivation of the ideal of the general scholar, the man who had a good grounding in the whole field of human learning, and the cultivation of a deep love for the Classics. Both of these emphases are evident in Owen's writings. The notion of the general scholar, of course, promoted an ideal of learning in which students were expected to be able to converse in a thoughtful manner over a whole range of subjects, and candidates for theological degrees and for the ministry, such as Owen, were no exception to this. Theology was not to be pursued in isolation but to be studied in the context of intellectual engagement with the wider culture of learning and scholarship. As to the focus on the Classics, the one thing which an Oxford education was designed to achieve above all else was familiarity with the languages and literature of Greece and Rome. Commenting on this, Feingold makes the following illuminating observation:

> For contemporaries who believed in the constancy of human nature, the classics offered more than merely the foundations of knowledge. Students developed an emotional commitment to antiquity and its repository of useful knowledge, which illuminated the human condition and guided behaviour.[39]

Given such a world, it is not surprising that Owen's works are replete with quotations from, and allusions to, classical authors.In addition, we might note that this attitude to the Classics has a certain theological impact. First, without elaborating in any detail a notion of the 'seed of religion' in fallen humanity or the later doctrine of common grace, seventeenth-century theologians such as Owen were at ease with citing pagan classical authors in support of theological position. Second, the impact of such a culture of classical learning reinforced the belief which we find in the Reformers, themselves in part products of Renaissance humanism, that the past was a useful source of guidance and wisdom for the present. Respect for tradition was not simply a theological point; it was embodied in the very culture of wider learning in which Owen was involved; and this respect, as hinted at above by Feingold, was predicated upon a certain ahistorical attitude to texts, whereby the wisdom which they contained could be extracted without paying great attention to the historical context in which such texts were produced.[40] Indeed, it was only in the later

---

39 Feingold, 229.

40 Quentin Skinner makes the following illuminating comment regarding Tudor attitudes to classical texts: 'Having dusted down the ancient texts, they [scholars] exhibit almost no interest in reconstructing their historical contexts as a way of making better sense of them. On the contrary, they approach them as if they are contemporary documents with an almost wholly unproblematic relevance to their own circumstances.' *Reason and Rhetoric in the Philosophy of Hobbes* (Cambridge: Cambridge University Press, 1996), 40. This, of course, means that the scholars of the sixteenth and seventeenth centuries felt no difficulty in appropriating and

seventeenth and early eighteenth centuries, with the success of, among others, John Locke's assault upon the ideal of the scholarly generalist, his advocacy of a more practical, utilitarian education, and the wider development of a more acute historicist sensibility among intellectuals, that this respect for tradition and for the past began to die out. This point is particularly important in two areas: first, in understanding the attitude of Owen and his generation to texts from previous historical eras; and, second, in delineating the relationship between the Reformed Orthodoxy of Owen's generation and the rise of the modern world. In this latter context, characters such as Owen occupy a transitional position: they are aware of the changes that are starting to take place; many of them were interested in the rise of new science, with a growing realization of the iconoclastic nature such developments would bring in their wake; yet they held strongly to premodern approaches to the relationship of contemporary theological reflection and past theological tradition.[41] Indeed, Puritanism thus has a somewhat Janus face as regards modernity, something which perhaps helps to account for some of the problems which surround it in the secondary literature.[42]

It was in this world in which Owen received his education in the liberal arts and then in divinity, and a glance at his library catalogue indicates the breadth of his education and continuing interests. In addition to the expected massive holdings in theology (where patristic, medieval, Catholic, Lutheran, Reformed and heretical authors are all well-represented), we also find extensive lists of Rabbinical and Jewish works, philosophical books, from the classical era to Hobbes, Descartes, Gassendi and Spinoza, books on philology, history, geography, law, classical literature (both primary sources and critical studies), and a large number of miscellaneous volumes covering subjects from parliamentary procedure to mathematics, gardening and music theory. There are even a few volumes on very arcane subjects such as

---

juxtaposing the works of, say, a Plato or a Cicero with those of a contemporary author, as if they were all engaged in essentially the same arguments.

41   The most (in)famous example of this is probably Gisbert Voetius, who opposed the inroads of Cartesianism at the University of Utrecht: see Theo Verbeek, *Descartes and the Dutch* (Carbondale: Southern Illinois University Press, 1992).

42   Perceptions of Puritanism have been shaped by a number of factors. At a popular level, the lens of Victorian non-conformity, reinforced by the republication of Puritan texts by later pietistic groups, has led to it being regarded as an early form of Protestant fundamentalism; at a more sophisticated level, the work of Marxists such as Christopher Hill has attempted to forge a link between the ideology of Puritanism and the rise of the early modern bourgeoisie, thus giving it a more progressive image: see, for example, Hill's *Intellectual Origins of the English Revolution* (Oxford: Clarendon Press, 1980). In fact, Puritanism, at least in its Reformed Orthodox manifestation, embodied both pre-modern and early modern elements. For example, a figure such as Joseph Alleine, known to generations of non-conformists for his popular evangelical work, *An Alarme to Unconverted Sinners*, was also an intimate friend of many of the early pioneers of the Royal Society, and even produced a (now lost) work of philosophical theology, *Theologia Philosophica*. Another example might be Stephen Charnock, whose work *On the Existence and Attributes of God*, deploys many medieval-style metaphysical arguments with regard to God and yet also shows evidence of up-to-date knowledge of medical science, for example the arterial valve system of the heart. Clearly, the middle decades of the seventeenth century are difficult to categorise using the unnuanced taxonomy of historical periodisation.

magic, the social life of silk worms and the virtues of 'warm beer'. Stereotypical ideas of Puritans as somehow divorced from the wider culture, as those who read only theological books, or as reactionary obscurantist defenders of the past who based their beliefs on willful ignorance of the present are simply unsustainable in the light of such a catalogue. That Owen was clearly an accomplished generalist in the Renaissance fashion is clear, right down to his apparent Lutheran leaning with regard to the merits of beer drinking. In no way did he or the majority of his contemporaries pursue their theological work in isolation from the wider cultural context. Rather, he was culturally a man of the Renaissance who happened to use his intellectual powers and learning in the context of Reformed theology, and there are, as one might therefore expect, many points in his work where his wider reading and cultural engagement show through.[43]

Owen and Theological Polemic

The translated title of Owen's earliest (and now lost) treatise gives a clear indication both of one of the central constructive theological concerns of his life's work and also of the polemical targets which result from that concern: *On the Priesthood of Christ, against Papists, Arminians and Socinians*. From the start of his career to its end, Owen consciously directs most of his polemical fire against these three targets – to different degrees, it has to be admitted, but always to the three basic targets.

As the title of his lost manuscript suggests, at the heart of his dispute with these groups is his attitude to the priesthood of Christ. Put simply, the Catholics undermine the biblical teaching about Christ's once-for-all sacrifice through their insistence upon the Mass and upon the intermediary role of human priesthood; the Arminians undermine the efficacy of Christ's priestly work through their understanding of a universal atonement and their semi-Pelagian notion of free will which means Christ's priesthood establishes salvation only as a possibility, not as an actuality; and the Socinians undermine Christ's priesthood by denying that Christ is very God of very God and thus reconfiguring the priesthood as little more than a moral paradigm for others to follow. To understand the concerns in more detail, however, it is worth tracing some of the wider background to these polemics in order to be able to place Owen more clearly in a particular context.

Roman Catholicism

In approaching Owen's attitude to Roman Catholicism, we need to be aware of the need for careful nuance in order to bring out the subtleties of his position, subtleties which might easily be obscured by the typical anti-Roman rhetoric which was staple

---

43   To make a somewhat polemical – and obvious – methodological point here: it follows from what I say above that the worst books on Puritan thought are those written by individuals who take no time to read and learn about the wider culture of which men like Owen were a part. Basic to a sound understanding of Owen's own mind is a thoroughgoing acquaintance with the kind of books and culture with which he was himself engaged.

for Reformed Orthodox theologians.[44] Thus, on one level, his attitude to Roman Catholicism is utterly straightforward: he regards it as an apostate, idolatrous, bloodthirsty, heretical institution headed by a figure who can be straightforwardly identified with the biblical figure of the Antichrist.[45] In addition, Owen articulates in his writings all of the usual Protestant objections to Romans Catholic theology: a faulty view of authority and the church; the error of transubstantiation; a sacrificial view of the Mass which undermines Christ's once-and-for-all sacrifice on Calvary; a mediatorial human priesthood; a denial of justification by faith; an unbiblical worship of the Virgin Mary; and other dubious doctrines such as those of sainthood, purgatory, and so on. In all of this, Owen stands foursquare with the mainstream Reformed Orthodox tradition.

In addition to the usual doctrinal objections, Owen also places central to this basic anti-Roman polemic his understanding of worship. Such a preoccupation with worship as a hallmark of true religious reformation was fairly typical of the Reformed stream of Reformation thought, where the purification of worship in line with perceived biblical teaching was seen as absolutely central to the reform program. Thus, while Martin Luther saw himself primarily as recovering the gospel and providing individual Christian consciences with comfort, leaving much of the aesthetics of worship relatively unchanged (the move to vernacular liturgy and the centrality of the pulpit being the most significant innovations), the Reformations of Zwingli, Calvin and Knox were focused much more closely on the reform of worship. This is most clearly evident in a man like Knox, for whom the idiom of Old Testament prophecy was basic to his own theological productions and self-identity. The issue, of course, spilled over into struggles within Protestantism itself, and England had been the scene of numerous bitter controversies over the use of ceremonies and vestments in the formal worship of God, as exemplified in those surrounding the consecration of John Hooper as Bishop of Gloucester in 1550 and John Knox's role in the so-called Black Rubric of 1552, which was a late addition to the second Book of Common Prayer, clarifying that kneeling at communion did not imply worship of the elements. Both crises were arguably influenced by the continental theological sympathies of Hooper and Knox.[46] This kind of controversy continued into the seventeenth century. With the high espiscopal policies of the House of Stuart and the various liturgical implications that carried with it, Reformed opposition within Anglicanism to all forms of ceremonial religion, including the very notion of any kind of formal liturgy, grew apace – a distinct departure from the

---

44   For a carefully nuanced and highly detailed study of attitudes to the Church of Rome among Protestants in England in the years immediately prior to Owen's public career, see Anthony Milton, *Catholic and Reformed: The Roman and Protestant Churches in English Protestant Thought, 1600–1640* (Cambridge: Cambridge University Press, 1995).

45   For example, *Works* 14, 547. Owen's major anti-Roman writings are: *Animadversions on a Treatise Entitled 'Fiat Lux'* (1662), *A Vindication of the Animadversions on 'Fiat Lux'* (1663), *The Church of Rome No Safe Guide* (1679), all three reprinted in *Works* 14; and Sermons 14 and 15 in *Works* 8.

46   For the relevant controversies in Edwardian England, see Diarmaid MacCulloch, *Thomas Cranmer* (New Haven: Yale University Press, 1996), 471–85 and 525–33; Jasper Ridley, *John Knox* (Oxford: Clarendon Press, 1968), 108–10.

position of the earlier Reformers.[47] Yet, while the liturgical practices of Anglicanism were of concern to Owen, he regarded the aesthetic worship of Rome as the ultimate perversion of Christian worship. Owen's own view was that worship was primarily a spiritual activity, that this spiritual activity focused upon the word preached, and that concern with increasingly elaborate aesthetics was indicative of a decreasing confidence in, and experience of, the power of the word. This goes a long way to explaining his theological objections to formal Protestant liturgies in 1662, to justify which he constructs an historical/theological narrative which portrays the liturgical development of Roman Catholicism as part and parcel of Rome's general apostasy and idolatry, to the point where she maintains the name and appearance of Christianity but has entirely lost its content and power.[48]

Nevertheless, Owen's attitude to Roman Catholic theology is somewhat more nuanced than his attacks on the institution as a whole might at first glance suggest. First, we should note that the blunt attacks on the idolatry of the church stand alongside highly sophisticated engagement with individual Roman Catholic thinkers and theologians whom Owen clearly takes very seriously as intellectually able and accomplished theologians and whose work is to be engaged in a serious, albeit polemical, fashion. Foremost among these figures are the great representatives of Jesuit theology such as Francis Suarez (1548–1617) and above all, Robert Bellarmine (1542–1621). Bellarmine's work, particularly the massive *Disputationes de Controversiis Christianae Fidei adversus huius temporis Haereticos* (Ingolstadt, 1586–93), represented the most significant sixteenth-century response to Reformation theology to emerge from Rome after the Council of Trent. Bellarmine was extremely well-versed in Protestant theology, and thus his work on the whole avoided the kind of straw-man argumentation which was the hallmark of so much controversial literature in this (and perhaps we might add, any other) period of history. In this context, he made significant contributions to anti-Protestant polemics in the areas of justification, Christology, authority and church history. Given that Bellarmine died in 1621, it is a testimony to his brilliance that he remained the Roman Catholic whom Protestants felt it necessary to refute until very late in the seventeenth century. Indeed, Anthony Milton has pointed out that attacking Bellarmine became a conventional means for

---

47   For example, William Ames, *A Fresh Suit Against Human Ceremonies in Gods Worship* (Amsterdam, 1633). For Owen's own major attack on formal liturgy, see *A Discourse concerning Liturgies* (London, 1662).

48   See his *Discourse on Liturgies* in *Works* 16 where he seeks to unite the liturgical Reformers of earlier generations with the Puritan campaign of his own day by interpreting their liturgies as temporary moves designed to wean the people off Roman ceremonial in small, easily disgestible stages. He also argues in quasi-Platonic fashion that the beauty and power of worship is located in the heavenly tabernacle and that the purpose of earthly worship is to be as simple as possible so as not to hinder contemplation of the exalted Christ. On the apostasy of Catholicism see the following quotation: '[H]aving lost all experience of this power [of the Holy Spirit working through the Word] in themselves, they wrested them unto things quite of another nature, – destructive to the truth, as well as devoid of its power; hereon it came to pass that there was a dead image made and set up of religion in all the parts of it, called by the name of that which was true and living, but utterly lost.' *Works* 8, 549. The whole sermon (*Works* 8, 547–91) is essentially an elaboration of this point.

Protestants to demonstrate their orthodoxy in the late sixteenth and early seventeenth centuries, with such heterodox Reformed figures as Arminius and Vorstius offering broadsides against the Jesuit as a means of trying to persuade others that they were doctrinally sound.[49]

Owen certainly owned a set of Bellarmine's works – that published in Cologne in 1628 – as well as other individual volumes.[50] In addition, he makes constant references to the Jesuit's works throughout his writings, clear evidence of the seriousness with which he takes Bellarmine's challenge to the Reformed faith. Most of these references occur in the context of typical debates between Protestantism and Catholicism, such as those surrounding justification or relating to issues of church power and authority, particularly in relation to the interpretation of scripture.[51] Other issues are raised, however, such as those which divide Reformed Protestantism from Roman Catholicism on the matter of Christology.[52]

These polemics against Catholic thinkers such as Bellarmine indicate that Owen was quite prepared to engage the opposition not simply with the broad-brush approach that attacked the institution and practices of the Roman church in general but also at the requisite academic level as set by its finest theological defenders. The increasing sophistication, methodological, metaphysical, linguistic and so on, was as much a function of the needs imposed on both Protestants and Catholics by the brilliance of their opponents; and crude caricatures and sneers only went so far in helping to defend the faith in the elaborate world of seventeenth-century polemics. Thus Owen, as a typical seventeenth-century theologian, was required to produce a finely-tooled and precise theological response to Catholicism. Yet even this acknowledgment of polemic gives only a partial picture of Owen's relationship to Roman Catholic thought. At another level, Owen himself, in common with his Reformed Orthodox contemporaries, actually appropriated much of established Roman Catholic thought in a positive fashion and brought it into the service of his own Protestant theology. Indeed, much of the recent scholarship in the area of Reformed Orthodoxy has sought to trace out the exegetical, theological and philosophical continuities between seventeenth-century Protestant orthodoxy and the late medieval period. Therefore, before turning to Owen in particular, it is perhaps worthwhile making some general observations on this approach as a whole.

First, and most basic, it is necessary for the contemporary reader of Reformed Orthodox texts to realize that the kinds of historical periodisation with which historians routinely work are themselves the constructs of a later era. Thus, while it

---

49   See Milton, 15. F G M Broeyer, *William Whitaker (1548–1595) Leven en Werk van een Anglocalvinistisch Theoloog* (Utrecht, 1982) provides a brief list of the principal anti-Bellarmine works of the late sixteenth and early seventeenth centuries: 319, n. 531. On the English scene, the most significant work specifically aimed at Bellarmine was undoubtedly that of William Ames, *Bellarminus enervatus a Guilielmo Amesio* (Amsterdam, 1628). Owen owned a set of the 1629 edition, published in Oxford: *Bibliotheca Oweniana: Libri Theologici*, 16, no 293.

50   *Bibliotheca Oweniana: Libri Theologici*, 4, no. 124.

51   See *The Doctrine of Justification by Faith* in *Works* 5 and the anti-Roman writings in *Works* 14.

52   For example, *Works,* 3, 170.

may be helpful for the historian to distinguish between, say, patristic and medieval sources, the boundaries between these two groups are even now somewhat fluid and, for theologians of the seventeenth century, such categories themselves certainly do not represent hard and fast divisions with significant methodological implications. The quest for theological precedent in Reformed Protestantism, so important to a church keen to allay any suspicions that it was introducing novelties of any kind, was not restricted to a canon of authors who wrote before the sixth century, even though such early authors might in general be given slightly more weight than those writing after the great period of Trinitarian and Christological creedal formulation and the dramatic rise of papal power. When exactly the rot set in to the Catholic Church, and to what extent this rot vitiated all the work done by her loyal theologians, was a moot point with no single answer enjoying general approval; but, while earlier was to an extent regarded as better, the Reformed never regarded the Catholic Church, even in the seventeenth century, as not containing theologians and philosophers who had something useful to say.

Second, it is important to realize that the intellectual developments of the Renaissance and the theological contributions of the Reformation did not require a wholesale abandonment of all the scholarly and theological work of the Middle Ages, no matter what the rhetoric might sometimes suggest. After all, it is a perennial truth that the quickest way to establish one's own importance is to disparage all that has gone immediately before, even when the break with the past is perhaps not quite as clear-cut as the protagonists might like to think. Thus, we now know that even Luther's doctrine of justification, and indeed his theology as a whole, stands in a more ambiguous relationship to his medieval background than he himself seems to have realized, or certainly acknowledged.[53] When we come to the later sixteenth and early seventeenth centuries, when the increasing sophistication of Roman Catholic polemic and the establishment of Protestantism in the university context both made demands upon Protestant theology, it is not surprising that theologians should return to the work of the medieval schoolmen to find wisdom on issues such as metaphysics, necessity, contingency and so on – issues which had been discussed by the medievals in great detail and for many years, with the result that a highly useful technical vocabulary and tradition of debate had developed which was not rendered immediately redundant by Protestant claims with regard to justification, authority, and worship. Then as now, there is no point in reinventing the wheel every generation. Technical vocabulary and even the general trajectories of metaphysical discourse remained useful to the Reformed even as medieval notions of, say, transubstantiation were rejected. In addition, there were numerous streams in medieval theology which embodied the development and defence of theological positions which were meat and drink to the souls of Reformation and post-Reformation Protestants. Thus,

---

53   See Heiko A Oberman, *The Harvest of Medieval Theology* (Durham: Labyrinth, 1983); *idem*, '*Facientibus quod in se est Deus non Denegat Gratiam:* Robert Holcot O P and the Beginning of Luther's Theology' in Heiko A Oberman, *The Dawn of the Reformation* (Edinburgh: T&T Clark, 1992), 84–103); also David C Steimetz, *Luther in Context* (Grand Rapids: Baker, 1995); David V N Bagchi, '*Sic et non*: Luther and Scholasticism,' in Trueman and Clark, *Protestant Scholasticism*, 3–15.

for example, medieval discussions of God, the Trinity, the nature of theological language and logic, and, perhaps most important of all, anti-Pelagian trajectories on predestination, grace and human freedom, all proved fields ripe for the harvest to later Protestants who found their rejection of Rome on certain key issues did not prevent their positive use of Catholic theologians in these particular areas.

Again, a glance at Barlow's *Autoschediasmata* is instructive at this point. Barlow considers a knowledge of school divinity to be crucial to any well-rounded theological education. Historically, he divides scholastic theology into three basic historic periods: 1020 to 1220, marked by the development of sophisticated rationales for the Roman supremacy and doctrines such as transubstantiation; 1220 to 1330, when the church came to terms with the impact of Aristotle's metaphysical treatises in the realm of theology; and 1330 to 1517, the worst (*pessima*) age, when theologians became increasingly absorbed in abstract and speculative questions.[54] Yet this dark historical picture is qualified in a number of ways. For example, he claims that medieval Catholic theology was, on the whole, rather agreeable when dealing with those areas (such as morality) which belong to the area of natural theology and do not require revelation.[55] More significantly, he clearly regards a thoroughgoing knowledge of Peter Lombard and Thomas Aquinas as basic to any understanding of the distinctions which are central to the premodern theological task, particularly in its polemical manifestations.[56]

Consistent with the approach of his tutor, Owen is also typical of the Reformed Orthodox tradition on this point, using the language and distinctions of medieval theology for his own particular theological purposes.[57] In addition, he drew deeply upon the medieval metaphysical tradition, with a particular liking for the thought of Thomas Aquinas. This is evident even in his earliest extant work, *A Display of Arminianism*, where Aquinas is explicitly cited on a number of occasions, and where the Thomist tradition clearly stands in the background of much of his argumentation. For example, Thomas is used as the source for the common late medieval technical distinctions and definitions such as the divine knowledge of simple intelligence and the knowledge of vision, and also the will of the sign (*voluntas signi*).[58] He is also cited, alongside Augustine, in defence of the simultaneous mode of God's knowing.[59] He provides Owen's basic definition of the crucial twofold division in the concept of providence between God's intentional ordering of everything in his eternal knowing and his execution of that order in time.[60] He is also useful to Owen in relation to

---

54   *Autoschediasmata*, 37–38.

55   *Autoschediasmata,* 40–41.

56   *Autoschediasmata*, 35–37.

57   For an excellent discussion of the importance and use of medieval distinctions in Reformed theology, see Willem J Van Asselt, 'The Theologian's Tool Kit: Johannes Maccovius (1588–1644) and the Development of Reformed Theological Distinctions,' *Westminster Theological Journal* 68 (2006), 23–40.

58   *Works.* 10, 23, citing *ST* 1a.14.9; *Works* 10, 45, citing *ST* 1a.19.11. For defintitions and brief histories of these terms, see Richard A Muller, *A Dictionary of Latin and Greek Theological Terms* (Grand Rapids: Baker, 1985).

59   *Works*, 10, 28, citing *ST* 1a.14.7

60   *Works*, 10, 31, citing *ST* 1a.22.3.

argument concerning the simplicity of God with regard to the relation between the divine intellect and the divine will,[61] in arguing that election is materially as well well as formally determined,[62] and in pointing to sin as a defect of nature and not simply of an individual.[63] In addition, the work also shows evidence of dependence upon more recent Dominicans, such as Diego Alvarez, and on arguments which, while not credited to any specific source, clearly exhibit typical Thomist patterns.[64] For example, in defence of an anti-Pelagian understanding of grace, Owen deploys arguments rooted in precisely the same kind of causal metaphysics that we find in Aquinas's famous Five Ways.[65] What is clear in all of this is that the thought of Aquinas, particularly as articulated in the First Part of the *Summa Theologiae* and developed by the later Dominican and Thomist tradition, is extremely useful to Owen from the earliest time of his career as a source of argumentation for defending Reformed understandings of God and his sovereignty against Jesuit and Arminian attacks. Yet Owen's Thomism is not restricted to the issue of anti-Pelagianism. In a later work, *A Dissertation on Divine Justice*, Owen uses Thomist approaches to theological language and natural theology in order to defend the idea that retributive justice is an essential part of God and that, once God decided to forgive sin, the incarnation and death of Christ became necessary, not just convenient; and he does this in explicit disagreement not simply with the Socinians but even with Reformed Orthodox writers such as Twisse and Rutherford who are more influenced in their doctrine of God by a kind of Scotist voluntarism, with all the theological and linguistic implications that contains. Here again, the tradition of theological reflection on God and on God-talk of which Thomas is the classic representative, is of crucial importance to Owen.[66]

Owen's Thomism cannot, of course, be equated with a wholesale partisan Thomism as one might have found within an organized body such as the Dominican Order. For a start, the appropriation of medieval terminology and argument by Reformed theologians such as Owen was both eclectic and pressed into the service of a theology which was more historically oriented, particularly with regard to Christological considerations, than was typical of medieval systems. This eclecticism should also caution modern interpreters in making sweeping and generalized statements about the precise commitment of Reformed theologians to medieval trajectories of thought.

---

61 *Works*, 10, 44, citing *ST* 1a.19.1.

62 *Works*, 10, 57, citing simply 'Aquinas' but probably referring to his arguments in *ST* 1a.23.7.

63 *Works*, 10, 73, citing *ST* 1a.2ae.81.1.

64 For Owen's use of Alvarez, an anti-Pelagian Dominican of the seventeenth-century and notable commentator on Thomas, see *Works* 10, 52 (citing the commentary on Thomas), 73, and 131.

65 See *Works*, 10, 117–20. For further discussion of this passage, see Trueman, *Claims of Truth*, 119 n. 50.

66 See *Works*, 10, 481–624. For an analysis of Owen's arguments, his differences with the Socinians, Twisse and Rutherford on this issue, and his use of Thomist patterns of argumentation, see Carl R Trueman, 'John Owen's *Dissertation on Divine Justice*: An Exercise in Christocentric Scholasticism', *Calvin Theological Journal* (hereafter cited as *CTJ*) 33 (1998): 87–103.

For example, it has been argued with some passion by the Dutch scholar, Anton Vos, that Reformed theology is essentially Scotist in its metaphysics, but this approach seems to depend upon a narrow definition of Scotism which restricts it to a particular view of the nature of contingency, rather than the more obvious points of difference with Thomism, such as Scotism's insistence upon the univocity of being and the rejection of the real distinction between being and essence. In fact, the appropriation of Scotus even by those Reformed theologians who emphatically rejected Thomist intellectualism, was highly eclectic: William Twisse, for example, imbibed a clearly voluntarist approach to God from Scotist sources yet emphatically rejected both the univocity of being and Duns's denial of the real distinction.[67] Then, when one comes to a theologian such as Owen who is clearly dependent upon Thomas for large areas of his metaphysics, on Vos's reading one would still be forced to conclude that he is somehow not Reformed on the grounds not that he did not stand within the confessional trajectory of Reformed theology or held to the Christology and soteriology of the Reformed church, but simply because he was not committed to a medieval tradition on contingency.[68] The conclusion to which a close reading of Owen and his use of Thomas and Thomist sources would seem to lead is that his thought is, on one level, not to be legitimately described as Scotism but as a modified and eclectic Thomism.[69]

Medieval theologians in general, and Thomists and Dominicans in particular, are not the only Catholic authors whom Owen is prepared to use positively in his theological program. It is also clear that he had a deep personal interest in the controversies that raged on the continent between the Jesuits and the Jansenists over the nature of God's grace, a controversy which was important to the Reformed such as Owen because it paralleled in certain crucial ways the debate between the Arminians and the Calvinists in Protestant circles, parallels which, as it happens, were not entirely accidental.[70] The Jansenists owed much of their intellectual and spiritual vigour to

---

67   See his *Vindiciae Gratiae* (Amsterdam, 1632).

68   For Antonie Vos's arguments regarding Scotus and synchronic contingency, particularly as these relate to Reformed theology, see 'De kern van de klassieke gereformeerde theologie,' *Kerk en Theologie* 47 (1996): 106–25; also 'Scholasticism and Reformation,' in Van Asselt and Dekker, *Reformation and Scholasticism*, 99–119. Vos's ideas have been applied to the thought of Gisbertus Voetius by Andreas J Beck, 'Gisbertus Voetius (1589–1676): Basic Features of His Doctrine of God,' in Van Asselt and Dekker, *Reformation and Scholasticism*, 205–26. On Vos's stress upon synchronic contingency as defining the essence of Scotus's contribution, the point upon which his Scotism-Reformed theology argument depends, see the criticism of Richard Cross, *Duns Scotus* (Oxford: Oxford UniversityPress, 1999), 154 n. 6. Nevertheless, despite this, Vos's contribution to the recent revival of scholarly interest in Reformed Orthodoxy has proved outstanding and creative.

69   This was my own earlier conclusion: see *The Claims of Truth*, 148; cf. the similar conclusion of Rehnman, *Divine Discourse*, 182, who sees Owen's basic Thomism as *modified* in a Scotist direction.

70   On the history of Jansenism, see Augustin Gazier, *Histoire générale du mouvement janséniste depuis ses origins jusqu'à nos jours* (Paris, 1922); Louis Cognet, *Jansénisme* (Paris, 1961); Alexander Sedgwick, *Jansenism in Seventeenth Century France: Voices from the Wilderness* (Charlottesville: University Press of Virginia, 1977).

the life and work of two men, the Abbé de Saint-Cyran (1581–1643) and Cornelius Jansen (1585–1638), the latter of whom was greatly influenced by the writings of Michel Baius (1513–89) on the anti-Pelagian works of Augustine. Jansen provided much of the creative intellectual input into the movement, while Saint-Cyran, in alliance with the politically powerful Arnauld family, exerted tremendous influence as a spiritual counselor at the convent at Port-Royal, which became the spiritual centre of the movement. Its significance for Reformed Orthodoxy lay in its conflict with the Jesuits over the interpretation of the writings and legacy of Augustine, and in its development of arguments against the all-important Jesuit concept of middle knowledge, with the various implications for human agency and contingency which this carried with it.[71]

It would be wrong, of course, to see Jansenism as a form of quasi-Protestantism within the fold of the Roman Catholic Church. In addition to being anti-Pelagian in its view of grace, Jansenism was highly sacramental in terms of its soteriology, and thoroughly orthodox in its view of the Mass; it also exhibited a much stronger interest in miracles than was typical of Reformed Protestantism; and, of course, its adherents were also careful to emphasize that there was no point of contact between their doctrine and that of the heretical Calvinists.[72] Nevertheless, their interest in anti-Pelagian notions of grace, and the struggles they engaged in with the Jesuits, appear to have endeared them to John Owen. Now, it is true that there are very few explicit references to the movement in his writings, and that Dominican theology would appear to be the major anti-Pelagian Roman Catholic tradition upon which he draws, but there is evidence that lack of explicit citation does not mean that he was not interested in and fully conversant with the issues at hand. For example, his library catalogue shows, as we might have expected, that he owned a copy of a 1652

---

71   The major authoritative text in the interpretation of Augustine along Jansenist lines was Jansen's own massive three volumes, *Augustinus* (Louvain, 1640). On the theology of Jansenism, see Henri de Lubac, *Augustinisme et théologie moderne* (Paris: F Aubier, 1969); also Leszek Kolakowski, *God Owes Us Nothing* (Chicago: University of Chicago Press, 1995). There is a demonstrable dependence of Arminian theologians upon Jesuit theology, particularly with regard to the crucial category of divine middle knowledge, or *scientia media*, which is the concept that allows for the metaphysical construction of the Arminian understanding of the relationship between divine foreknowledge and human free agency: see Eef Dekker, 'Was Arminius a Molinist?' *Sixteenth Century Journal* (hereafter cited as *SCJ*) 27 (1996), 337–52; Richard A Muller, *God, Creation and Providence in the Thought of Jacob Arminius* (Grand Rapids: Baker, 1991), 143–66; W J Van Asselt, 'Scholastiek ten tijde van de vroege orthodoxie,' in W J Van Asselt, T T J Pleizier, P L Rouwendal and P M Wisse (eds), *Inleiding in de gereformeerde scholastiek* (Zoetermeer: Boekencentrum, 1998), 91–113, especially 93–95.

72   For example, the comments of Blaise Pascal on Calvinist views in his ''Treatise on Grace': 'That is the appalling opinion of these heretics, injurious to God and unbearable for men. These are the shameless blasphemies by which they establish in God an absolute will without foreseen merit or sin to damn or save his creatures.' *Pensées and Other Writings*, trans. Honor Levi (Oxford: Oxford University Press, 1995), 216. French Catholic iconography was not so sensitive to the distinction, frequently juxtaposing Jansenists and Calvinists in propaganda cartoons and engravings.

edition of Jansen's *Augustinus*.[73] More significant is the fact that he wrote a preface to Theophilus Gale's *The True Idea of Jansenisme*, a Protestant treatise expounding the history and tenets of the movement in a sympathetic manner; furthermore, he also claimed at one point that he has read all of the literature on the Jansenist–Jesuit controversy and intended to write a theological history of the same – a project which never appears to have been realized.[74]

Given the above, it is quite clear that any understanding of the relationship between Reformed Orthodoxy in general, and Owen in particular, with the Roman Catholic Church needs to be carefully nuanced. Of course, he regards the institution itself as hopelessly corrupt and idolatrous; but, behind the rhetoric lies a more subtle and eclectic approach. Clearly, he is widely read in medieval and contemporary Catholic sources; and it is obvious that he uses this knowledge in a careful manner which allows him to cite authors, particularly Thomas and writers of the Dominican tradition, in a way which supports the anti-Pelagian theology which he is articulating. Such is only surprising to those who do not understand either the intellectual context in which he is operating, or the relatively narrow range of disagreement between certain strands of Catholic thought and that of the Reformed. Of course, we must not understate the importance of even this narrow range of disagreements – as far as Owen was concerned, these disagreements were absolutely crucial to the integrity of the gospel message – but they did not mean that there was not much of value to be gleaned from a careful study of such authors on those issues where there was substantial common ground.

Arminianism and Socinianism

The two other polemical targets in Owen's writings were Arminianism and Socinianism. While these groups are today routinely distinguished as representing different theological trajectories, with Arminianism at least accepting the creedal tradition on the Trinity, in the seventeenth century the Reformed generally regarded both as essentially manifestations of the same heretical tendency towards notions of human autonomy. If the two were to be distinguished, it was as points on a sliding scale of heresy, with the difference being one of quantity, rather than quality, of error.

In terms of origin, the two movements had entirely different pedigrees. Arminianism originated with the thought of Jacob Arminius, a student of Beza who later went on to be professor at the University of Leiden. His thought represented a reaction to Beza's supralaparianism, a modification of the Reformed understanding of grace in a semi-Pelagian direction, and an appropriation of the modified Thomism of the Jesuits, particularly with regard to God's knowledge of future contingents.[75]

---

73   *Bibliotheca Oweniana: Libri Theologici*, 3, no. 90.

74   *Works* 12, 560.

75   For Arminius's life, see Carl Bangs, *Arminius: A Study in the Dutch Reformation* (Nashville: Abingdon, 1971); on his theology, see Muller, *God, Creation, and Providence*; also Eef Dekker, *Rijker dan Midas: Vrijheid, genade, en predestinatie in de theologie van Jacobus Arminius (1559–1609)* (Zoetermeer: Boekencentrum, 1993).

Socinianism, however, took its cue from the work of the Italian uncle and nephew, Laelio and Fausto Sozzini, particularly the latter whose book, *De Jesu Christo Servatore* (1594) came to be regarded as the definitive attack on orthodox Christology and soteriology.[76] Focusing on the practical, ethical life, Socinianism was vigorously anti-metaphysical in its theology and, while it later enjoyed the popular reputation of being an early rationalist movement, it is probably more accurate to see it as a blend of practical pietism and blunt biblical literalism, given its commitment to the reality of miracles.[77] Both Arminianism and Socinianism grew to become influential movements, particularly in the Netherlands and Poland respectively, and both received a form of creedal expression: Arminianism in the Remonstrance of 1610 to the States of Holland, and Socinianism in the Racovian Catechism of 1605.[78]

Despite the different origins of the two movements and the differing degrees of orthodoxy they exhibited in their basic theological commitments, there was, in fact, some historical evidence for the contemporary Reformed view that the two movements were closely related. In particular, the controversy surrounding the figure of Conrad Vorstius (1569–1622) at the University of Leiden indicated the close political and theological relationship that existed between Arminians and Socinians. Vorstius's appointment as Arminius's successor was driven by the political agenda of the Remonstrant party, headed by Oldebarneveldt, yet Vorstius's opponents managed to successfully tar him with the Socinian brush, with the result that he never actually took up the chair;[79] that such a theological connection did exist between Vorstius and Socinus, and that such smearing therefore had some basis in reality, has been clearly demonstrated by the work of John Platt in this area.[80]

While the European dimension of the Arminian/Socinian issue was clearly of relevance to the English situation, England itself had its own particular experience of these movements, and it is this that provides the immediate background to Owen's own reaction. First, Arminianism was, of course, far more than just a movement of semi-Pelagian soteriology. For the Reformed it also gave the impression of being somewhat more amenable to Roman Catholicism; after all, a semi-Pelagian notion of grace would seem to make faith into a kind of work and therefore to advocate that most offensive of Roman doctrines, justification by works; in addition, the Laudian party in England, responsible for the drive towards a form of church piety focused on sacraments and elaborate ritual, with an increasing hostility towards preaching,

---

76   On the life of Socinus, see D M Cory, *Faustus Socinus* (Boston: Beacon Press, 1932); on the history of Socinianism, see E M Wilbur, *A History of Unitarianism: Socinianism and its Antecedents* (Cambridge: Harvard University Press, 1945); H J McLachlan, *Socinianism in Seventeenth Century England* (Oxford: Oxford University Press, 1951).

77   On the theology of Socinianism, see Wilbur, *A History*, 408–19; Alan W Gomes, '*De Jesu Christo Servatore*: Faustus Socinus on the Satisfaction of Christ,' *Westminster Theological Journal* (hereafter cited as *WTJ*) 55 (1993): 209–31; Trueman, *Claims of Truth*, 152–98.

78   On events surrounding the Remonstrance, see Jonathan Israel, *The Dutch Republic: Its Rise, Greatness, and Fall 1477–1806* (Oxford: Clarendon Press, 1995), 421–32.

79   Wilbur, *History*, 541–44; Israel, *Dutch Republic*, 428–30.

80   See John E Platt, *Reformed Thought and Scholasticism; The Arguments for the Existence of God in Dutch Theology, 1575–1650* (Leiden: Brill, 1982), 204–07.

seeing it as a means of social subversion, was also commonly regarded as Arminian. While it would appear that Laud and many of his followers cared little for the details of soteriology and were thus not sophisticated representatives of Arminianism in that sense, their strong Erastianism, their contempt for the Reformed Orthodox, and their quasi-Roman ceremonialism all helped to reinforce the notion that they did represent an Arminian party within England and that the English struggles of the 1630s and 1640s paralleled in significant ways the Dutch struggles of the second decade.[81]

Given all this background, it is not suprising that Owen's polemic against Arminianism and Socinianism both tends to blur the differences between the two streams and operates at several levels: from the strictly doctrinal, with issues of God and providence, to the soteriological, with discussions of grace, to ecclesiological and political, with discussions of liturgy and toleration. Of all of these, however, it is those relating to soteriology which occupy most of his time and brings forth the most sophisticated of his theological polemics. Some of the relevant issues will be dealt with in subsequent chapters, but it is worth noting at this point the connection Owen makes between Arminianism and Socinianism in terms of the relative autonomy each tradition grants to the human agent. This is because it is the perceived common ground on this issue which Owen regards as relativising whatever other differences may exist between the two.

In Arminian and Socinian theology, human agents were regarded as having significant libertarian freedom relative to their actions. With a theologian like Arminius, this was defended with the concept of middle knowledge which allowed for the maintaining of a form of divine omniscience while yet granting real freedom to men and women in their choices.[82] With a Socinian such as Crellius, denial of God's knowledge of future contingents effectively precluded the kind of logical problem concerning divine omniscience and human freedom which had exercised theologians from at least the time of Boethius. For Owen, and for the Reformed in general, however, the metaphysical freedom which both systems granted appeared to remove human beings from the need for specific divine causality and this had a twofold effect: human beings were made into the equivalent of God, as they were themselves the source for the being of their own actions; and thus the advocates of these approaches were guilty of atheism. Both of these points are evident in *A Display of Arminianism*. As to the first, he offers several arguments all of which amount to the same metaphysical point. The most succinct expression of this is:

> All the acts of the will being positive entities, were it not previously moved by God himself, 'in whom we live, move, and have our being,' must needs have their essence and

---

81   See Nicholas Tyacke, *Anti-Calvinists: The Rise of English Arminianism c. 1590–1640* (Oxford: Clarendon Press, 1987); also D D Wallace, *Puritans and Predestination: Grace in English Protestant Theology* (Chapel Hill: University of North Carolina Press, 1982).

82   For Arminius theology, see Eef Dekker, *Rijker dan Midas: Vrijheid, genade en predestinatie in de theologie van Jacobus Arminius 1559–1609* (Zoetermeer: Boekencentrum, 1993); Richard A Muller, *God, Creation, and Providence in the Thought of Jacob Arminius: Sources and Directions of Scholastic Protestantism in the Era of Early Orthodoxy* (Grand Rapids: Baker, 1991).

existence solely from the will itself; which is thereby made αυτο ον, a first and supreme cause, endued with an underived being.[83]

The kind of causal scheme envisaged here is the same as that used by Thomas in the Five Ways, each of which famously ends with a self-caused cause, an αυτο ον, which Thomas declares by common consent to be called a god.[84]

Thus, the denial of the necessary and regressive logical causal chain between human action and God is tantamount to declaring that human beings are the ultimate source of specific, positive entities – in other words, human beings are creators, gods, with reference to their own actions. Owen's argument makes sense given the accepted Thomist background within which he is working, and points to the second objection to Arminianism and Socinianism: it is atheism, a charge he makes early in the treatise. Because human beings have been granted an autonomy of action which effectively allows them to create beings of their own in the form of positive actions, God himself therefore becomes subject to human action: his knowledge is contingent upon human activity, not ultimate in itself, and is therefore mutable. This, Owen declares, is 'transcendent atheism'.[85] It is atheism because it disrupts the creator-creature relationship, frees human beings from causal subordination to God, ontological and moral, and thus – to make the final move in the argument – indicates that Arminianism and Socinianism are really motivated by a desire to exalt human abilities and, perhaps even more significantly, to exempt human beings from divine jurisdiction. This is one of the reasons why Arminianism and Socinianism are consistently excoriated by Owen while theologians of the Roman Catholic Church who at least represent classic anti-Pelagian positions on the Creator-creature distinction are used positively throughout his works. In addition, we should note that Owen's take on atheism as being primarily a practical, rather than a speculative matter, places him squarely within the Reformed (and pre-modern) tradition of seeing atheism not so much as an intellectual problem but rather as a moral problem which involved not a theoretical rejection of God's existence but a willful suppression of that truth to facilitate license.[86]

While Arminianism and Socinianism are the major Protestant polemical targets for Owen, it is worth noting one other stream of such thought which some scholars have sought to regard as something against which the Reformed Orthodox reacted with vigour, namely Amyraldianism. Amyraldianism was a school of thought associated with the Academy at Saumur in France and developed by such theologians as Moses Amyraut and John Cameron as a means of obviating Arminian criticism of classic Reformed theology with regard to its apparent restriction of God's will to save. In a very influential book, Bryan Armstrong made such a case at some length and others

---

83   *Works*, 10, 120.

84   Thomas Aquinas, *Summa Theologia* (hereafter cited as *ST*) 1a.2.3.

85   *Works*, 10, 14.

86   At the start of *A Display*, Owen argues that Arminians are motivated by two desires: to exempt themselves from God's jurisdiction; and to clear human nature of the heavy imputation of being sinful and corrupt. See *Works* 10, 12–13. Both amount to what seventeenth-century divines called 'practical atheism:' see Stephen Charnock, *The Existence and Attributes of God* (Grand Rapids: Baker, 1979), 89–175; also F Turretin, *Institutes* 1.3.2 and 1.3.14.

have followed in his wake, arguing a fundamental opposition between Reformed Orthodoxy of the type represented by Francis Turretin and John Owen, and the theology which came from Saumur which, advocates of this thesis not infrequently argue, was in fact more faithful to Calvin.[87] The major problem with this scholarship is that it presupposes something which was basically not true: that the Reformed Orthodox regarded Amyraldianism as a heresy and therefore as essentially evil. Now, it is true that the kind of universal atonement proposed by Amyraut and his followers was considered incorrect, and that the re-ordering of the divine decrees demanded by the Amyraldian scheme was regarded as wrong, but Amyraldian authors were not on that score regarded as heretical – a crime which, in the seventeenth century, involved a basic denial of one of the central truths of the faith. The problem, as Richard Muller has pointed out, is that too many writers on the topic have confused the history of confessional orthodoxy with the history of doctrinal controversy.[88] For example, when we look at the work of Francis Turretin, one of the great opponents of Amyraldianism, we find that he specifically does not regard them as occupying the same heretical status as the Arminians. On the crucial issue of the ordering of the decrees, he declares the Arminian to be 'Pelagian' and thus clearly heretical;[89] the Amyraldians, however, are considered 'among the Reformed' and, while their system is regarded as biblically defective, they are nowhere decried as heretics.[90] Owen's attitude is similar. Obviously, his understanding of atonement and the ordering of decrees is emphatically particularistic, but on other issues he can quote Amyraldian authors with great respect and no hint of any discomfort. Thus, Amyraut himself is 'a very learned man' in whose opinion on a matter of the nature of the church Owen is happy to acquiesce,[91] while Cameron (along with the professors at Saumur) is a 'very learned' theologian whose careful and accurate work on the doctrine of God helped Owen change his mind on the nature of divine justice[92]. To misquote George Orwell, for the Reformed Orthodox, all errors are erroneous, but some errors are more erroneous than others; and the holding of views such as Amyraldian universalism which did not destroy the crucial dependence of the creature upon the Creator or undermine understanding of the sinfulness of fallen men and women, was not enough to qualify one as a heretic whose whole theology was thus vitiated. Thus, while Arminians and Socinians also held to a form of universal divine love and intention to save, it was their revision of God's sovereignty and the doctrine of sin which really pushed their theology beyond the pale, rendering them practical atheists and poisoning their theology in a deep, comprehensive manner; Amyraldian commitment to universalism, while, according to the Reformed Orthodox, thoroughly misguided, did not render their whole theology as worthless, nor did it necessarily

---

87   Bryan Armstrong, *Calvinism and the Amyraut Heresy* (Madison: University of Wisconsin Press, 1969); A C Clifford, *Atonement and Justification: English Evangelical Theology 1640–1790, An Evaluation* (Oxford: Clarendon Press, 1990); R T Kendall, *Calvin and English Calvinism to 1649* (Carlisle: Paternoster Press, 1997).

88   Muller, *After Calvin*, 8–9.

89   Turretin, *Institutes*, 4.18.6.

90   Turretin, *Institutes*, 4.18.13–20.

91   *Works*, 13, 138.

92   *Works,* 10, 488.

push them beyonds the bounds of what the Reformed themselves considered to be 'Reformed'. We should remember that Amyraldian issues postdated most of the great Reformed confessions and were only tangential even to the Westminster Assembly. As noted above, even a casual glance at, say, Francis Turretin's *Institutes of Elenctic Theology* reveals that, yes, it is true that Amyraldians, Arminians, and Socinians were the major Protestant targets of Turretin's polemics; yet the language used against Amyraldianism, while strong, is qualitatively different to that applied to the other two groups, indicating that the Saumurians were seen as erroneous on certain points but not as engaging in damnable heresy like the other groups. The lessons are clear: first, scholarship which fails to understand how the Orthodox themselves thought of Amyraldianism is doomed to anachronism and irrelevance;[93] and, second, as with the issue of Reformed attitudes to Roman Catholic theologians, scholars need to see the Reformed Orthodox as critically eclectic in relation to other Protestant theological trajectories, and as appreciating good theology when they see it, no matter by whom it might be written.[94]

Conclusion

From this sketch of Owen's intellectual background, it is quite clear that we cannot approach his theology in any way that reduces either the complexity of the cultural background from which he emerges, nor the theological method and approach which he adopts. The Puritans of seventeenth-century England ultimately lost the great battles of their day – politically to a Restoration government set on revenge for past wrongs, educationally to an establishment which excluded them and their ecclesiastical descendants from university education, and intellectually to an Enlightenment whose self-conscious iconoclasm called into question the theological

---

93 In the case of Alan Clifford's approach to Owen, this misunderstanding of Reformed attitudes to Amyraldianism would seem to lie at the heart of an analysis which tends to reduce the question of the relationship of Owen's theology to the Reformed tradition to two points: his methodological dependence on Aristotle; and his theological commitment to limited atonement. As to the former, 'Aristotelianism' in the seventeenth century is a term almost devoid of meaning except as it refers to a very diverse tradition which looks to the canon of Aristotle's texts as in some way authoritative; and as to the second, in addition to Clifford's basic misunderstanding of Reformed views of atonement, he fails to see that, in the seventeenth century, this single point of theology is not enough to establish the kind of traditionary, theological and confessional antithesis which his analysis seems to presuppose as true and which then appears as if by magic in the primary texts.

94 The Reformed Orthodox wrestled long and hard with exactly which items of the Christian creed were necessary to be believed for credible Christian profession and which found expression in the various lists of *fundamental articles* which exist. While there was no confessional consensus on exactly which articles, and how many, should be included, a representative list can be found in Turretin, *Institutes* 1.14.24. On the whole issue of fundamental articles, see Muller, *PRRD* 1, 406–30; Martin I Klauber, *Between Reformed Scholasticism and Pan-Protestantism: Jean-Alphonse Turretin (1671–1737) and Enlightened Orthodoxy at the Academy of Geneva* (Selinsgrove: Susquehanna University Press, 1994), 165–87.

premises, philosophical assumptions, moral absolutes, and cultural presuppositions of their work. They thus suffered the fate of all those who lose: as they did not control the writing of history, so they were either written out of that history or demonized by that history, dismissed variously as fundamentalists, pietist obscurantists, and moralizing kill-joys of no intellectual merit whatsoever – an image sadly reinforced by some of the republishing projects and cultural attitudes of well-meaning followers who, because they had no real access to the avenues of higher education available to the pre-1662 English Reformed, were incapable of really understanding the sophistication of the theology they produced.[95]

Much of the older scholarship surrounding Reformed Orthodoxy in general and John Owen in particular, suffers from one of two basic faults: it is either driven by doctrinal agendas which were simply irrelevant in Owen's day (for example, Hegelian historiography,or Barthian presuppositions, or the idea that Amyraldianism was regarded as heretical); or by categories that are either demonstrably nonsensical or too simplistic (for example, a concept of Aristotelianism which assumes it to be a monolithic school of thought, or a notion of scholasticism which conflates it with a nascent Enlightenment rationalism). The problem with such approaches is, of course, that they are methodologically disastrous for an historical-theological study. As Quentin Skinner has continually reminded intellectual historians, books are complex historical actions and need to be understood in terms of both synchronic and diachronic contexts. Of course, all historical analyses are provisional: the construction of such contexts is the task of the historian and is thus necessarily limited by the historian's own act of selection and exclusion; but that does not mean that all histories are equally valid. It is a fine line between using analytical categories as heuristic devices and using them as Procustean beds; and the more simplistic, anachronistic, or plain false such analytic categories are, the more distorted and misleading the historical conclusions drawn will be. What this chapter has demonstrated is that, whatever one thinks of the substance of Owen's theology, it is worthy of study as the product of a sophisticated seventeenth-century intellectual context which brought together strands of the theological tradition, contemporary philosophy, and church and state politics in a manner which requires that we avoid reducing our analysis of his thought to the level of sound bites.

Indeed, when a theologian such as Owen is set in context, it becomes apparent even before detailed engagement with his theology, that we are dealing with a theologian whose neglect over the centuries has more to do with who is writing the history, rather than the intrinsic mediocrity of his thought. Had he been born a Dutchman, there is no doubt, given the dominance of Reformed thinking in that country, that

---

95 A classic example would be Richard Baxter, who wrote on a wide variety of theological topics with sophistication and, it must be said, a varying level of clarity. Yet it was only his popular works of warm piety which enjoyed extensive republication after his death, leading to his current image as that of a man who was basically a pietist, interested in Christian experience rather than the niceties of Christian doctrine. This image completely obscures the fact that his more polemical and dogmatic works demonstrate extensive appropriation of and interaction with all manner of theological streams and philosophical trajectories: see Carl R Trueman 'A Small Step Towards Rationalism: The Impact of the Metaphysics of Tommaso Campanella on the Theology of Richard Baxter', in Trueman and Clark, 181–95.

he would have occupied a place alongside Johannes Cocceius and Gisbertus Voetius as a major contibutor to a significant theological tradition. The issues with which he engaged – Roman Catholicism, Arminianism, and Socinianism – were highly significant both theologically and politically (if one can reasonably talk of separating the two categories in the seventeenth century) and his contributions were perhaps the most significant made by an Englishman to these various controversies and therefore merit study as providing insights into the intellectual, theological and political life of early modern England. That later generations chose to label him and his colleagues as proto-fundamentalists and control freaks simply indicates a basic misunderstanding of what seventeenth-century culture was really like.

As we turn, then, to the actual substance of Owen's thought, we must keep in mind that he approached theology against the background of an education which exposed him both to medieval and Renaissance pedagogical trajectories; that he was well-schooled in logic, rhetoric and the other basic building blocks of an Arts education; that his theology was constructed in dialogue with patristic, medieval and contemporary writers from all Christian traditions; that, despite the anti-Roman rhetoric, his relationship to medieval theology, especially that of Thomas Aquinas, was far more nuanced if not generally positive than such rhetoric might have led us to suspect; that England and English problems often gave him his specific pretext for engaging in theological controversy but that the debates in which he engaged were of much wider European significance; and that he deserves to be taken seriously as a leading proponent not simply of English Puritanism – far too parochial and narrow a category – nor simply of Reformed Orthodoxy, but of the ongoing Western anti-Pelagian and Trinitarian tradition that stretched back from the seventeenth century, past the Reformation, through the Middle Ages, and back to the writings of the early church Fathers.

Chapter 2

The Knowledge of the Trinitarian God

Introduction

As with the other aspects of Owen's theology, his doctrine of God is not *his* in any real sense of the word; rather, the doctrine of God articulated by Owen belongs, in a narrow sense, to the Reformed Orthodox tradition, a tradition which, as already noted, itself needs to be understood within the Western Christian tradition. Owen had no intention of developing his own doctrine of God; nor did he ever do so. What he did was to give specific voice to, and occasional elaboration and nuancing of, the established trajectories of thinking on the doctrine.

In addition to noting this essential lack of originality in his work, we also need to acknowledge at the outset that Owen's articulation of the doctrine of God occurred at a point in history from the 1640s to the 1680s when many of the certain and established truths about God were subject to increasing polemical pressure, and when there was a need to mount careful defences of many positions which had previously been regarded as unassailable. Given the truism that the identity of God was absolutely central to all other aspects of Christian faith and life, the same polemical opponents – Romanists, Arminians, Socinians – have to be addressed across the whole spectrum of theological discussion; and when the centrality of Trinitarianism to Reformed Orthodoxy as a whole is acknowledged, it is clear that the principle opponents in polemic will be those who push hardest for the refinement or even abandonment of this basic Christian tenet. Thus, radical Arminianism and especially Socinianism received a considerable amount of attention in Owen's defence of the orthodox view of God. This is significant among other reasons on the grounds that both of these traditions subscribed to Protestantism's scripture principle and thus their aberrations from established Reformed positions raised in an acute form the question of scriptural interpretation and, perhaps more significantly, that of metaphysics and the nature and utility of philosophical arguments in theological discussion. As Protestantism had experienced its first crisis of authority and interpretation in the 1520s, when Luther and Zwingli had clashed over the meaning of the phrase, 'This is my body,' so the seventeenth century saw it slowly disintegrate under the impact of new challenges to orthodoxy which were self-consciously rooted in the scripture principle.

Prolegomenal Issues

Before addressing the doctrine of God in Reformed Orthodoxy, it is necessary to look briefly at a couple of prolegomenal aspects of such theology. This matter has been dealt with in exhaustive detail elsewhere, both in terms of Reformed Orthodoxy in general and John Owen in particular, so nothing of any great originality can be added at this point; it is, however, important that a few basic points be grasped in order to set Owen's narrower teaching on the doctrine of God within its wider theological and methodological context.[1] While the quest for a *Centraldogma* to Reformed theology has proved an inappropriate and anachronistic activity, it is yet true to say that Orthodoxy does embody two basic principles which have a profound impact upon the way theology is understood. Ontically speaking, the Reformed are clear that it is God himself who is the author of theology: were there no God, or if that God had decided that he would not reveal himself, then there could be no theology. Noetically speaking, the Reformed are agreed that scripture is the cognitive ground of theology. This is not to say that God has not revealed himself outside of scripture, in his mighty creative acts, for example, or supremely in the Incarnation; it is not therefore to reduce revelation to scripture; but it is to establish as basic the point that scripture is now the norming norm of all theological statements: revelation in nature or in the Incarnation is only comprehensible when grasped through the teaching of scripture; and all theological statements have to be judged by their consistency with what scripture teaches.

Reformed Orthodoxy makes a basic distinction between archetypal and ectypal theology. The specific terminology was coined by Francis Junius, but it has its origins in late medieval Scotism.[2] The basic point is a simple one: as God is infinite, only he can have perfect knowledge of himself, or *archetypal* theology. This is entirely consistent with the basic Reformed premise that the finite cannot contain/ grasp/comprehend the infinite. Human beings, as finite creatures, can thus only have access to a finite theology which co-ordinates with their finite capacity to know God, a theology which is characterized as *ectypal*. In the hands of the Reformed, of course, this capacity for knowing God is further limited by an understanding of the noetic effects of sin.

Three significant effects flow from this. First, human theology becomes self-consciously radically dependent upon God's revelation of himself. There can be no autonomous access to God because the infinite God is, in himself, unknowable by finite creatures, and his revelation of himself, over which he has sovereign control, becomes the only basis upon which such creatures can know him. Thus, accusations of *rationalism* or of the development of an autonomous natural theology in the Enlightenment sense are misguided in the context of Reformed Orthodoxy. This basic conceptual distinction guards Reformed theology against such; and failure to spot the significance – and even the existence! – of this distinction has led to some incorrect and misleading criticism of Reformed Orthodox theology.[3]

1   See Muller, *PRRD* 1; Rehnman, *Divine Discourse*.

2   See Francis Junius, *De Vera Theologia* IV–V in *Opera Selecta*, ed. A Kuyper (Amsterdam, 1882), 51–56; cf. *Synopsis purioris theologiae*, I.3–4; Turretin, *Institutio* 3.2.6; for discussion in the secondary literature, see Muller, *PRRD* 1, 225–38; Willem J Van Asselt, 'The Fundamental Meaning of Theology: Archetypal and Ectypal Theology in Seventeenth-Century Thought' in *Westminster Theological Journal* 64 (2002), 319–35.

3   See Clifford, *Atonement and Justification*.

Second, theological language is delimited in terms of its scope and claims. All that ectypal language can really claim is that this or that is how God has willed to be in relation to his creation; the ability to extrapolate from the ectype to the archetype is cut off by the logical and ontological gulf between the finite and the infinite; and there can be no one-to-one correspondence between human words and realities as they exist in God and are known by God. This gives all theological discussion a contingent nature – not contingent in the sense that theological statements are not true and binding (this is no community language game that is being played); but contingent in that they are utterly dependent upon their relationship to God's voluntary act of revelation and have no autonomous status of their own.

The third effect, an inference from the first two, is that God in himself is not subject to the logical and ontological limits of human language and thought. This is crucial in Owen when it comes to his defence of the Trinity. The unknowability of the essence of God by any but God himself, rules out of bounds any claims about what is and is not possible for that essence, outside of what has been revealed in the ectype. The boundaries of possibility for God from a human perspective are based solely upon what has been revealed, not upon some higher logic or ontology which can be imposed upon God and to which he must conform in some Procustean manner.

The second major prolegomenal issue is that of the scripture principle. If God can only be known via his revelation, then Reformed Orthodoxy identified scripture as the sole normative cognitive foundation for theology. Again, this matter has been dealt with in exhaustive detail in recent secondary scholarship. The key things to grasp in the context of our study of John Owen are as follows. First, the Reformed notion of scriptural authority actually drives the development of highly sophisticated linguistic studies in the seventeenth century. A high view of the authority and integrity of the biblical text as God's word written was major factor in fuelling the development of careful attention both to the biblical languages and other cognate tongues, and to issues of textual history and criticism. The idea that the seventeenth-century Reformed were interested neither in careful exegesis nor in the literary and linguistic contexts of the Bible is simply untrue. Indeed, the linguistic and exegetical work of this century was far more elaborate than that which had marked the earlier Reformation. Second, and related to this first point, the exegesis of the Reformed Orthodox is far from the dogmatically-driven Procusteanism of popular mythology. Again, this has been documented in impressive detail by Richard Muller, but will become very clear as we examine specific doctrinal-exegetical points in the writings of John Owen. Of course, the move from exegesis to doctrinal synthesis is never an entirely straightforward one, and it has to take place within an historical context which itself provides a certain traditionary vocabulary and framework, but this does not in any way require mindless, decontextual proof-texting, nor the shoe-horning of texts into doctrinal patterns which they simply do not fit.

It is against this background, the noetic distinction between archetypal theology and ectypal theology, and the central importance and authority of scripture, that the Reformed Orthodox understanding of God must be set. As with so many other areas of theology, the Reformed build positively upon the patristic and medieval traditions at hand in order to understand God; but all is ultimately subject to the critical perspective supplied by these basic premises.

Divine Simplicity

In common with Reformed theologians from Calvin onwards, Owen holds to the doctrine of the simplicity of God.[4] This doctrine is, at least in intention, not the basis for speculative philosophizing about the being of God but rather a way of expressing the fact that God is not a composite being and cannot cease to exist. For this reason, the notion was questioned only by the most heterodox in the sixteenth and seventeenth centuries.[5] Owen himself is clearly aware of the implications of a denial of divine simplicity, a denial which he sees lying at the heart of Socinian reconstruction of the doctrine of God in a manner which radically limits divine being and power.[6] He is also aware that the language of divine simplicity, while apparently positively assertive, is, in fact, part of the *via negationis* and asserts truths about God through denial:

> [T]hough simplicity seems to be a positive term, or to denote something positively, yet indeed it is a pure negation, and, formally, immediately, and properly, denies multiplication, composition, and the like. And though this only it immediately denotes, yet there is a most eminent perfection of the nature of God thereby signified to us; which is negatively proposed, because it is in the use of things that are proper to us, in which case we can only conceive what is not to be ascribed to God.[7]

Thus, the point is as much a logical and linguistic one, acknowledging the need to be critically aware of the limits of finite language and human concepts in their application to God. To support this point, Owen makes marginal reference both to the Spanish Jesuit thinker, Suarez, and to Cajetan's commentary on Aquinas's work, *On Being and Essence*. As is apparent throughout Owen's articulation of the doctrine of God, he is heavily indebted to the work of medieval and Renaissance Catholic thinking. This is neither a surprise, nor something which makes his theology somehow sub-Protestant; it merely indicates that, when it comes to significant areas of theology, he is operating self-consciously within a tradition much larger than that contained within the bounds of confessional Reformed Protestantism.

Owen draws four conclusions from his notion of divine simplicity. First, God has absolute ontological priority over everything else and enjoys total independence.

---

4   See Muller, *PRRD* 3, 273–75.

5   Summarizing sixteenth and seventeenth-century thinking on this point, Muller states, 'It belongs to the very nature of composite things that they come into being and perish – and Scripture certainly indicates that God cannot either be made or destroyed!' *PRRD* 3, 276.

6   'That God is *simple act* is the next thing excepted against and decried, name and thing; in the room whereof, that he is compounded of matter and form, or the like, must be asserted. Those who affirm God to be a simple act do only deny him to be compounded of divers principles, and assert him to be always actually in being, existence, and intent operation.' *Works* 12, 71. Cf. Aquinas, *Summa contra Gentiles* 1.14.

7   *Works*, 12, 71.

Second, God is absolutely and perfectly one and the same; his essence is what it is, and contains nothing that is accidental to it or which differs from it. Third, all his attributes enjoy perfect oneness and unity in God, since all attributes are infinitely perfect and thus essentially identical with the being of God. Fourth, God contains no potency to be other than that which he is; he is perfect and self-existent and can never be any different.[8]

The third point is of particular interest in light of Reformed theology's elaboration of formal discussion of the so-called divine attributes. As noted above, there was general agreement on the simplicity of God; and, at first glance, this would appear to generate problems for talking about God in terms of attributes since such talk might appear to presuppose or imply divine complexity. In general, this was defused by careful reflection upon the nature and variety of distinctions. Just because God was simple did not mean, to cite a modern philosopher, that he was a 'property' and that his love was really the same as his wrath, that every attribute was the same as every other.[9] Instead, the Reformed regarded distinctions between the attributes as formal, not real, and as reflecting necessary linguistic conventions that allowed finite, complex human beings to speak of God. Thus, the subsistence of love and wrath in a God who was in himself absolutely simple was mysterious on the grounds of the divine simplicity; but language which distinguished the two was not in and of itself at best merely metaphorical, at worst meaningless nonsense.[10]

As mentioned previously, Owen never wrote a formal systematic theology, but he does offer significant discussion of particular divine attributes in two major works: *A Dissertation on Divine Justice* (1653) and his refutation of John Biddle, *Vindiciae Evangelicae* (1655). Again, the context for both works was basically the perceived threat to orthodox theology posed by Socinianism; however, in *A Dissertation*, Owen also took on two stalwarts of the Reformed faith, William Twisse and Samuel Rutherford, revealing that even within the bounds of confessional orthodoxy there were significant disputes concerning some fairly basic theological commitments.

The Attribute of Immensity

In the *Vindiciae Evangelicae,* Owen uses his understanding of God's being and attributes to combat the Socinian claims of John Biddle. The kind of antimetaphysical theology represented by Biddle raises critical philosophical questions with which earlier generations of Protestant theologians had not had to wrestle, and in this context we find Owen articulating a doctrine of God which positively connects to

---

8   *Works*, 12, 71–72.

9   See Alvin Plantinga, *Does God Have a Nature?* (Milwaukee: Marquette University Press, 1980), 47. Useful clarifications of the meaning(s) of divine simplicity which, in part, respond to Plantinga can be found in Brian Davies, *The Thought of Thomas Aquinas* (Oxford: Clarendon Press, 1992), 51–54; and Muller, *PRRD* 3, 40–42.

10   For example, see *Synopsis purioris theologiae* VI.xxi; William Twisse, *A Discovery of D Jacksons Vanitie*, 72–76; Edward Leigh, *A Body of Divinitie*, 163, 208; Turretin, *Institutes* 3.7.14–15.

earlier medieval paradigms in its utilization of philosophical notions as a means of reinforcing the results of biblical exegesis.

Key to Biddles's attack on classical orthodoxy is his assertion of the spatial limitation of God. Spatial limitation, of course, at least implies embodiment; and embodiment in turn implies mutability and also epistemological limitation, both geographically and chronologically. Thus, Biddle's point about such spatial limitation is, from the perspective of Owen, the foundation of his whole defective doctrine of God; and this is surely why Owen chooses to use the problem of presence as the entry point for his refutation.[11]

Owen starts his response by highlighting the implications noted above of spatial limitation. Indeed, he cannot resist a sarcastic comment on Biddle's claim that one can see from God's left hand to his right: Mohammed, he notes, claimed it was a three days journey between God's eyebrows; this would seem to make Biddle's God even smaller than that of Islam.[12] Of course, Owen is aware that Biddle cites plenty of scriptures which speak of God being in heaven; and this underlines the need for seventeenth-century theologians to connect their exegesis to broader philosophical considerations in order to be able to defend established orthodox positions. This is not to say that exegesis becomes subordinated to philosophy but rather that theologians such as Owen need to give more careful attention to the necessary philosophical implications or presuppositions of the biblical text which allow it to speak with one voice and in a coherent fashion. In other words, commitment to the unity and perspicuity of scripture requires a measure of philosophical synthesis; indeed, it rises out of this commitment, since unity and perspicuity demand that scripture offer a coherent view of the realities about which it speaks; and that requires consideration of broader questions about the nature of God and of the world he created; just hurling texts back at the Socinians will simply not achieve very much.

Thus, Owen's first line of response is to argue that those verses which speak of God being in heaven are not speaking in a restrictive manner which denies God's presence elsewhere; instead, scripture here uses such language to underline the eminence of the manifestation of God's glory in heaven, and the fact that this place is the focus of eschatological expectation.[13] This argument is well-established in Christian tradition, going back to the early church, and is also a key element of the response of Owen's friend and Oxford tutor, Thomas Barlow, to Conrad Vorstius's assertion, essentially identical to that of Biddle, that God is restricted to heaven.[14]

Second, Owen draws on traditional distinctions about place, which he defines as a space which can receive and contain a body (*spatium corporis ambientis*). In doing so, he notes that he regards the traditional definition of space as *superficies*

---

11   Owen summarizes Biddle's view of God as follows: 'The description of God which he labours to insinuate is, that he is "one person, of visible shape and similitude, finite, limited to a certain place, mutable, comprehensible, and obnoxious to turbulent passions, not knowing the things that are future and which shall be done by the sons of men; whom none can love with all his heart, if he believe him to be 'one in three distinct persons.' " ' *Works* 12, 86. This would appear to be a fair summary of *Twofold Catechism* (London, 1654), 6–22.

12   *Works*, 12, 89.

13   *Works*, 12, 90–91.

14   *Exercitationes Aliquot Metaphysicae de Deo*, (Oxford, 1658), 292–93.

corporis ambientis as now outmoded, again reflecting the position of a contemporary scholastic philosopher such as Thomas Barlow. He then distinguishes between imaginary place and real place, the former being a hypothetical conception of a space that is apt to receive a particular body, the latter being the space when it has indeed received the body;[15] and he further distinguishes between *being* in a particular place and *being present* in a particular place. The former applies to any body, since all physical objects have an existence in a particular space; *presence*, however, is a predicate of *persons*.[16]

Having said all this, Owen then argues for God's omnipresence on the basis of his immensity, though his treatment of this issue has a profoundly negative quality about it. First, Owen denies that God's presence is the same as those of beings with dimensive properties. Then, he makes a basic distinction between God's absolute and relative attributes: absolute attributes are those which are absolute, subsist in God himself and require no external object, and include, for example, God's immensity; relative attributes are those which require some external object for their egress, and include such things as ubiquity and punitive justice.[17] Immensity is one of the former, because it refers to his unbounded nature as God; ubiquity is one of the latter because it refers to the relationship that exists between his immensity and the created world. This leads Owen to a statement of God's omnipresence which is remarkable not for its philosophical speculation, but for its implicit rejection of precisely such speculation:

> God, who in his own being and essence is infinite and immense, is, by reason thereof, present in and to the whole creation equally, not by a diffusion of his substance, or mixture with other things, heaven or earth, in or upon them, but by an inconceivable indistancy of essence to all things, though he exert his power and manifest his glory in one place more than another; as in heaven, in Zion, at the ark, etc.[18]

The central words here are negative: *inconceivable* and *indistancy*. Owen is really telling the reader how God is not to be conceived of as present rather than offering a positive affirmation of how he is. Philosophical arguments and distinctions are thus used to produce an anti-speculative notion of divine presence.[19]

---

15 *Works*, 12, 91–92; cf. Barlow, *Metaphysicae*, 242–44.

16 *Works*, 12, 92.

17 'The properties of God are either *absolute* or *relative*. The absolute properties of God are such as may be considered without the supposition of any thing whatever, towards which their energy and efficacy should be exerted. His relative are such as, in their egress and exercise, respect some things in the creatures, though they naturally and eternally reside in God.' *Works* 12, 93.

18 *Works* 12, 93.

19 Cf. the discussion of immensity and omnipresence by Edward Leigh: 'Immensity is such a property of God, by which he cannot be measured nor circumscribed by any place, he fills all places without multiplying or extension of his essence. He is neither shut up in any place, nor shut out from any place, but is Immense; he is without place, and above place, present everywhere, without any extension of matter, but in an unspeakable manner.' *A Systeme or Body of Divinity*, 173. As with that of Owen, the effect of Leigh's apophaticism is to exert a profoundly anti-speculative influence on discussion of the divine attributes, in this

Owen rounds off the discussion with four further arguments to make his point. First, God's perfection demands his omnipresence, as absence from any given place would mark a limitation or imperfection in God. Second, if God's immensity requires space, then that space becomes either prior to, or equally ultimate with, God; and, if he creates space and is then confined by it, he must have ceased at some point to be infinite. Third, God's infinite essence requires omnipresence; and, of course, as Owen holds to the simplicity of God, any restriction on his essence is an immediate restriction on his individual attributes. Fourth, if God is confined to heaven, then he must have at least quasi-corporeal extension, and thus differ in terms of being from creatures only quantitatively, not qualitatively. Interestingly enough, each of these arguments is also negative, pointing to the unacceptable consequences of Biddle's assertions.[20] In this manner, his argument about presence is a textbook example of the outworking of the basically negative thrust in theological language which is rooted in his notion of divine simplicity, as noted above.

The Attribute of Vindicatory Justice

Owen's most extensive discussion of a single divine attribute is his *A Dissertation on Divine Justice*, the purpose of which was to argue that, given the existence of sin and of God's decision to save a people for himself, the incarnation of Christ was necessary. In other words, it would have been impossible for God to have forgiven sin by a mere act of his will. Interestingly enough, Owen had articulated this latter position in 1647 in *The Death of Death*, underlining his point by dismissing the position for which he was to argue in 1653 as an unwritten tradition with no scriptural warrant.[21] It would seem that this significant change in his thinking was probably precipitated by his perception of the rising threat of Socinianism in England of the early 1650s; and the reason for pursuing Twisse and Rutherford on this point was not, of course, that he regarded them as crypto-Socinians. Rather, he seems to have considered their essentially Scotist grounding of the necessity of incarnation and atonement purely on the will of God as providing an inadequate basis for maintaining an orthodox Christology and soteriology in the face of Socinian critiques. To attenuate or even break the connection between God's attributes, incarnation, and atonement, and thus to make the atonement unnecessary, even when considered logically subsequent to a divine decision to save sinful humanity, was half-way to making it unnecessary in any objective sense and to leave the door open for merely moral or exemplary understandings of incarnation and atonement.[22]

---

case immensity, relative to the created world, and to underscore the profound ontological gulf that exists between Creator and creature.

20 *Works*, 12, 95–97. Finally, Owen uses the argument that Biddle's claims about God's circumscription fly in the face of the common consent of the nations, indicating that, for all of his use of the philosophy of the schoolmen, he is also a thoroughgoing man of the Renaissance, steeped in rhetorical strategy.

21 *Works*, 10, 205.

22 Owen notes in the preface that his new position places him at odds with Augustine, Calvin, Musculus, Twisse and Vossius, while bringing him into line with Paraeus, Piscator,

The arguments which Owen deploys after his change of heart demonstrate a strongly Thomistic tendency in his thought at this time, with close connections being made between the way the world is and the way God is.[23] We should note, however, that the arguments for this 'natural theology' are not all of a metaphysical kind, with the standard 'consent of the nations' argument, a basic element of Renaissance rhetoric, being used with more emphasis and to greater effect than philosophical arguments about the relationship between uncreated and created being.[24] Of more significance to us here, however, is the way in which the discussion of the necessity of the atonement sheds light on Owen's understanding of the attributes.

At the heart of the issue are two separate but related problems. First, to what extent can human beings know how God must act in certain circumstances? To put it another way, to what extent can human beings know the limits of God's absolute power, the range of possible worlds of the knowledge of simple intelligence; for, in asserting the absolute necessity of atonement if God is to redeem sinners, Owen is effectively denying that God can even hypothetically conceive of a possible world where such remission takes place without atonement. And, second, how does human language about attributes of God actually refer to God, since it would appear on the surface that such language ascribes complexity to one who is purely simple? One might say that both problems resolve into the linguistic issue: how is human language about God meaningful?

The basis of Owen's argument is the idea that divine justice, as it is inherent in God, is simply one way of describing God's overall perfection; and hence provides the basis for all of God's external acts: as they are governed by his being, so they are inevitably governed by his justice. In other words, to say 'God' is just is to make a point about his claim of right over his creation, a point for which Owen's main explicit authority is the Jesuit philosopher, Francisco Suarez.[25] This has obvious implications for the understanding of the language of divine attributes: as we noted above, Owen routinely distinguishes between absolute and relative attributes, and punitive or vindicatory justice belongs to the latter category since it requires the existence of something external to God which contravenes God's perfection and thus requires punishment. In other words, punitive justice refers to the outworking

---

Molinaeus, Lubbertus, Rivetus, Cameron, Maccovius, Junius, and the professors at Saumur 'who, after the spreading of the poison of Socinianism, have with great accuracy and caution investigated and cleared up this truth' and that their names and reputation gave him confidence in his convictions. The presence of the Amyraldian theologians such as Cameron and those others at Saumur, on this list, and Owen's not untypical praise for them, should serve as a salutary warning about the complexity of theological relationships and politics in the seventeenth century, a warning all too often left unheeded by later writers on the history of Reformed thought *Works*, 10, 488.

23   See Trueman, John Owen's *Dissertation*, *passim*; Rehnman, *Divine Discourse*, *passim*.

24   For example, *Works*, 10, 497, where Owen establishes universal consent with regard to divine justice as a basic premise of all that is to follow; also Chapter 4 on human sacrifices: *Works*, 10, 525–41; in my earlier treatment of this work, cited above, I missed the significance of rhetoric for the overall argument.

25   *Works*, 10, 502–03.

of God's perfection relative to a fallen creation, an outworking which has two basic elements: first, the publication of a legal code which clearly defines God's sovereign rule over his creation; and, second, particular punishments inflicted upon those creatures which break the terms of the legal code. That such punishment is necessary is established by Owen on the basis that for God not to do so would be to relinquish and to contradict his ontological status as Creator.[26] God inflicts such punishment freely, because he is moved to do so by his own being, and not by something prior to him or above him; but he still inflicts punishment necessarily because he cannot do otherwise without contradicting himself. For God not to punish contravention of the legal code which defines his status would be for him to abandon being God.[27]

The linguistic implications of this approach are clear: Owen is following the Suarezian pattern of referring certain of the attributes of God to God's action in the world rather than to formally distinct attributes in God himself: we talk of God being angry with sin and of punishing sin; but we do not thereby impute human emotions to God; rather, we are describing the way in which God's perfection works out and reasserts his authority and order in the context of the chaotic and sinful actions of creatures. We should not, however, read Owen as implying that this process of punishment is an impersonal, mechanistic process: we shall see later how Owen's Trinitarianism involves him in seeing the divine action to save humanity as being deeply personal vis-à-vis the intratrinitarian relations of Father, Son, and Holy Spirit in the context of the soteriological economy; and even here, in the context of the necessity of punishing sin, Owen is careful to stress the language of divine will relative to divine action. As such, the inevitability of God's punishment of sin, required by God's necessity to be sovereign over his creation, does not obviate the fact that this is an act of his free, personal will.

This discussion of the ascription of emotions to God is a critical point in Owen's debate with Biddle. The biblical literalism and strongly anti-metaphysical thrust of the latter's theology leads him to a straightforward, basically univocal, application of the language of human emotion to God.[28] In Biddle's theology this is closely connected to his understanding of God being finite, and having a local, physical, spatially circumscribed and material, body.[29] Christian theology had long understood the need to understand language about God, particularly that regarding emotion and

---

26　*Works*, 10, 508–10.

27　'[T]hat God punishes sins with a concomitant liberty, because he is of all agents the most free, we have not a doubt. Thus, his intellectual will is carried towards happiness by an essential inclination antecedent to liberty, and notwithstanding it wills happiness with a concomitant liberty: for to act freely is the very nature of the will; yea, it must necessarily act freely.' *Works* 10, 510. This is one of the aspects of Owen's theology to which William Sherlock will take strong exception in the 1670s. In opposition to Owen, he argues (along lines very similar to Thomas Aquinas) that the remitting of sins is generally regarded in human societies as a virtue; thus, God's decision to punish sin must rather be rooted in the fact that such punishment is, according to God's infinite wisdom, the best means of dispensing his grace: see his *A Discourse Concerning the Knowledge of Jesus Christ and Our Union and Communion with Him* (London, 1674), 45–46.

28　*A Twofold Catechism*, 11–14.

29　*A Twofold Catechism*, 7–11.

suffering, within the context of God's infinity and incorporeality and utter difference in these matters from his creation. Aquinas, for example, posits change as a function of potency, which is itself linked either to material corruptibility, locational change, the order to an end, or the possibility of ceasing to exist, all of which do not apply to God, and, by inference therefore, the language of which cannot therefore be applied univocally to God. [30] Thus, Owen, following the line of argument articulated by Thomas Aquinas, established it as basic in his *A Dissertation on Divine Justice*, that language about God's attributes needed to be understood as operating in a manner which took account of the analogy, not univocity, of being between God and his creatures:

> [I]n ascribing the perfection of excellencies to him, we exclude the ratio of habit or quality, properly so called, and every material and imperfect mode of operation. [31]

Given this, when Owen comes to speak about divine attributes which seem to imply emotions in God, he is concerned to guard God's status as creator by ensuring that such language is applied in a manner which takes account of the basic ontological distinction between the immaterial creator and the material creation. In the *Vindiciae Evangelicae*, Owen thus proceeds from arguments about God's incorporeality to his perfection, a perfection which he points out requires that God is perfectly blessed. From this, he infers that the attribution of emotion to God is made complicated by four basic theological needs: (i) the need to avoid implying that God's will is somehow frustrated; (ii) the need to avoid making God subject to something outside of himself; (iii) the need to avoid implying change and mutability in God; and (iv) the need to avoid implying impotence in God. [32]

Owen then proceeds to discuss a series of scriptural attributions of emotion to God as test-cases for these four concerns. When ascribed to God in the Bible, anger, Owen claims, refers to one of two things: either God's immutable will to punish sin; or the effects of that punishment when delivered, a distinction which corresponds to the argument made in *A Dissertation on Divine Justice*. [33] He then supports this by turning one of Biddle's own interpretative principles against him: in the preface to his catechism, Biddle claims that what is ascribed to God in one verse and denied of him in another cannot therefore be understood as being ascribed properly to God; [34] and, as Owen points out, anger is indeed denied of God in Is. 37:4. [35] Then, Owen turns his attention to repentance and to fear, both of which he sees as intimately connected to God's prescience: a prescient God cannot be a God who repents or fears in the human sense of the word, but such emotions in mortals are associated

---

30 *ST*, 1a.9.2.

31 *Works*, 10, 504; cf. Aquinas, *ST* 1a.13.5.

32 *Works*, 12, 109–10.

33 *Works*, 12, 111.

34 The hermeneutical problem faced by the Orthodox (which texts to take literally, which to take figuratively) is indeed acknowledged by Biddle, the difference, of course, being which texts the respective sides consider to be straightforward: *Twofold Catechism*, Preface, 8–9 (no pagination in original).

35 *Works*, 12, 112.

with lack of knowledge, and lack of control, of the future. This, then, requires that we understand such biblical language in terms of divine condescension to human capacity and not in some univocal way, a point which he supports with marginal quotations from Manasseh Ben Israel and Nicholas of Lyra. The point is, in other words, a common one and Owen is saying nothing outrageous or exceptional. This point also paves the way for Owen to move to the discussion we noted earlier on God's knowledge of future contingents.[36]

In assessing Owen's approach to God's attributes, it is important to remember that, at base, the practical importance of the argument for Owen is a soteriological one: the clear articulation of God's immutable relationship to his creation is not constructed with a view to developing an impersonal, 'unmoved mover' model of deity, but is rather aimed at drawing out the ontological presuppositions of the anti-Pelagian way of salvation which the West inherited from Paul, via Augustine, and then modified in significant but not entirely discontinuous ways during the Reformation. Owen's discussion of God and his attributes, while drawing heavily for some of its conceptual content on the work of Suarez, yet stands within the overwhelming stream of anti-Pelagian exegesis on the Bible. Modern theology, of course, with its equally philosophical and scholastic (according to the accepted canons of the academy) commitment to an anti-metaphysical approach, along with its close cousin, a radical narratival reading of scripture, is likely to dismiss Owen (and thus most of Western Christianity prior to Kant) as being hopelessly in thrall to Greek thought. Nothing could be further from the truth: it is unlikely that Aristotle, Plotinus, or many of their followers, would have recognized in Owen's God much or anything of their own thought. And that Owen sees the scriptural texts as implying an ontology is scarcely surprising or radical: it simply reflects the overwhelming thrust of the exegetical and theological work up to his day. Attempts to argue that such approaches mark a break with the Reformation, or a fundamental perversion of the Reformation, a regression to pre-Reformation theology, or a dramatic move towards the rationalism of the Enlightenment are all overstated, unhistorical, methodologically dubious, and more often than not driven by the eisegetical concerns of modern theologians desperate to find justification for their particular hobby-horses in earlier texts. As regards the basic contours and substance of his doctrine of God, Owen is a rather typical figure of the seventeenth century, building on a long-standing Christian heritage; and, moreover, his doctrine of God is ineradicably Christian, as will become increasingly clear as we turn to the next section in our study of Owen on God: the doctrine of God as Trinity.

---

36   *Works*, 12, 112–14, 119–20. In this latter section, Owen sees language of repentance in the Bible not to changes in God's inner being but to changes to his relation to outward works and created entities. This position, akin to the modern logical notion of a Cambridge Change, was a standard medieval solution to the problem of such language and places Owen within the overwhelming mainstream of Western theology on this point: cf. Thomas Aquinas, *ST* 1a.9.1.

God as Three and God as One: Defending the Trinity

As we turn from Owen's discussions of God's existence and attributes to his statements on God as Trinity, it is worth noting at the outset that this particular doctrine was, unlike say, the scripture principle or justification by faith, an ecumenical dogma; it had been clearly formulated in early church creeds which were questioned neither by Catholics nor by orthodox Protestants; and, as a result, the contributions of the Reformed Orthodox to Trinitarian theology are not marked so much by innovative critique of the dominant tradition but rather defence of that tradition in the face of radical attacks by those who rejected the creeds and who saw patristic theology as reflecting declension from, and perversion of, the pristine gospel of the New Testament. Having said that, it will become clear that Owen's approach to the Trinity, particularly in terms of intratrinitarian relations relative to the economy of salvation and of this to piety, does indicate the way in which the Reformed Orthodox elaborated and applied the traditional doctrine within the new doctrinal and practical frameworks of Protestantism.

The Reformation scripture principle always had the potential to be used in a way which did not simply critique the traditional teachings of the church but could also overthrow them wholesale. That this was the case is clear from the Socinians, whose radical scripture principle manifested itself in a major anti-metaphysical reconstruction even of those theological topics left substantially unchanged by the Reformers, such as the doctrine of the Trinity and that of the Incarnation. So radical was their critique that even hallowed patristic authors who both Catholics and Protestants had regarded, in their different ways, as authoritative, were dismissed as Platonic perverters of true Christian theology. In place of either the teaching magisterium of the church, or the careful exegesis of scripture in critical relation to historical church traditions of exegesis and synthesis, the Socinians urged a literal and, over time, increasingly rational, biblicism which had little or no place for the collective wisdom of the church through the ages and which exhibited a strong anti-metaphysical tendency, lethal to classical Christian theism.

Richard Muller has noted three basic characteristics in Reformed Orthodox discussion of the Trinity in polemical context: a careful appropriation and deployment of patristic vocabulary; a vigorous struggle over the exegetical ground of the doctrine; and the struggle to find a set of philosophical categories for the expression of the doctrine, given the increasingly problematic conception of substance in the seventeenth century. All three are significant for understanding the thought of John Owen on this matter.[37]

While Socinianism was a preoccupation of John Owen from his earliest days as a theological writer, and is rarely far from the surface in almost all of his works, his major exposition of Trinitarian doctrine in polemic against them was the *Vindiciae Evangelicae* (1655). As noted before, this was produced as the result of Parliamentary commission to refute the *Twofold Catechism* of John Biddle, the translator (and modifier) of the *Racovian Catechism* which had recently been published in English. Whether Socinianism was a major cultural force is highly debatable, but certainly the

---

37 *PRRD*, 4, 58–62.

perception among the orthodox theologians and politicians of the Commonwealth was that it represented a significant threat. Trinitarian controversy had been in the air in England since the 1630s and 1640s, when there had been considerable controversy over the matter generated in main part by William Chillingworth's *Religion of Protestants a Safe Way to Salvation* (Oxford, 1638). Thus, for example, Parliament had previously arranged in 1652 for all copies of the *Racovian Catechism* to be seized and burned. Three years later, Owen's own response was less incendiary in a literal sense but still marked with heat of theological passion; and, while his work is, theologically, as wide-ranging as Biddle's work and the *Racovian Catechism* itself, of particular interest in this chapter is his articulation of the doctrine of the Trinity.

In engaging with Biddle, Owen does not underestimate the ability of his opponent, warning that no one should try to combat the Socinians who is not adept in the biblical languages and well-trained in logic and rhetoric. Clearly, the production of effective anti-Socinian polemic is the task of a Renaissance man in the truest sense of the word.[38] In addition, Owen prefaces his point-by-point polemic with a long history of Socinianism, which sees the origins of the heresy in the Cerinithianism and Ebionitism of the early church. As such, he lays out at the very start the principle that Socinianism, far from being a legitimate reaction against the patristic perversion of Christianity, was, in fact, ruled out of bounds as heresy as far back as the close of the apostolic era.[39] He then charts the history of the heresy from Cerinthus until his own day, with particular attention to Faustus Socinus, the most brilliant representative of the movement.

When Owen tackles Biddle's text proper, he starts with a surprisingly brief comment on the *Twofold Catechism*'s doctrine of scripture, with which he has little disagreement. The very brevity of the chapter, along with its somewhat petulant *ad hominem* nature, indicates the problem: the Socinians appear to hold to a basic scripture principle in a formally similar manner to the orthodox. The differences, in fact, are significant, and go straight to the heart of why Owen can see scripture as teaching the doctrine of the Trinity and the Socinians reject such a conclusion: the point at issue is not simply whether scripture is the authoritative noetic foundation for theology, but how that scripture is to be interpreted, a point which draws in matters of logic, of metaphysics, and of how individual passages of scripture are mutually related in the act of interpretation.

The place where the theological pinch is really felt most immediately in this matter is, of course, the doctrine of the Trinity, where the different metaphysical and logical frameworks of Biddle and Owen are most clearly demonstrated. Biddle offers three basic reasons why the orthodox doctrine of the Trinity cannot be true. First, he points to the epistemological impossibility of framing the concept of more than one person in one substance in the mind without falling into bitheism etc. Second, he argues that to distinguish persons within the Godhead requires either that the persons be finite, in which case it is required that God himself is finite, given the insistence of the orthodox of that everything in God is God himself; or that the persons be infinite, which then requires the logical impossibility of multiple

---

38 *Works*, 12, 50–51.
39 *Works*, 12, 13.

infinities in God. Third, the idea of a substance behind the persons opens the door to speaking of God impersonally, and this flies in the face of biblical teaching and sane theology.[40] Underlying each of these points is Biddle's belief that it is logically and ontologically impossible to distinguish personhood and essence, and that the two must be identified in such a way that a difference in number or person demands a distinction in essence. This, of course, is a lethal supposition as regards the doctrine of the Trinity: when scripture asserts there is one God but also teaches a distinction between Father, Son, and Spirit, then Socinianism is the obvious and only conclusion to be drawn.[41]

Owen deals with this objection in a single paragraph, where he relies heavily upon there being a fundamental difference between the logical constraints to which a finite substance is subject, and those which apply to an infinite substance:

> Distinction of persons (it being an infinite substance) doth no way prove a difference of essence between the Father and the Son. Where Christ, as mediator, is said to be another from the Father or God, spoken *personally* of the Father, it argues not in the least that he is not partaker of the same nature with him. That in one essence there can be but one person may be true where the substance is finite and limited, but hath no place in that which is infinite.[42]

Richard Muller has noted how defining *substance* and *essence* in the seventeenth century became an increasingly problematic activity, and how the two terms were often roughly equivalent.[43] Here, however, it would appear that Owen is operating with a subtle nuance between *substance* and *essence*. Essence as a term strictly indicates *quiddity* or the 'whatness' of a thing, while substance indicates more the concretion or actual being. Thus, when a substance or concrete being is finite, it does not permit of more than one person; but when infinite and spiritual, Owen does not regard this as interfering with the presence of more than one person or hypostasis.[44] The subtlety of the distinction is crucial to the argument's validity, but also indicative of the logical pressure under which Trinitarian language was being placed in the seventeenth century by critics such as Biddle and others. The radical biblicism of the Socininians was, in effect, cutting the very ground away from under the traditional doctrine and forcing its exponents to greater degrees of precisely the kind of conceptual and linguistic subtlety which the Socinians decried as betraying the straightforward teaching of scripture.

The other point which underlies Biddle's critique is his overarching emphasis on the economy of the history of salvation as giving clear, logically prior and determinative insights into the being of God. God is, in himself, if you like, exactly what he appears to be. This, of course, is basic to the kind of argumentation displayed

---

40 John Biddle, *The Apostolical and True Opinion concerning the Holy Trinity, revived and asserted* (London, 1653), 2–3.

41 Muller, *PRRD* IV, 95.

42 *Works*, 12, 170–71; cf. *Works*, 12, 237.

43 *PRRD*, IV, 171–75.

44 I am most grateful to Richard Muller for a useful email discussion on this passage in Owen.

in his catechisms: leading questions answered by selections of biblical quotations isolated from context and from any notion of the analogy of faith. To the extent that ontology is at all important, it is entirely subordinated to the flux of history and no overarching synthesis is either desirable or even possible. By contrast, an elaborate Trinitarian ontology is basic to Owen and is, indeed, the only means whereby history itself can be given any coherence or significance: the voluntary intratrinitarian relations of Father, Son and Holy Spirit relative to creation and then to the history of salvation is his basic means of articulating a relationship between time and eternity which makes the former the ontic ground for the latter, and the latter the noetic ground for the former. Thus, in addressing Biddle's claim that the subordinationist language of scripture demands an ontological subordination of the Son to the Father, Owen responds by reading these passages against the background of the covenant whereby Christ is established as Mediator according to both natures, thus defending a subordination that is merely voluntary and economic. This, of course, points towards Owen's defence of the deity of Christ.[45]

The Deity of Christ

One of the *Racovian Catechism*'s major contentions is that the Incarnation is a nonsense because it posits the idea that two substances of contrary properties can meet in a single person, and that two persons cannot be incarnated as one person. Owen's response is to distinguish between natures and person: the various properties of Christ as divine and human are properties of the separate natures; they are not properties of the person. This is classic Chalcedonian orthodoxy, set within the context of the Reformed understanding of the communication of attributes. Further, Owen rejects the 'two persons' criticism by pointing to the anhypostatic nature of Christ's humanity: it was not a human person who was assumed in the Incarnation, but a human nature which received its personhood in union with the divine. Again, a classic post-Chalcedonian Christological point is deployed to answer the Socinian objection, indicating how self-consciously the Reformed Orthodox appropriated the theological heritage of the ecumenical creeds and discussions to meet the specific exigencies of their own particular polemics.[46]

In addition to discussion of substance and the appropriation of patristic concepts such as that of the anhypostasis, Owen also utilizes other well-established doctrines to argue for the deity of Christ. Thus, he speaks of the eternal generation of the Son by the Father, a point which he sees as rooted in passages such as Jn 5:19–23 and as clearly demanding that the Son is God as well as the Father.[47] He also points to the demands created by God's justice in the light of sin for a mediator who was not simply human but also divine. The argument is reminiscent in structure of that offered, 'with

---

45 *Works,* 12, 171, 173–78. For detailed discussion of Christ's appointment as mediator, along with the dogmatic and exegetical issues which drive this discussion, see Chapter 3 below.

46 *Works*, 12, 209–10. For more detailed discussion of Owen's Christology in general, and these points in particular, see Chapter 3 below.

47 *Works*, 12, 214.

Christ removed', by Anselm in *Cur Deus Homo* (1098), but the use of soteriology as a means of establishing Christ's divinity is typical of much Christian theology right from the early patristic debates. It also serves to highlight that the differences between Orthodoxy and Socinianism are as much moral as epistemological; and indicates clearly that Owen thinks always in holistic, theological terms which require each scripture passage, and each piece of doctrinal synthesis, to comport with the analogy of faith and the overall teaching of scripture.[48]

Owen vindicates the traditional doctrine not simply by a re-examination of the term *substance* relative to Socinian objections, by the application of patristic and ecumenical concepts and vocabulary, and by setting Christology within the overall soteriological framework of scriptural teaching, but also by careful analysis of individual scriptural passages. Central to this task are those which refer to pre-existence. This particular doctrinal point opens up the very heart of the difference between the Socinians and the Reformed Orthodox, since the former wish to ascribe a decisive significance to the particulars of history and the economy of salvation which the latter wish to set against the background of a divine Trinitarian ontology. In this context, Owen deals with objections with the typical Reformed combination of exegesis and theology. Thus, for example, one major element of his defence of pre-existence is based on texts such as Jn. 1:1, which the *Racovian Catechism* refers to the start of the subject matter of the gospel and thus as having no significance whatsoever for Christ's pre-existence.[49] Owen offers various lines of response, but one of the most interesting, given the common idea of Reformed Orthodox theologians as, variously, logic choppers or blunt proof-texters, is the way in which he insists upon reading Jn. 1:1 in a literary context. He argues that the apostle clearly wished to make an allusion to Gn. 1:1, and he then looks at Gn. 1:1 in the Syriac version, which Owen translates as 'In the beginning, the Word made all things.' The reading may not prove pre-existence for a modern reader, but it is worth noting that the way in which Owen constructs his argument is far removed from the rigid approach to the biblical text which popular mythology ascribes to the seventeenth-century divines.[50]

Owen's defence of pre-existence is not dependent on this one text, however: for example, he also uses arguments from the historical dynamic implied in the act of Incarnation.[51] More importantly, he deals with a number of Old Testament passages routinely applied by the Reformed Orthodox to Christ as God. Thus, he pushes the identification of Wisdom in Pr. 8 with the Logos, for which he provides six reasons: the description of Wisdom here can only apply to Christ; the same things are affirmed of Christ in the New Testament; Christ is called the Wisdom of God; Solomon intended to speak of the Wisdom of God; Christ is called Wisdom in an

---

48 *Works*, 12, 214.

49 *Works*, 12, 215–17.

50 *Works*, 12, 218. Another, negative, example of this is the way in which Owen rejects Ps. 110:3 as evidence for pre-existence, because the passage has only been used for such because of the influence of the mistranslation of the verse in the Vulgate, 'tecum principium in die virtutis tuae in splendoribus sanctorum ex utero ante luciferum genuite,' *Works*, 12, 243.

51 *Works*, 12, 225–36.

absolute sense in the New Testament; and the language Solomon used was personal, referring to a person, not an abstraction.[52]

In addition to the passage from Proverbs, Owen also spends considerable time addressing predictive prophecy vis-à-vis the Messiah. In this context, and, additionally, from the point of view of seeing the sophistication of Owen's approach to scripture in action, his discussion of Is. 9:6 is extremely important. The *Racovian Catechism* applies this passage to God the Father and Grotius applies it to Hezekiah.[53] Owen's response is careful, nuanced, and embodies a series of arguments. First, noting that some of the rabbis agree with Grotius, he yet argues that the dating of the prophecy at the time of invasion of Judah by Rezin and Pekah requires that Hezekiah must already have been born, and so could scarcely be predicted in the passage. Second, he indicates that the Chaldee paraphrast identifies the prophecy as speaking of the Messiah, and also applies the title 'the God of Counsel' to him. Third, he claims that the consensus of ancient rabbis held the same basic view as the Chaldee paraphrast. Fourth, Owen outlines the lack of agreement among those rabbis who see the prophecy as referring to Hezekiah, citing Hillel, Joseph Olbo, and Tanchum. This is then followed by a discussion of the titles of Is. 9:6 in the original Hebrew, and the extent to which they can only be applied to the Messiah and to which they demand his deity. The whole discussion is indicative of the variety of sources, the subtlety, and the sophistication of Reformed Orthodox approach to the interpretation of scripture in the seventeenth century; and, in its technical complexity, it is indicative of the polemical pressure being exerted on the exegetical underpinnings of orthodox theology by its most brilliant opponents.[54]

One final note to Owen's defence of orthodox Christology relates to his discussion of the term Logos and also the references in scripture to Christ as the image of God. To the first, Owen shows a clear grasp of the different biblical and theological uses of the term, and draws once again on patristic conceptual vocabulary to express himself: the Word is either *prophorikos*, that is, the word which is outwardly spoken by God, or *endiathetos*, God's eternal, essential Word. Christ cannot be the former literally, as he is clearly a person; nor can he be the former metaphorically (as the one who speaks the words of God); instead, he must be *Logos endiathetos*, with the exegetical proof being Jn. 1:1, where Christ is characterized as Logos and as being God; and Rev. 19:13, where Christ is depicted as executing judgment on his enemies as king, a clear function of deity.[55] Owen combines this point with the references to Christ as divine image in Col. 1:15 and Heb. 1:3. As to the first, he makes a distinction between essential image and accidental image, the former referring to person the latter to office. The Socinians routinely refer such verses to Christ's office, but Owen argues that the context of the verse demands that it be understood of the person. As to the second, Owen does little more in *Vindiciae Evangelicae* than refer the Socinians to the earlier clause in the same verse, referring to the Father's glory.[56] That this is

---

52   *Works*, 12, 243–44.
53   *Works*, 12, 314–15.
54   *Works*, 12, 315–21
55   *Works*, 12, 321.
56   *Works*, 12, 322.

far from mere mantra-like repetition of a verse in the face of heretical exegesis, is demonstrated by Owen's treatment of the same verse in his massive *Hebrews*. Here, he connects the language of *express image* to that of *glory*, but then engages in a detailed discussion of the use of such *glory*-language in the Old Testament, cross-referenced to Kimchi, Rashi, the Targum, and Elias Tishbi, as well as to equivalent Greek usage in the New Testament. Again, the sophistication of Reformed Orthodox exegesis, particularly in the context of verses contested by heretics, is remarkable.[57]

The Deity of the Spirit

The final piece in the Trinitarian jigsaw is, of course, the deity of the Spirit. There is a significant difference on this matter between Biddle and the general consensus of Socinians. The former, whilst denying the Spirit's deity, yet affirmed his personality; the latter generally regarded the Spirit merely as a way of referring to the impersonal powers of God. Indeed, in a letter written to a member of the House of Commons, Biddle states that he believes:

> The Holy Spirit to be the chief of all ministering Spirits, peculiarly sent out from heaven to minister on their behalf that shall inherit salvation; and I do place him, both according to the Scripture, and the Primitive Christians, and by name Justin Martyr in his Apologie, in the third rank after God and Christ, giving him a preeminence above all the rest of the heavenly host.[58]

Biddle defends his position with twelve arguments. The first is his contention, already noted above, that those things which are personally distinguished must have separate essences; and as the Spirit is so distinguished from God, thus he must have a separate essence.[59] In the twelfth argument, Biddle points to a distinction of wills between God and the Spirit. This has a twofold impact: the Spirit is, once again, shown to be not God as he must be essentially distinct from him; but, because he possesses a will, he must have personhood, the point which marks Biddle off from mainstream

---

57 *Works*, 20, 93–95. The discussion is preceded by Owen criticizing the traditional analogies of the Father–Son relation to that of the sun and its beams (92); and is followed by discussion of Philo and further Hebrew usage (95–96).

58 John Biddle, *The Apostolical and True Opinion concerning the Holy Trinity revived and asserted* (London, 1653), 8 (the prefatory material, to which this statement belongs, has no pagination in original); also the comment of Stephen Nye, 'They [the Socinians] say, the Spirit is the Power and Inspiration of God, saving that Mr Bidle, and those that follow him, take the holy Spirit to be a person, chief of the Heavenly Spirits, prime Minister of God and Christ, and therefore called *the Spirit* by way of excellence; and the *Holy* Spirit, to discriminate him from Satan, Prince and Chief of the wicked and Apostate Spirits.' *A Brief History of the Unitarians, called also Socinians* (n.p., 1687), 33–34.

59 *The Apostolical and True Opinion*, 1–3. Biddle makes the same point in his eleventh argument, when he points to the separate understandings that are ascribed to God and to the Spirit, again requiring separate essences: *The Apostolical and True Opinion*, 11–13.

Socinianism.[60] Biddle's deviation on this point is not lost on Owen, who opens his chapter on the Spirit's deity by connecting him to the ancient Macedonian heresy.[61]

In the *Vindiciae Evangelicae*, whose primary target is Biddle, Owen therefore spends most of his time defending the deity of the Spirit as the point at issue. This he does primarily with reference to the work which scripture ascribes to him: he creates; he regenerates; he indwells believers as God in a temple; he makes and appoints ministers of the church; he is sinned against in such a way that the sin is unforgivable; he is the object of worship, specifically as mentioned in the baptismal formula; and the attributes of ubiquity and omniscience are directly ascribed to him (Ps. 139:7; 1 Cor. 3:16; 1 Cor. 2:10; Jn. 16:13) and his omnipotence and eternity can be inferred from his work in creation.[62]

The functional argument is powerful, and has its Christological corollary in Owen's use, noted above, of a modified Anselmic argument to prove the necessity of Christ's deity from the work he had to perform relative to God's justice combined with his desire to save. Elsewhere in Owen's writings, however, he engages in a much more elaborate discussion and defence of the Spirit's deity in his *Discourse on the Holy Spirit*. This latter discussion has been singled out by Richard Muller as exemplifying both the continuity between Reformed Orthodoxy and earlier Reformation discussion of the Spirit, and the need to address the subtleties and nuances of biblical usage, given the way these were being exploited by Socinians and others.[63] Thus, Owen prefaces his defence of the Spirit's deity with careful examination of the names given in Scripture to the Spirit. Central to this is analysis of the use of *ruach* and *pneuma*, along with their cognates, in the Old and New Testaments, and the Septuagint. Owen is aware that these words are often used to describe things other than the third person of the Trinity; indeed, he lists no less than six categories of meaning for the terms: wind; vanity; a part or quarter of the earth; something intangible; the affections of the soul; and angels.[64]

With his general linguistic background, Owen turns his attention to the specific term, *Holy Spirit*, and from this infers a number of things about him. First, he argues that the appellation *Spirit* clearly indicates his immaterial nature.[65] Second, the use of the adjective *Holy* refers to his eminent nature, not his work (Owen citing Justin Martyr and Chrysostom as his theological authority for these points). This is significant because, in the contrast drawn between the Holy Spirit and unclean spirits

---

60   *The Apostolical and True Opinion*, 13–16. The argument from will to personality is tangential and inferential in this work, but made clearer elsewhere: *A Confession of Faith touching the Holy Trinity, According to the Scripture* (London, 1648), 6–7, 51–52.

61   *Works*, 12, 334.

62   *Works*, 12, 337.

63   *PRRD*, 4, 338–41.

64   *Works*, 3, 47–53.

65   *Works*, 3, 56–57. Owen acknowledges that in passages such as Jn. 4:24, the term *Spirit* is applied to the Godhead in general, not exclusively to the Holy Spirit, but also points out that the language of Spirit is consistently and persistently applied elsewhere to the third person of the Trinity, and thus that the implications of the term are particularly relevant to understanding his nature and work.

in Mk. 3:29–30, and the possibility of blaspheming the Spirit therein described, Owen sees key evidence for the Spirit's personality.[66]

The Spirit's personality is not, of course, a point at issue with John Biddle; yet Owen sees personality and divinity as inextricably connected. Indeed, he regards the order of subsistence within the Trinity as indicating the personality of the Spirit: as the Son is eternally generated by the Father, so the Spirit proceeds from the Father by eternal procession. Owen sees hints of this in the use of the plural *Elohim* in Gn. 1:2, but more important in that verse is the connection between *ruach* and *Elohim*, which he regards as structurally parallel to the genitive in Jn. 20:17, and thus as legitimating a reading of *ruach* which refers to the Spirit in hypostatic terms. The Spirit is the Spirit of God (the Father) as the Son is the Son of God (the Father). In reading the passage this way, Owen is not innovating but standing within a well-established tradition, as evidenced by him supporting this view with a marginal quotation from John Chrysostom.[67] He then proceeds to flesh this position out by arguing for the distinctively Western order of procession, with the Spirit proceeding from both Father and Son, the key pieces of scriptural evidence being verses such as Gal. 4:6, 1 Pe. 1:11, Rom. 8:9, as well as such passages as Jn. 14:16–17.

Perhaps more significant for Owen in his dual defence of personality and divinity, however, are the implications of his epistemology. Given that Owen regards God as in himself incomprehensible, and thus all human theology as built upon the ectype of revelation, conclusions regarding the essential nature of Father, Son, or Holy Spirit are ultimately based upon inferences drawn from descriptions of their revealed properties and actions.[68] On this basis, Owen proceeds to show that the Spirit is described in scripture in such a way that his personality and his divinity are inextricably connected. First, he is included in the Great Commission's baptismal formula, Mt. 28:19. The key for Owen here is not simply the inclusion of the Spirit, but the fact that all three, Father, Son and Spirit, are connected to the one name, singular, which he sees as a direct reference to the Godhead, or essence, of God.[69] Second, his appearance like a dove at Christ's baptism also indicates personality and divinity. In this context, Owen connects the New Testament accounts of the dove descending with connotations which he finds in Gn. 1:2. This is no baseless juxtaposition, as he justifies the connection both linguistically and historically. First, he indicates that the Hebrew word translated as 'hovers,' also carries implications of 'growth,' and which he therefore reads as implying the communication of life, as from a mother bird in laying and hatching eggs. Indeed, Owen offers the Latin translation 'incubabat' as equivalent. Second, he quotes the text in the original of Severinus's Syriac ritual of baptism which forges a clear liturgical connection between Gn 1:2 and Christ's baptism. Once again, the sophistication, subtlety and catholicity of the Reformed Orthodox approach to exegesis and doctrinal formulation is in evidence.[70]

---

66 *Works*, 3, 55–56.
67 *Works*, 3, 60.
68 *Works*, 3, 69.
69 *Works*, 3, 72–73.
70 *Works*, 3, 74–75.

Finally, Owen points to the fact that scripture ascribes understanding and wisdom, a will and power to the Holy Spirit, all of which are characteristics which are properly ascribed only to persons. Of course, Biddle would have no problem with this; indeed, the scriptural ascription of a will to the Spirit is that which leads him to break with the dominant Socinian tradition. Owen, however, points out that each of these things is attributed in scripture to the Spirit in a way which indicates his divinity. As to understanding and wisdom, Owen connects the Greek of 1 Cor. 2:10–12, with the Hebrew of Is. 40:28, and also to Ps. 117:5. If the Spirit knows all things, he must therefore be God.[71] As to the will, he is careful to reject the relevance of Jn. 3:8 in this context, arguing that the purpose of the verse is merely to deny that the wind is not subject to human guidance or direction; he also indicates that Jas. 3:4 cannot be taken strictly literally, as the rudder is not the ultimate source of its direction; instead, he argues that this implies the existence of an active helmsman, a person, and thus connects willing to personhood; and he then clinches the Spirit's personality with reference to 1 Cor. 12:8–11. Finally, he points to power, not in some raw sense of the capacity to achieve an effect, but in terms of that which is put forth and exercised by understanding and according to the will; as creation is ascribed to the Spirit, and creation is by necessity the action of a divine person, thus the Spirit is a divine person. In this context, Owen takes to task the exegesis of the Socinian author, Schilchtingius, who refers the language of spirit in the text under discussion, Job 33:4, merely to the human spirit. In typical fashion, Owen cites the Hebrew text and shows how the verse breaks into two basic units, and how the action of the first is specifically ascribed to the Spirit of God, the second to his breath, which Owen takes a synonym for Spirit. The verse teaches the creative act of the Spirit, and thus implies both his divinity and his personhood.[72] God is one substance, but three persons, Father, Son, and Holy Spirit.

What is clear, therefore, in Owen's discussion of God as Trinity is the complexity of the task in hand: Owen is keen to defend the traditional orthodoxy of Trinitarian faith, yet he does not do so in any simplistic or off-hand manner. Careful logical distinctions and discussion combine with soteriological, exegetical, and linguistic concerns to elaborate a defence of the Trinity at a point in time when the doctrine is coming under fire on each of these fronts. Again, the caricature of Reformed Orthodoxy as involving a tiresome repetition of hackneyed dogmatic arguments is exposed as highly inaccurate: the position defended and expounded may well be traditional, but the tools with which this is done represent the best that were then available, both drawn from the wider Western tradition and current scholarship, and are deployed in a manner which makes accusations of apriorism and proof-texting somewhat misplaced.

---

71   *Works*, 3, 78–79.

72   *Works*, 3, 81–82. Owen continues to list other actions which the Spirit performs in scripture which require personhood: teaching, comforting, ministering, assuring and so on.

God and the World of Creation

Before moving on from Owen's discussions of the doctrine of God proper, it is necessary at last to spend some time looking at how he articulates the basic relationship between God and his creation. Again, we should not expect originality here, but nor should we assume the truth of the mythology about this topic which has grown up around Reformed Orthodoxy in the secondary scholarship. Modern theology, under the impact of the anti-metaphysical tenets of Kantianism and its various philosophical offspring, has tended to disparage the era of Reformed Orthodoxy as one which saw the alleged kerygmatic or humanist or biblical (choose your own tendentious characterization!) theology of the Reformers subverted by an infatuation with, among other things, philosophical patterns of thought. More recent scholarship has attempted to overcome these kind of caricatures by both a rejection of the kind of anti-metaphysical and anachronistic a priori assumptions with which such studies have tended to operate, and by a careful attention to texts in context, which avoids the imposition of the concerns of later theological paradigms on the seventeenth century. This has led to a renewed concern with the metaphysics of God as articulated in Reformed Orthodoxy. Prominent among those in this field has been Utrecht philosopher-theologian, Antonie Vos, who, as we noted in Chapter1, has done significant work in demonstrating the dependence of Reformed theology upon medieval metaphysics right from its inception in the work of men such as John Calvin. Vos has argued consistently for a strong Scotist dimension to Reformed thought, particularly as this manifests itself in a commitment to what he has called *synchronic contingency*, a way of construing the relation between God and creation which allows for divine sovereignty and yet avoids both the Scylla of determinism and the Charybdis of the human autonomy.[73] While Vos's work has proved to be of immense value in opening up discussion of Reformed theology in a manner not tainted at the outset with the anti-metaphyisical prejudices of modern thought, my own view is that his case for the absolutely fundamental importance of Scotism, almost to the exclusion of other options, needs to balanced by acknowledgment of other influences and issues. For the historian, Vos's systematic interests place tremendous emphasis upon the one issue of synchronic contingency, while other philosophical commitments which would have been considered in the seventeenth century as more definitive of a Scotist position are perhaps not as emphasized. Thus, William Twisse, who would no doubt be regarded as Scotist in his construction of contingency, yet rejects the univocity of being and accepts the real distinction between existence and essence, positions which, in the Middle Ages and early modern period, were hallmarks of Thomism in distinction to Scotism, and which would have been considered as much more definitive of one's philosophical identity than the somewhat marginal issue of synchronic contingency. For this reason, I myself am convinced that, whatever the undoubted contemporary systematic gains to be made by emphasizing Scotist

---

73   See A Vos, 'De kern van de klassieke gereformeerde Theologie,' in *Kerk en Theologie* 47 (1996), 106–25; also 'Scholasticism and Reformation,' in Van Asselt and Dekker, *Reformation and Scholasticism*, 99–119; cf. Andreas Beck, 'Gisbertus Voetius (1589–1676): Basic Features of His Doctrine of God' in the same volume.

contingency in such a vigorous fashion, the historian needs to be open to a more flexible, eclectic model of metaphysical influence when approaching the Reformed Orthodox in order to produce a proper contextual and historical account. The Scotist model may have much to commend it systematically, and maybe even historically, but it still leaves us in danger of producing analyses which might be vulnerable to the criticism that they are too neat and tidy to provide an historical understanding of the subtleties, complexities, or even, one might say, the messiness of Reformed Orthodox theology, especially in its relationship to medieval antecedents.

A nuanced historical approach which is properly sympathetic to the work of Vos but which also seeks to do justice to the eclectic nature of Reformed Orthodoxy is thus offered by Sebastian Rehnman, the Swedish scholar, in his study of John Owen's theological prolegomena. He helpfully characterizes his subject as holding to a Scotistically modified Thomism.[74] Elsewhere, I have myself noted the strongly Thomistic nature of much of Owen's thought, particularly in terms of his understanding of the nature of God, of God-talk, and of the analogy between human concepts of justice and the divine attributes.[75] While this Thomistic dimension does not mark Owen out as distinctive, being typical of theological discourse which was sensitive to the revitalized Thomism of the Renaissance, Rehnman suggests that the specific source of Owen's own philosophical commitments would seem likely to be his education at Oxford, where he studied metaphysics under the vigorously anti-Pelagian though avowedly conformist Anglican thinker and future Bishop of Lincoln, Thomas Barlow, and also undoubtedly came into contact with the work of John Prideaux. Both men are, on occasion, mentioned explicitly in Owen's writings.[76] Both men were also stalwarts of the Established Church, reminding us that commitment to Reformed Orthodox views of God, grace and salvation were not the monopoly of the Puritan party in seventeenth-century England.[77]

Barlow, a Fellow of Queen's, Oxford, and lifelong friend of Owen, published his metaphysical lectures on God and we thus have fairly comprehensive knowledge of the kind of philosophical theology to which Owen would have been exposed as an undergraduate. In these lectures he discussed God as the object of metaphysics, and the means by which he was naturally knowable; in addition, he also offered a defence of the orthodox doctrine of God against the critique of the same by Conrad Vorstius.[78]

---

74   Rehnman, *Divine Discourse*, 62–64, 181.

75   See Trueman, 'John Owen's *Dissertation on Divine Justice*', *passim*.

76   For Barlow's thought in general, see *The Genuine Remains of that Learned Prelate Dr Thomas Barlow* (London, 1693). This posthumous collection of his works contains important statements of his vigorous Reformed Orthodoxy (for example, his letter to John Goodwin on particular redemption, *Genuine Remains*, 122–30) and his earnest commitment to conformity (for example, his letter to dissenters in his diocese, 641–643).

77   We could add to this list other names such as those of Archbishop Ussher and Daniel Featley. The tendency to conflate Reformed Orthodoxy, a broad and variegated confessional tradition, with narrow ecclesiological or political positions is an unfortunate one, leading to ahistorical claims belong made about *the* Reformed view of church and state – as if James I, George Gillespie, and John Owen – all Reformed by conviction – shared any significant common ground on the matter.

78   *Exercitationes aliquot metaphysicae de Deo* (Oxford, 1658).

Barlow is insistent that God can be discussed within the bounds of metaphysics, a point which he significantly supports with frequent reference to Thomas and others in the Thomist tradition.[79] This, of course, then allows him considerable scope for discussing the existence and the attributes of God from a metaphysical perspective, in other words a natural theology based upon ontology. If the content of Barlow's published exercises are a reliable guide to the kind of metaphysical theology which he taught his students at Oxford, then it is not surprising that we see significantly Thomistic patterns of thought in Owen's writings from an early stage when he faces off against the same Arminian and Socinian opponents as his Oxford friend and mentor. Thus, in his *Display of Arminianism* (1642), he will argue for the positive nature of being and thus for the necessity of a single, self-existent source of being for all other positive entities, including acts of the human will, within the created realm.[80] While Owen uses this to establish the dependence of creation and all creatures upon God, the basic presuppositions are the same as those undergirding Thomas's arguments for God's existence, and also as those found in Barlow.[81] Indeed, he is happy in the same work to refer to God variously as *Actus Simplex*, First Cause, and Pure Act, not to depersonalize God but to emphasize his absolute ontological priority over creation.[82] Of course, the commonplace nature of such argumentation and language makes it impossible to argue that Owen derived his thinking from Barlow; but the parallels in the teaching of his Oxford metaphysics mentor offer both a probable line of broad influence and an indication of the basic unoriginal, traditionary yet highly sophisticated nature of Owen's thinking.[83] We should also note at this point that the use of metaphysical argumentation such as this is not simply a rehashing of the medieval tradition but also involves the refraction of that tradition through the lens of Renaissance rhetoric: the argument from the consent of the nations, such a key element of Renaissance argumentation, is frequently deployed by Owen as a means of strengthening the metaphysical argumentation.[84]

The continuation and development of medieval metaphysical discussion, along with its technical conceptual vocabulary, was to prove a most useful phenomenon for the Reformed Orthodox, and Owen's exposure to this at Oxford was to bear significant fruit in his own theology. For example, take the issue of contingency. Owen's use of an established Thomistic argument from the nature of being to the necessity of all created being deriving its reality from one supreme entity, points

---

79　Barlow's main argument is found in *Exercitationes*, 91–117.

80　*Works*, 10, 120; cf. Trueman, *The Claims of Truth*, 118–19.

81　Thomas Aquinas, *Summa Theologiae*; Barlow, *Exercitationes*, 118–179 *passim*, especially 128–29, 158–62.

82　*Works*, 10, 20, 119, 120.

83　These notions, of course, undergird Aquinas's Five Ways and are thus commonplaces of subsequent Western theology: *ST* 1a.2.3.

84　For example, *Works* 10, 517–24; cf. Barlow, *Genuine Remains*, 524; *Exercitationes*, 123. A good example of the fusion of rhetoric and metaphysics in discussing the existence and attributes of God is provided by Stephen Charnock: see his lecture on the existence of God in *Several Discourses upon the Existence and Attributes of God* (London, 1682) 1–46, where frequent resort is made to various rhetorical tropes in order to reinforce the standard metaphysical arguments; see Muller, *PRRD* 3, 185–87.

clearly towards a basic determinism, one which is most conducive to what he sees as the Bible's teaching about the sovereignty of God, and for which he is happy to offer exegetical justification. Yet use of specifically metaphysical argumentation and medieval distinctions enables Owen to nuance this determinism in a way which represents a clear advance on the somewhat bald statements of earlier generations of Protestants.[85] Drawing on medieval distinctions, he discusses God's knowledge of entities as being either that of simple intelligence or that of vision. The former refers to the set of all possible entities which God could, according to his absolute power, choose to actualize; the latter refers to that set of entities which God has actually decided to actualize.[86] These concepts are important among other things for maintaining the ontological distance and distinction between God and creation: if it is arguable that Thomas's God is required by his very being to create a world external to himself, at least with this conceptual distinction within the divine knowledge, one can argue that God did not have to create *this particular world* and thus underline the difference between the absolute necessity of God's existence and the contingent necessity of the existence of any given creation. And this distinction fulfils a similar purpose within Owen's Reformed Orthodox construction of the Creator–creature relationship: created entities are contingent precisely because they do not have to exist in the way that God, the one *necessary* being has to exist.[87]

It is worth noting at this point the observation of Richard Muller that the Reformed Orthodox frequently used the traditionally more intellectualist, Thomistic terminology of the knowledge of simple intelligence/knowledge of vision in manner which represented the kind of voluntarist, Scotistic modification which we noted above as typical of the eclectic approach to metaphysics exhibited by the Reformed. Thus, in his *Vindiciae Evangelicae*, he accents the fact that the objects of the knowledge of vision are things past, present and future; the measure of it is the divine will; and the manner of it is free, grounded in an act of the will. To underline the correlation with Scotist thought at this point, Owen casually mentions that the *scientia visionis* is also called the *scientia libera*, a typically more Scotist term, though we must beware of exaggerating the difference between Thomists and Scotists on this point: as mentioned above, even for Thomas, *this particular world* is contingent and thus the result of an act of God's will.[88]

---

85   The literature on these issues in Luther and Calvin is vast, but two recent works are of particular help in this regard: for Luther and Lutheranism, see Robert Kolb, *Bound Choice, Election, and Wittenberg Theological Method: From Martin Luther to the Formula of Concord* (Grand Rapids: Eerdmans, 2005); and for Calvin, see the discussion in Chapter 4 ('Providence and Evil') in Paul Helm, *John Calvin's Ideas* (Oxford: Oxford University Press, 2004).

86   *Works*, 10, 23–24; 12, 127–28. By Owen's day, the terminology is a commonplace in Western theology: cf. Barlow, *Genuine Remains*, 569–70.

87   Owen does not use the precise term 'knowledge of simple intelligence' in the main text of *A Display of Arminianism*, though he does provide a marginal quotation from Aquinas which uses the term.

88   *Works*, 12, 128. Barlow also identifies the Thomist terms *scientia simplicis intelligentiae* and *scientia visionis* with the Scotist *scientia naturalis et necessaria* and *scientia libera* respectively, and grounds the latter on his free decree: see *Original Remains*, 570.

This conceptual distinction provides the basis for Owen's understanding of contingency. Ever since the publication of Luis de Molina's work on contingents in the sixteenth century, much debate had raged around the status of created entities vis-à-vis the divine willing.[89] Indeed, Molina's basic position had been seized upon with a vengeance by Arminians who had developed the concept in a manner which had led to views of God as being subject to succession, and, in the hands of certain figures such as the Socinian, Crellius, to the idea that God had dramatically restricted knowledge of the future. This view then manifested itself in works such as that of Biddle, where it was given a more straightforward biblicist form.[90] In particular, middle knowledge, as developed by the Jesuits and adopted by the Arminians had proved a focus of Reformed polemic. Developed by Molina from the work of Fonseca, this is a species of divine knowing between the knowledge of simple intelligence and the knowledge of vision which has as its object future conditionals or contingents which depend upon the free willing of human agents.[91]

Owen himself spends very little time at all in directly refuting middle knowledge. Indeed, in *Vindiciae Evangelicae*, he merely informs the reader at the relevant point that he does not intend to deal with 'that late figment' at this point.[92] By the time he was writing in the mid-seventeenth century, the pathways of Reformed critique were well-established: for example, a rejection of the idea that God could even hypothetically conceive of a world where he was not the determining cause of all that happened; an anti-Pelagian affirmation of the nature of human sinfulness such that, in no possible world would individuals turn to God without the intervention of prevenient and irresistible grace; and careful articulation of the nature of God's knowledge relative to future contingents.[93] He does, however, hint at considerable interest in the work of Jansenius and his followers, the major proponents of repristinated Augustinianism and opponents of the Jesuits, at one point even indicating an intention to write a major analysis of the history and theology of the Jansenist controversy.[94] The reason for the silence on middle knowledge may well be that Owen's major polemical focus is not so much classical Arminianism as Socinianism, compounded by his tendency, evidenced from his earliest work, to conflate the two groups and consider them as

---

89 See Luis de Molina, *On Divine Foreknowledge*, trans. A J Freddoso (Ithaca: Cornell University Press, 1988); on the history of this issue in general, see William Lane Craig, *The Problem of Divine Knowledge and Human Freedom from Aristotle to Suarez* (Leiden: Brill, 1980).

90 See Muller, *PRRD* 3, 120–21; *Twofold Catechism*, 14–21; Owen, *Works* 12, 115–40.

91 Muller, *PRRD* 3, 417–20; perhaps the most significant contemporary Reformed Orthodox response to this concept was that of William Twisse, *Dissertatio de scientia media tribus libris absoluta* (Arnhem, 1639).

92 *Works*, 12, 128.

93 For example *Synopsis purioris theologiae* XI. The notion was also well established in confessional literature by Owen's time: for example, The Bremen Consensus of 1595, Chapter 6; and the Westminster Confession of Faith (hereafter cited as WCF) (1547), Chapter 3.1.

94 *Works*, 12, 560; cf. his preface in Theophilus Gale, *The True Idea of Jansenisme* (London, 1669).

representing essentially the same moral problem: the desire to deny that human beings are subject to God's sovereignty and to the impact of sin.[95]

Given this, it is clear why the issue of contingency should be of particular importance to the Reformed, such as Owen, in their conflicts with Arminians and Socinians, because the question of contingency raised questions about the ontological status of created entities with reference to God, both in terms of His knowledge and His will. In his very first treatise, *A Display of Arminianism*, Owen argues that, given the absolute ontological and causal priority of God, and the origin of the created realm in an act of the divine willing, all objects of his knowledge – all created entities – are certain precisely because they depend utterly upon Him for their being. For this, he does not simply offer a metaphysical defence, but also presents scriptural verses: Acts 15:18; 2 Sam. 12:11–12; Job 1:21; Acts 4:28; Eph. 1:11. He is astute enough, of course, to see that the real problem with contingency is thus with the nature of the divine knowledge; and that it is the problem of divine knowledge of future contingents which creates the difficulty. If God knows now a future contingent, then that contingent is already predetermined, or else the divine knowledge is uncertain. This logical problem is hard to avoid; and Owen thus insinuates that 'in their most secret judgments' all Arminians are at one with the Socinians in making God's foreknowledge merely conjectural.[96] He then proceeds to outline his own understanding of God's knowledge of contingents: God knows all things (i) by knowledge of his decree; (ii) in their immediate causes (iii) in their own nature as future, but to God's infinite knowledge always present.[97]

This basic scheme receives more detailed elaboration in the later *Vindiciae Evangelicae*, where Owen responds to Biddle's litany of biblical texts which imply both God's ignorance of future events and the future's essentially open and undetermined nature. In responding, Owen divides things contingent into two classes: those things that are only contingent, and those that are also free. As examples of the first class he offers the case of a stone falling from a roof and killing a man: the fall of the stone was necessary, being pulled down by its own weight, but the man's death was contingent in that it is not necessarily included in the falling of a stone. As the prime example of the second class, he gives the soldier piercing Christ's side: both effect and cause were contingent, the soldier being able to will or not will the specific action.[98] He then argues as follows: God knows everything which can be known (that is, everything that is possible); everything which has a cause may be known, and indeed known as future by the one who knows the cause which determines the thing to exist at some future point in time. At this point, Owen makes a statement which is worth quoting in its entirety:

> Now, whatever is at any time was future; before it was, it was to be. If it had not been future, it had not now been. Its present performance is sufficient demonstration of the

---

95   *Works*, 10, 27; Trueman, *The Claims of Truth*, 19–23.

96   *Works*, 10, 22–28.

97   *Works*, 10, 28.

98   *Works*, 12, 129. Owen's distinction between the two types of contingency closely parallels that offered by Barlow in his disputed question on whether the prescience of God denies contingency: *Genuine Remains*, 571.

futurition it had before. I ask, then, whence it came to be future, – that that action was rather to be than a thousand others that were as possible as it? For instance, that the side of Christ should be pierced with a spear, when it was as possible, in the nature of the thing itself and of all secondary causes, that his head should be cut off. That, then, which gives any action a futurition is that determinate cause wherein it may be known, whereof we speak. Thus it may be said that the same thing that is contingent and determined, without the least appearance of contradiction, because it is not spoken with respect to the same things or causes.[99]

Owen thus solves the problem of contingency to his own satisfaction by making the issue one of the use of language: the same entity can be contingent relative to its immediate causes (for example, the decision of the soldier to pierce Christ's side) and yet be determined according to that which determined that it would have existence at some point in time. And this, in Owen's thinking, is the will of God himself. He is, however, clear that the language of freedom and contingency can still be applied to all things, even though determined by God's will, precisely because of the liberty they have with respect to secondary causes.[100]

One key Socinian objection to the position outlined by Owen is that future contingents, being future, do not presently have any existence or truth-value and thus cannot be objects of divine foreknowledge. The kind of question raised was familiar to Christian theology from at least the time of Boethius's *Consolation of Philosophy* where he grappled with the kind of problem raised in Aristotle's *On Interpretation* 8. Aristotle had raised the question of the truth-value of future tensed propositions, a problem which could be defused (as it was by Aristotle) by appeal to logic when confined to the area of linguistics but which took on dramatic metaphysical implications when connected to a God who, with infinite and perfect knowledge, by definition knew the truth-value of any given statement which was past, present or future relative to any given point in time. The problem for the Arminians, of course, was that this meant that God's knowledge of the future could thus appear as deterministic as any Reformed Orthodox formulation; and this is surely one of the reasons why radical Arminianism tended to blend into Socinianism: denial of God's exhaustive knowledge of the future, and the positing of succession in the divine knowing, solved the logical problem and preserved human freedom.

One avenue of response in the English context was offered by the mercurially brilliant autodidact, Richard Baxter in his *Catholick Theologie*.[101] Baxter is interesting for a number of reasons, not least because of his rather strident ecumenicity, built around a radical delimitation of what could and could not be known about God; and also because of his attempt to reconstruct Christian theology around a metaphysics

---

99   *Works*, 12, 130.

100   *Works*, 12, 131. Of course, it might be objected that Owen is playing here with words; but he makes it clear that, given the choice of a completely autonomous human free will creation or a determining Deity, he would rather opt for the latter 'ten thousand times' before he would countenance the former: *Works* 12, 132.

101   *Richard Baxter's Catholick Theologie: Plain, Pure, Peaceable: for Pacification of the Dogmaticall Word-Warriors* (London, 1675). For a discussion of Baxter on divine knowledge, see Muller, *PRRD* 3, 414–17.

borrowed from the brilliant and controversial Renaissance philosopher, Tommaso Campanella, who drew heavily on the Neoplatonic tradition to offer a view of reality which divided being into three parts, power, wisdom and love or will.[102] Baxter applies this to the knowledge of God, arguing not for a threefold knowledge along the lines of simple/necessary, middle knowledge, and vision/free but rather power, wisdom, and will: according to his power, God knows all possibles; according to his wisdom, he knows all things that are fit to be willed; and according to his will, he knows all things that he will will. In the case of things not yet existent but future, Baxter is adamant that we need to understand that it is God himself, in his power, wisdom, and will, who is the object of God's knowledge.[103] When it comes therefore, to the problems associated with future contingents, Baxter offers two lines of particularly significant argument: first, future entities have no existence and thus they cannot be the cause of God's knowledge of them, i.e., he can know that they will be at some point in time, but this is not because they will be at some point in time. Thus, the priority of God's knowledge over created being is maintained.[104] Second, he presses the radical difference between divine and human knowing in such a way as to bring into serious question the way in which the issue of future contingency has been discussed in terms of Aristotle's conundrum regarding the truth value of future propositional statements. According to Baxter, propositions are a function of human minds, not the divine mind: God is simple and transcendent and does not think in terms of propositions; sure, he knows propositions, because he knows human beings as knowing them; but he does not think in such terms and is, crucially, therefore, not subject to the same kind of logical problems which beset the human mind when asking questions such as those regarding the truth value of future propositions.[105] The bottom line for Baxter is that distinctions in divine knowing can be useful for finite humans, but divine simplicity demands that these are used as no more than subordinate heuristic devices and must not be allowed to take on a life of their own and generate unnecessary logical (and ontological) problems.[106]

---

102 See Carl R Trueman, 'A Small Step Towards Rationalism: the Impact of the Metaphysics of Tommaso Campanella on the Theology of Richard Baxter' in Trueman and Clark (ed) *Protestant Scholasticism*, 147–64.

103 *Catholick Theologie*, I.iv.40–43. He then proceeds to dismiss the standard terminology thus: 'From what is said, you may see, that the Common School distinction of all Gods knowledge, into *scientia simplicis intelligentiae*, and *purae visionis*, is not accurate, and the terms too arbitrary and dark to notifie the thing intended; and that the *scientia media* added doth not mend the matter.' *Catholick Theologie* I.iv.45.

104 '1. Futurity is nothing; and Nothing hath no Cause. 2. Nothing is eternally in God but God: and God hath no Cause nor is an Effect. 3. At least that which is Nothing cannot be the Cause of God. 4. It is not true that God foreknoweth things, *because* they will be, but only that he foreknoweth *that* they will be.' *Catholick Theologie* I.v.85.

105 *Catholick Theologie*, I.v.74–78;

106 'The feigning God to have in himself so many acts of knowledge, *really distinct*, and to lye in *such an order*, is intolerable, seeing God is most simple. But by extrinsecal denomination, his Knowledge may by us, through our weakness and necessity, be distinguished according to its respect to diversity of objects, by inadequate conceptions: But on that pretence to feign so many *needless distributions*, is profane.' *Catholick Theologie*, I.xii.262.

Owen's solution is somewhat different, running along typical Reformed Orthodox tracks and offering a less convoluted defence of divine prescience. He does not opt for the solution in terms of God's own way of knowing; instead, he focuses upon the logical properties of statements in terms of their referentiality. He established this referentiality by pointing to scripture: the Bible contains determinate predictions of future contingent events; therefore, such statements must be susceptible of a truth–value prior to their realization (and, implicitly, God must know their truth value and thus have them as objects of his knowledge). Once he has made this basic point, the logical arguments are straightforward: all propositions making a truth claim must be either true or false; and such future propositions must be true or false from eternity. In this way, the straightforward appeal to biblical prophecy combines with basic logic to circumvent the need for sophisticated metaphysical arguments about whether future contingents have a reality which allows them to be objects of knowledge. This is important: the Reformed commitment to God's knowledge of future contingents is not exclusively, or even primarily, a metaphysical one. Rather, it is rooted in the statements of scripture, with the theologian then having the task of elaborating the necessary ontological framework and logical consequences of such statements. This is not autonomous metaphysics and logic gone mad; rather, it is them being used to explain how and why these scriptural statements can be said to be coherent and what they can be said to imply.[107]

Of course, what is being expounded in all this discussion of contingency and divine foreknowledge is a metaphysical foundation for making sense of the Bible's teaching on divine sovereignty and human freedom. While, for Aristotle, the discussion of the truth value of future tense propositions was an interesting logical conundrum, for Owen (as for the Reformed in general; indeed, for medieval Catholics, for Arminians, and for Socinians as well) the issue was one raised by the text of scripture and motivated by deep religious concerns for understanding the nature of God and his creation. Owen's solution, far from being the kind of determinist synthesis and harsh hyperlogical departure from earlier Christian teaching which some have considered it to be, is, in fact, representative of a continuing anti-Pelagian tradition in the seventeenth century, whose religious roots go right back to Paul and whose theological and philosophical roots lie in the work of Augustine and then of the great medieval schoolmen such as Aquinas and Scotus. The result is, one might say, a theological framework for anti-Pelagianism, arising directly out of an understanding of the ontological relationship which exists between the Creator and his creation. If all events are foreknown and foreordained by God, even if contingent in terms of their secondary causality, then predestination, whether election to glory or reprobation to damnation, must also come under that category.

There is another side to this particular coin, of course, and that is the economic, connecting as it does to the nature of human sin and, particularly, to the covenantal identity of Adam and of Christ. It is to this that we shall turn in the next chapter.

---

107 *Works*, 12, 139–40. Barlow also uses the basic biblical premise of scripture's prophecies regarding future contingents as the basis for asserting God's knowledge of the same: *Genuine Remains*, 572–73. Cf. Turretin, who also prioritises the biblical testimony as his basic premise: *Institutes* 3.12.11–14.

A Concluding Postscript

As a final note to Owen's articulation of Reformed Orthodoxy on the topic of God in refutation of Socinian revisions, it is worth quoting the first seven questions from his satirical catechism, appended at the end of *Vindiciae Evangelicae*, and drawn from inferences from the work of John Biddle:

> **Qu. 1:** What is God?
> **Ans.** God is a spirit, that hath a bodily shape, eyes, ears, hands, feet, like to us.
> **Qu. 2:** Where is this God?
> **Ans.** In a certain place in heaven, upon a throne, where a man may see from his right hand to his left.
> **Qu. 3:** Doth he ever move out of that place?
> **Ans.** I cannot tell what he doth ordinarily, but he hath formerly come down sometimes upon the earth.
> **Qu. 4:** What doth he do in there in that place?
> **Ans.** Among other things, he conjectures at what men will do here below.
> **Qu. 5:** Doth he, then, not know what we do?
> **Ans.** He doth know what we have done, but not what we will do.
> **Qu. 6:** What frame is he upon his knowledge and conjecture?
> **Ans.** Sometimes he is afraid, sometimes grieved, sometimes joyful, and sometimes troubled.
> **Qu. 7:** What peace and comfort can I have in committing myself to his providence, if he knows not what will befall me tomorrow?
> **Ans.** What is that to me? See you to that.[108]

'What is that to me? See you to that.' With this biting punchline, Owen makes the point with his characteristic wit: theology was a complicated business, and Owen was among the most able men in the seventeenth century when it came to bringing the riches of the Western tradition, theological and philosophical, to bear on its most subtle problems; but the issues at stake when it came to the doctrine of God had profound pastoral implications; and the Arminian and Socinian proposals were not simply intellectually disastrous; they were also disastrous for the economy of salvation, and thus for Christian pastoral practice, and for the experience and aspirations of the ordinary believer as well. Thus, it is now necessary to move on from discussing God and his relationship to creation in general to the specifics of how Owen understands the human condition and the economy of salvation which the Trinitarian God establishes to bring his people to glory.

---

108 *Works*, 12, 588.

Chapter 3

Divine Covenants and Catholic Christology

Introduction

If Owen's doctrine of God is remarkable in the main because it is so unremarkable, merely being in large part a repristination of much that had gone before in patristic and medieval theology, albeit in the context of rather intense and specific contemporary polemics and challenges, the details of his understanding of God's relationship with humanity and of his Christology do represent distinct developments from the earlier established patterns. This is not to say at the outset that Reformed Orthodox thinking in these areas represents in any sense an absolute break with the past. On the contrary, some of the conceptual innovations which Reformed theology introduces (such as the covenant of works) have close structural and functional parallels in established theological systems; while others represent attempts to resolve problems created either by those prior systems or by the need to correct those systems in the light of specific Protestant insights. Of the latter kind, as we shall see, is the notion of the covenant of redemption between Father and Son as being the basis of the Son's mediation.

Central to all of this is the notion of *covenant*, a concept and a term which became increasingly significant for Reformed Protestantism in the later sixteenth and seventeenth centuries. For Owen, as for many contemporaries, covenant is a remarkably useful term: it facilitates articulation of the basically relational nature of theology, as something which is to be considered in terms of God's relation with his creation; it allows for the bridging of the ontological chasm that exists between an infinite, self-existent Creator and a finite, dependent creation; and it picks up terminology that reflects a basic biblical motif. For all of these reasons, covenant or federal theology proved remarkably attractive to the Reformed.

Before the Fall: Natural Theology

Typical of the Reformed Orthodox, Owen's major discussion of theology as it existed in creation prior to Adam's fall is critical if one is to understand other areas of his theology, such as Christology, soteriology and so on. That Owen is specific that the second person of the Trinity becomes Incarnate only on account of the need to deal with the problems generated by Adam's fall, renders it crucial to understand the exact nature of Adam's relationship to God before the Fall, indeed,

Adam's *theology* before the Fall. The major discussion of this occurs in his Latin treatise, *Theologoumena Pantodapa*, the purpose of which is to outline the varying dispensations of God's revelation to his creatures. Thus, the overall point of Owen's discussion is epistemological; and, in dealing with the world before the Fall, Owen utilizes a series of basic ideas which are typical of the Reformed Orthodox tradition in distinguishing between the various types of natural theology, the instruments by which this theology is grasped, and how these connect to the free action of God in creation. Central to this is the notion of the covenant of works, but the discussion is not restricted to this point for one simple reason: the covenant is an act of condescension on God's part and thus not necessary even upon the supposition of God's free act of creation.

In the state of unfallen nature, Owen sees Adam as possessing a knowledge of God which can be characterized in a very particular sense as natural. It is still supernatural in its origin, in that it depends entirely upon God's revelation of himself and thus on his initiative, but it is natural in the sense that it was part of Adam and of the created realm from the very beginning. This natural theology is also itself to be nuanced, and Owen does this using two Greek terms of classical/patristic vintage. Adam's theology is *endiathetos*, or *internal*, but not entirely *emphytos*, or *innate*.[1] The use of the term *endiathetos* is particularly interesting as this has strong connotations of the second person of the Trinity, especially given its use in patristic discussion. By Owen's time, the word had become an accepted part of Reformed Orthodox idiom when discussing theology, often contrasted with theology that was *prophorikos*, again a patristic term, this time referring to theology that is built on external revelation.[2]

Owen connects this internal theology to his notion of illumination: God himself gives Adam an intrinsic light, or 'spiritual wisdom' so that he can understand God as Creator, Lawgiver, Ruler, and Rewarder; but he also reveals himself in an external fashion in the sacramental command relative to the Tree, and required of Adam that he increase his knowledge on a daily basis by considering his works. This was then to issue a response of obedience in accordance with the stipulations of the covenant of works.[3] Adam's life was thus in a sense to be one of increasing perfection, or, perhaps better, increasing maturity, even though he was pure from his very creation.[4] What is important to note here is that this natural theology is actually supernatural in terms of its causal ground (the revelation of God), and only 'natural' in the sense that it is Adam as unfallen who has access to this knowledge by natural means: the light God has implanted in him used to reflect upon God's commands and actions in the wider world. This is not natural theology in the Enlightenment sense of theology rooted in some kind of autonomous human access to God, and to be opposed to revealed

---

1   'In eo statu theologia erat *endiathetos* et naturalis: non tamen usquequaque *emphytos*.' *Works* 17, 39.

2   See M Muhl, 'Der *logos endiathetos* und *prophorikos* von der alteren Stoa bis zur Synode von Sirmium 351, '*Archiv für Begriffsgeschichte* 7 (1962), 7–56. For Reformed use of the terms, see *Synopsis purioris theologiae* I.xv.

3   *Works*, 17, 39.

4   Cf. *Synopsis purioris theologiae* XIII.vi.

theology; it is revealed theology rooted in the ongoing, free activity of God, and it is inappropriate to impose later categories of critique upon it. Owen himself uses the term *natural*, but explains exactly what he means by it: he does not use the term to imply that the light of which he speaks was a necessary, structural part of being human; but he argues that it can be called natural because it relates to the original righteousness which Adam possessed and the end for which he was designed. It is thus not an essential property of humanity, considered in the abstract, but something nonetheless with which Adam was created.[5] Elsewhere, in his 1674 work on the Holy Spirit, Owen argues that Adam can be considered in two ways: naturally, in terms of those elements essentially constitutive of human nature; and morally, in terms of principles of obedience, the law given to him, and the end proposed.[6] Both are the work of the Holy Spirit, as the divine agent in works *ad extra*. The moral qualities are then connected to three specific capacities given to Adam by the Holy Spirit: an ability to discern the will of God; a free and uncoerced disposition to legal duties; and a psychological readiness for doing good and abstaining from sin. This uprightness of nature, Owen stresses, is logically separable from the essential faculties of the human soul but was in fact concreated with them. Thus, they were neither superadded or infused into Adam at creation.[7]

The background to Owen's argument at this juncture is the Reformed rejection of the medieval notion of Adam as created *in puris naturalibus*.[8] The point here is not that the Reformed reject the idea that humanity cannot be conceived as consisting solely in terms of essential properties, without reference to moral categories (a point which was not disputed), but whether humans *as created by God* were in fact such beings, which Owen clearly denies in the passage referred to directly above. To answer in the affirmative would be to give significant ground to an understanding of human nature which came to be a basic element in the semi-Pelagian anthropology of certain late medieval trajectories of theology.[9] Turretin offers a thorough critique of this position in his *Institutes*, noting that such a view of Adam as created *in puris naturalibus* is contradicted by the facts that: he was created in the image of God; he was made to glorify God; he can never be indifferent to righteousness or sin; and the notion of pure nature is incoherent as an actual reality.[10]

The point in Owen connects very closely to notions of original righteousness in Adam as being made in the image of God, consisting of wisdom, righteousness and holiness. In this context, Owen speaks of the law as being the *verbum endiatheton* and as being *emphytos*, thus making explicit the moral structure and obligation which natural theology placed upon Adam.[11] Reformed discussions such as that of

---

5   *Works*, 17, 40; cf. Turretin's distinctions regarding the use of the term *natural* in *Institutes* 5.IX.ii.

6   *Works*, 3, 100.

7   *Works*, 3, 102.

8   Owen's final sentence makes it clear that he is consciously writing against this background: 'Sed de hisce contra *pontificios*, alibi satis superque disputatum est.' *Works*, 17, 40.

9   See Oberman, *Harvest*, 47–50.

10   *Institutes* 5.IX.v.

11   *Works*, 17, 41–42.

Owen on these issues, thus stress that such elements of wisdom and righteousness are not, in the way in which they existed in Adam before the Fall, essential properties of humanity, but that Adam never existed without them. In so doing, not only is the alleged semi-Pelagianism of certain patristic and late medieval conceptions avoided, but a structural point is introduced which corresponds to medieval notions of the *donum superadditum* as a means of preserving the radical distinction between the creature and the Creator and thus safeguarding against Pelagianism even before the Fall.

The Reformed connection to notions of a *donum superadditum* is a point of some interest, especially given the fact that it highlights the critical nature of the relationship between Reformed Orthodoxy and medieval Catholic theology: Reformed theology frequently has to respond to the same problems as medieval theology, even if its answers are often very different; and the fact that both medieval anti-Pelagian theology and Reformed Orthodoxy operate within the same basic Augustinian parameters, the answers given by the latter often contain structural parallels to those of the former. Turretin's discussion of whether original righteousness is supernatural or natural, for example, stresses in opposition to Catholic theology (as epitomized by Bellarmine) that Adam's righteousness in creation is natural, not supernatural. This is because he regards the Catholic position, whereby the supernatural righteousness serves to perfect and stabilize nature, as reflecting an inadequate understanding of the intellectual and moral integrity of humanity in the state of creation.[12] Yet he still offers a position which, as noted above, makes the righteousness more than an essential property of human nature, in the strict sense of the word.[13] The same applies to Owen, who stands in the same tradition of emphasizing that natural theology is yet not natural to humanity in the sense that is not constitutive of human nature and logically separable from it in the abstract.

The whole notion of such creation of humanity *in puris naturalibus* is, of course, excluded by various of Owen's other doctrinal commitments. First, Owen's mature position on the nature of divine justice means that any relationship between God and a rational creature is going to be defined in large part by the non-negotiable nature of the way in which God, as creator, must relate to his creation: law, as we have noted, is an egress of God's being and reflects that being in relation to creation. Thus, any rational creature must necessarily exist in a state of moral obligation to God as Creator, a moral obligation which will have a certain legal content which cannot be a matter of simple divine whim; it has to embody those elements such as obedience which reflect the ontological Creator–creature distinction and relationship which must necessarily exist once God has acted to create.

The second point which precludes any notion of the creation of Adam *in puris naturalibus* is Owen's belief that Adam is designed for a supernatural end to which his natural endowments were not adequate. For the Reformed such as Owen the distance between Creator and creature was so great that the idea that human obedience could, in itself, merit an eternal reward was simply inconceivable. One part of Owen's answer to this problem is the original righteousness which was

---

12   *Institutes*, 5.XI.v.
13   *Institutes*, 5.XI.xvi.

outlined above and which, on occasion, he can refer to as being supernatural.[14] Just as significant, however, is Owen's articulation of a covenant of works between God and Adam which serves to bridge the distance between the two and make eternal reward possible on the basis of covenantal obedience.

The Covenant of Works

By Owen's day, the concept of a pre-Fall covenant arrangement between God and Adam in the Garden of Eden was a commonplace of Reformed theology, particularly in the British tradition.[15] Indeed, the idea enjoyed confessional status in the Westminster Confession and Catechisms, though the Westminster divines used a number of terms to refer to the idea.[16] Thus, when Owen comes to use the idea, he stands once again against the backdrop of decades of significant doctrinal reflection, and must therefore be set within that traditionary context.

The idea of the covenant of works is interesting in part because scripture itself does not apply the term *covenant* to the arrangement with Adam; yet to assume that its use in Reformed Orthodoxy is therefore the result either of Procustean dogmatic eisegesis or of bald proof-texting or of a brutal imposition of a legalistic or commercial doctrine of God on creation would be wrong. Underlying the seventeenth-century articulation of the concept is a world of careful linguistic and theological reflection. In this context, one of the most useful discussions of covenant language in the seventeenth century is provided by the pen of Patrick Gillespie, a good friend of John Owen and brother of the more famous George, the youngest and one of the

---

14 'That habitual grace and original righteousness wherewith he was invested was in a manner due unto him for the obtaining of that supernatural end whereunto he was created. A universal rectitude of all the faculties of his soul, advanced by supernatural graces, enabling him to the performance of those duties whereunto they were acquired, is that which we call the innocency of our first parents.' *Works* 10, 85. The use of the term *supernatural* here may be the result of this quotation being from Owen's earliest published work, *A Display of Arminianism* (1642) and thus an example of youthful imprecision; or it could be a deliberate contrast with the bare constitutive elements of human nature; but the choice of word is not of overall dogmatic significance. Cf. *Works* 3, 102, where Owen specifically rejects the adjective *supernatural* with regard to these moral endowments.

15 There is substantial controversial secondary literature on the origins and development of covenant theology in general, and of the covenant of works in particular: see especially: Lyle D Bierma, *German Calvinism in the Confessional Age* (Grand Rapids: Baker, 1996); R Scott Clark, *Caspar Olevian and the Substance of the Covenant* (Edinburgh: Rutherford House, 2005) R W A Letham, 'The *Foedus Operum*: Some Factors Accounting for Its Development,' *SCJ* 14 (1983), 457–67; Richard A Muller, 'The Covenant of Works and the Stability of Divine Law in Seventeenth-Century Reformed Orthodoxy: A Study in the Theology of Herman Witsius and Wilhelmus A Brakel,' in *idem*, *After Calvin*, 175–89; Willem J Van Asselt, 'The Doctrine of the Abrogations in the Federal Theology of Johannes Cocceius (1603–1669)', *Calvin Theological Journal* 29 (1994), 101–16; *idem*, *The Federal Theology of Johannes Cocceius* (Leiden: Brill, 2001).

16 For example, WC F 7.2 ('covenant of works'); Larger Catechism 20 ('covenant of life'), 30 ('covenant of works'); Shorter Catechism 12 ('covenant of life').

most brilliant delegates to the Westminster Assembly. Patrick Gillespie wrote a five-volume work on covenant theology, two volumes of which survive: *The Ark of the Testament Opened* (London, 1661), a treatise on the covenant of grace; and *The Ark of the Covenant Opened* (London, 1677) on the covenant of redemption.

Gillespie's *The Ark of the Testament Opened* lays out in clear fashion much of the basic linguistic and conceptual groundwork for the discussion of covenant in Reformed Orthodoxy, particularly in Chapter 2, 'Of Covenants in Generall,' where the author engages in significant discussion of the linguistic issues surrounding the Hebrew word *berith* and its cognates. Here, Gillespie shows a clear understanding of the debates concerning the origins of the Hebrew term,[17] and of the different rites and ritual practices associated with the idea of covenant.[18] He also offers five elements which must be present in order for an arrangement to be of a covenantal nature: there must be two or more parties; they must involve agreement; there must be conditions; these conditions must be mutually binding; they must be mutually beneficial; and they must be strictly binding, to the extent that any breach of covenant is tantamount to a breach of the law of God.[19] In this context, Gillespie argues that covenants are sacred, irrevocable, grounds of absolute assurance of the fidelity of the parties involved vis-à-vis the covenant stipulations, utterly binding to the extent that those who break covenant know no moral bounds, and inviolable according to the law of nature.[20]

What is significant about this preliminary discussion of covenants in general is the appreciation which Gillespie exhibits for nuance and sophistication within the concept. *Pace* the criticism of a writer such as James B Torrance, who regards federal theologians as making the simplistic mistake of confusing the biblical notion of covenant with the commercial notion of a contract, Gillespie (and he is not untypical of the Reformed Orthodox tradition at this point) shows clearly that he understands the term covenant to be both linguistically and conceptually complex. Thus, while arguing that all covenants involve some sort of condition and mutual obligation, he yet recognizes that some covenants are between equals, others are between a superior and an inferior; some involve explicit conditions, other implicit; some antecedent conditions, others consequent; some are meritorious, some gratuitous; some of justice, some of grace.[21] Then there are different types of covenant in terms of substance: civil, concerning social, political or commercial arrangements between parties; sacred, pertaining to religious matters; and mixed, which are partly religious and partly civil in the way they relate to both heavenly and earthly matters.[22] And the list goes on: Gillespie argues that covenants can be further distinguished according to extent, annexes and adjuncts, nature, terms and conditions, natural influences,

---

17   *The Ark of the Testament*, 43–45.
18   *The Ark of the Testament*, 43–49.
19   *The Ark of the Testament*, 49–51.
20   *The Ark of the Testament*, 52–59.
21   *The Ark of the Testament*, 50.
22   *The Ark of the Covenant*, 63.

predominant influences (for example justice or grace), scope and ends, and divine approbation.[23]

Such discussion as that of Gillespie is significant for demonstrating the linguistic and conceptual nuance of the Reformed Orthodox in discussing covenant and its various uses in the Bible and elsewhere, and is typical in the seventeenth century, as shown, for example, by similar sections in earlier works by John Ball and Thomas Blake. Ball in particular stands as another example of such linguistic care and exegetical sensitivity: his work on the covenant of grace offers a six page preliminary chapter analyzing the use of *berith* and its cognates in scripture, along with careful comparison to the Septuagint translation, the Syriac, and the textual work of Erasmus and Beza. In other words, Ball, in typical Reformed fashion, analyzed the terminology using the best textual and linguistic tools available at the time; and it is very clear from Ball that the Reformed understood *covenant* to be a term which could be used in a variety of ways. It could be conditional or unconditional; it could refer to an arrangement between equals or between a superior and an inferior; it could operate on strictly commercial or meritorious bases and as operating upon congruently agreed terms of merit.[24] The idea that one could have posed a question as blunt as that of asking whether the Reformed believed in 'covenant or contract?' and expect to have been taken at all seriously is absurd. Such a question is not simply anachronistic; it does not even begin to take account of the complexity, linguistic and otherwise, of Orthodox discussion.[25]

The identification of the arrangement in Eden with a covenant typically depends upon four things: that there are two parties to the arrangement (God and Adam); that there is an obligation imposed upon Adam; that there is a promised reward annexed to the fulfillment of this obligation; and that Adam acts in a representative capacity for the whole human race. This latter is critical for understanding the theological impulse behind the idea which is derived far more from the implications of the Adam–Christ parallel in Romans 5 than from a bald reading of Genesis 1–3.[26] Underlying the whole is an acknowledgement of divine condescension in the arrangement: God is beholden to no creature, and any arrangement which places him in the creature's debt requires an act of condescension on his part.[27]

Having said this, the element of divine condescension in establishing the covenant as something beyond that required by mere natural relation does point to God's freedom in terms of both the covenant's origin in divine *fiat* and its particular stipulations and promise with respect to Adam.[28] This is certainly the case with Owen. First, he sets the covenant of works up as the structure which determines the nature

---

23 *The Ark of the Testament*, 63–74.

24 Ball, *A Treatise of the Covenant of Grace*; cf. Thomas Blake, *Vindiciae Foederis: A Treatise of the Covenant of Works and of the Covenant of Grace* (London, 1658), 1–10.

25 See James B Torrance, 'Covenant or Contract? A Study of the Theological Background of Worship in Seventeenth-Century Scotland', *Scottish Journal of Theology* 23 (1970), 51–76.

26 Ball, *A Treatise*, 11; cf. Ussher, *Body of Divinitie*, 127; *Westminster Annotations* (1645) on Rom. 5:12; also *Synopsis purioris theologiae* XIV.v.

27 Thomas Watson, *A Body of Practical Divinity* (London, 1692), 75.

28 Cf. Herman Witsius, *Economy of the Covenants* I.xi.

of Adam's obedience;[29] then he uses the covenant of works as a means of explaining the way in which natural endowments and the obedience based thereon was able to achieve a supernatural end. Though the theology on which it was based was natural, in the special manner outlined above, yet the covenant itself (and implicitly therefore its terms) was established by a most free act of God (Owen using the superlative) which therefore established the terms of merit and reward.[30]

Owen does not expand upon this latter point at any length in his works, but given his comments about condescension, and the Christological counterpoint which we shall discuss below, whereby the covenant of redemption determines the nature of Christ's death as sacrifice, it is clear that he is assuming the kind of position articulated by, among others. Francis Turretin. In his *Institutes*, Turretin argues the following regarding the covenant of works (or nature, as he prefers to call it): it is not a covenant in a strict sense, in that it is not a mutual pact between equals. As we have noted, the Reformed Orthodox are aware that the term *covenant* is not used univocally either in scripture or in the wider world, and that, when used of God and Adam, it involves deep condescension on God's part.[31] In this context, Turretin underscores the freedom of God by stressing that, even if Adam had remained fully obedient, the Lord would not have been obliged, outside of the context of specific covenant determination, to give any reward to that obedience.[32]

This is a point of some diversity within the Reformed tradition, as exemplified by Herman Witsius in his *Economy of the Covenants between God and Man* (1693). Witsius is quite clear that God owes nothing to his creatures on the basis both of his status as their creator and his infinite exaltation above his creation.[33] Like Turretin, he is also clear that Adam had no claim on his Creator prior to, or outwith, the covenant of works;[34] but Witsius goes on to argue that the nature of God means that it would have been a contradiction of his own being to act in certain ways. Thus, for example, it is impossible to conceive of a world where God would have allowed a creature who had been obedient and faithful simply to sink back into a state of non-existence because this would contradict his goodness and, quite possibly, his justice, a position which is clearly at odds with the view of, for example, David Dickson on the same point.[35] Significantly, Witsius presents his arguments in explicit opposition to the

---

29 *Works* 17, 39.

30 'Quamvis ideo natura sua, usumque et finem quod attinet, plane supernaturale fuerit (nam ut Deo homo, secundum foedus praemium aeternum pollicitans, obediret, ex Dei liberrima erat consitutione; tamen quia *endiatheton kai emphyton*, id ei naturale fuisse dicimus).' *Works* 17, 40.

31 *Institutes,* 8.III.i. It is important to note here that, while the Reformed Orthodox will routinely use language of *grace* when referring to this condescension, this is to be understood not in a redemptive sense, for there could be no redemption where there is nothing to be redeemed before the Fall, but simply as underlining God's freedom in the establishment of the covenant.

32 *Institutes,* 8.III.ii.

33 *Economy*, trans. W. Crookshank (2 vols), repr. Den Dulk Foundation, 1990, I.4.11.

34 *Economy*, I.1.14.

35 *Economy*, I.4.14–23 (Crookshank I, 77–82). Cf. with Dickson, *Therapeutica Sacra* I.5, 74.

extreme theological voluntarism of William Twisse, whose own doctrine of God, as noted above, was deeply indebted to Duns Scotus; thus one can read Witsius's own argument at this point as representing a more intellectualist stream within Reformed theology than that of his chosen opponent. Given Owen's own tendency towards intellectualism, and especially his opposition to Twisse on the issue of divine justice, it is reasonable to assume he would side somewhat closer to Witsius than to Dickson or Turretin on this precise point. Nevertheless, we must beware of accentuating the differences between the two approaches in a manner which might imply that this is a confessionally significant disgreement: both are represented within the bounds of the Reformed confessional community, and so this is an intra-confessional matter; it also reflects the eclectic origins of Reformed Orthodoxy in both the Thomist and Scotist streams of late medieval thought; and the central point – that the reward of eternal life in the covenant of works is the result of God's goodness in establishing a covenant, not the absolute priority and intrinsic merit of human works considered in the abstract – is the common ground upon which such confessional consensus can be maintained.

Turretin continues by arguing that the covenant involves the imposition of a law upon Adam and the promise of a reward for obedience.[36] The key element then becomes the nature of the merit which Adam can earn within the context of the covenant: we know that obedience to the Creator, considered purely in itself, is both required of human beings, as creatures, and incapable of earning eternal life; that is why a covenant of condescension is necessary; yet, once the covenant has been established through divine condescension, Adam has a legal right to the reward promised by that covenant. In other words, he is able to claim eternal reward not because of any intrinsic merit but because of covenantally determined merit. This allows Turretin to call the covenant both gratuitous (from God's standpoint in terms of his condescension), but also absolute (from Adam's standpoint in terms of the reward that is covenantally attached to his obedience; a debt of fidelity, as Turretin calls it).[37]

This view of legal, covenantal merit has obvious similarities with the notion of congruent merit as developed in the late Middle Ages in the *via moderna*. There, the notion was tied to a semi-Pelagian structure of salvation and connected to other parallel notions, such as the creation of Adam *in puris naturalibus* and the pactum principle *to the one who does what is in them, God does not deny grace*. In the hands of the Reformed, the notion is used to safeguard the radical difference between Creator and creature, and the notion that the Creator cannot, in any absolute, unqualified sense, ever be a debtor to his creatures. In other words, in the hands of Turretin, Owen, Witsius and company, it becomes a vital part of an anti-Pelagian, Protestant soteriology.

One further aspect of the covenant with Adam which is of central importance to the Reformed is its representative nature. Adam stands not simply as private individual but, as the first human being, he is also the representative of the whole race which is to follow. Turretin expresses this representative relationship as being

36 *Institutes*, 8.III.iii–xiv.
37 *Institutes*, 8.III,xvi.

twofold: a natural one, on the grounds that all subsequent humanity is biologically connected to Adam as the father of the race; and forensic, rooted in the specific covenant relation which establishes Adam as the legal representative of humanity.[38] This representative relation is, interestingly enough, not rooted so much in the exegesis of Genesis, although it would surely be arguable that the exclusion of Adam and Eve, and thus their posterity, from Eden, and the advent of death for all humanity in the wake of their sin, would provide a basis for some basic notion of federal representation in Adam. In fact, however, the relation is in large part an inference from Paul's teaching on sin in Rom. 5. For example, in *A Display of Arminianism*, Owen makes it very clear that this passage is the key to understanding the relation that exists between Adam's sin and all subsequent humanity:

> The scripture is clear that the sin of Adam is the sin of us all, not only by propagation and communication ... but also by an imputation of his actual transgression unto us all, his singular disobedience being by this means ours. The grounds of this imputation ... may be all reduced to his being a common person and head of all our nature; which investeth us with a double interest in his demerits, whilst so he was: 1. As we were then in him and parts of him; 2. As he sustained the place of our whole nature in the covenant God made with him; both which, even according to the exigence of God's justice, require that his transgression be also accounted ours. As St Paul is plain, not only that 'by one man's disobedience many were made sinners,' Rom 5:19, by the derivation of a corrupted nature, but also that 'by one man's offence judgment came upon all,' verse 18.[39]

Humanity sinned in Adam, Owen continues, because 'his transgression in God's estimation is accounted ours' In other words, the terms of the covenant of works are such that, when Adam disobeys, the whole of humanity is placed in a position of having sinned against God. Thus, Romans 5 provides a key piece of the puzzle with regards to the covenant of works and, of course, in the parallel which Paul there draw between Adam and Christ, we can see that the Reformed understanding of the covenant of works must have significant implications for the construction of the way whereby the problem of sin, or covenantal transgression, can be rectified.

The Post-Fall Situation

With Adam having broken the covenant of works, human beings are is now faced with the reality of the vast distance between God and humanity which the condescension involved in the covenant of works had been designed to overcome. They thus had the status of covenant breakers, a point not without significance: the covenant of works underlined the basic Protestant perspective on human nature in relation to God, that

---

38   *Institutes*, 8.III.xi. Interestingly enough, given the wide variety of authors at his disposal, Turretin cites 'the illustrious Amyrald' as his supporting authority on this point; this is again evidence that attempts to characterize the Reformed Orthodox as putting Amyraldianism in the category of heresy, along with Arminianism and Socinianism, are wrong-headed and fail to take account of the way the Reformed understood confessional boundaries and theological diversity.

39   *Works*, 10, 75.

such was to be understood first and foremost in terms of status not substance. This finds its obvious counterpart in the Protestant doctrine of justification by imputation, where being justified is a status, not a change in substance.

Nevertheless, for Owen the status of covenant breaker does bring with it a significant change in humanity's abilities. For a start, free will is automatically excluded. Now, given Owen's position on divine sovereignty and the nature of contingency, it is clear that there are significant ontological reasons pertaining to the Creator–creature relationship for excluding free will in any radical, libertarian sense. For the Reformed such as Owen, freedom can only ever be conceived in terms of secondary causality and the absence of external co-action. In this sense, then, there is continuity between human freedom before and after the Fall, since Adam's progeny enjoy freedom from necessity.[40] The difference between pre- and post-Fall contexts is thus not to be located in what one might call the order of being vis-à-vis human action, but rather in the moral/spiritual sphere: human beings after the Fall still freely do what seems good to them; but their moral mind, intellect and will, has been so corrupted by sin that they are incapable of doing that which is good; and, of course, given the vast gulf that exists between God and his creation which the covenant of works was designed to bridge, they are incapable of meriting any favour from God, given that the covenant is now shattered.

The Christological Response

Typical of theologians in the Reformed Orthodox tradition, John Owen's understanding of Christ's person and Christ's work are inextricably connected. We have already seen in the previous chapters how his historical context meant that he was rooted, albeit critically, in ongoing and longstanding traditions of theological reflection which had their roots in the patristic and medieval periods; and we have also noted how his doctrine of God and creation shaped his understanding of the human predicament after the Fall, particularly in terms of God's justice and the breaking of the covenant of works by Adam as federal head of the whole of humanity. These points provide the essential matrix for Owen's Christology, which he develops in conscious relation to the salvific work which Christ performs.

All of this points to the fact that Owen regards salvation as a task which needs to be undertaken by God himself if it is to be at all effective, and the shift in his thinking on divine justice in the early 1650s serves to make this point yet more theologically secure. This is where the importance of the doctrine of the Trinity becomes so obvious: the Christian God is a the Trinitarian God and thus all matters relating to him, from creation to consummation, need to be understood in Trinitarian terms; and salvation is no exception to this.

Foundational to this is the role of Christ as Mediator, and Owen locates the eternal basis for this office in the covenant of grace, made by God the Father with

---

40 'We grant man, in the substance of all his actions, as much power, liberty, and freedom as a mere created nature is capable of. We grant him to be free in his choice from all outward coaction or inward necessity, to work according to election and deliberation, spontaneously embracing what seemeth good to him.' *Works* 10, 116.

the elect relative to the work of Christ, and of the covenant between the Father and Son by which the Son is appointed Mediator. The technical English term for this latter is *covenant of redemption* and the Latin equivalent is *pactum salutis*, and this is to be distinguished from the covenant of grace because it is refers specifically to the agreement between the Father and the Son relative to mediation, and not directly to the elect.[41] In this context, the covenant of grace, establishing and revealing as it does the divine will to save, has theological priority.

The Covenant of Grace

By Owen's day, the concept of the covenant of grace was well-established in Reformed literature and enjoyed clear confessional status, often in conjunction with statements on infant baptism if not explicitly in the main sections on soteriology.[42] As a soteriological point, the covenant of grace ties in closely with the particularism of election: as God chooses only to save some and not others, so those elected for salvation are those with whom, in Christ, God makes the covenant of grace. It is important to note this in order to understand that Reformed notions of predestination are not some crude metaphysical abstraction; rather, they involve the connection of Augustinian anti-Pelagianism to Christology to the growing recognition in Reformed circles of the usefulness of the language of covenant in expressing God's relationship with his creation both pre- and post-Fall.

Owen sees the exegetical basis of the concept in Gn. 17:7, Je. 32:38–40, and Heb. 8:9–12, with its extended quotation from Je. 31:31–34.[43] In *Hebrews*, Owen engages in careful comparison of the Greek of Hebrews with the Hebrew of Jeremiah, arguing that the berith/diatheke connection not only means *covenant* but also strongly connotes something unconditional or testamentary in its tendency.[44] This has soteriological significance: any merit or work prior to entry into the covenant is clearly excluded at the outset; the covenant of grace is, in other words, the outward manifestation of God's decree to save, a point which Owen makes in *The Doctrine of the Saints' Perseverance* by use of the typical scholastic distinction between *principia* of being and of knowing:

> The *principium essendi* of this truth [the covenant of grace], if I may so say, is in the decrees and purposes of God; the *principium cognoscendi*, in his covenant, promise, and oath, which also add much to the real stability of it, the truth and faithfulness of God in them being thereby peculiarly engaged therein.[45]

---

41   Owen makes this distinction clear in Exercitation XXVIII of his Hebrews commentary: *Works* 19, 78.

42   For example Hungarian Confession (1562), 17–19; Heidelberg Catechism (1563), 68, 73, 74; Bentheim Confession (1613), 9; Bohemian Confession (1609), 13.2; Irish Articles (1615), 29–30; WCF (1647), 7.

43   *Works*, 11, 205–10.

44   *Works*, 23, 135.

45   *Works*, 11, 205.

Of course, the inclusion by the Reformed of children within the covenant of grace in order to provide a federal basis for infant baptism stands somewhat at odds with this close identification of the decree with the covenant, but this does not seem to have caused Owen any great heartache or led him to modify this typical Reformed position in any way.[46]

What is significant, however, is that this close correlation of decree and covenant clearly drives Owen's understanding of the nature of conditionality as it touches salvation. For example, Owen is clear that, if the covenant of grace is conditional in the sense of the requirement of prior individual fulfillment of a condition before entry into the covenant, then it is not the covenant or the divine promise which provides the real basis for salvation but the individual's own action. This is something which would render the covenant of grace akin to the covenant of works and also relativize and marginalize the unique work of Jesus Christ, making salvation an unstable and unreliable synthesis of the action of God and the action of human beings.[47] Owen sees support for this in careful analysis of the biblical use of *berith*, which he sees used in an unequivocally unilateral and unconditional manner in Gn. 6:18 and 9:9; and he also (in a manner reminiscent of the passage in Augustine's *Confessions* which so upset Pelagius) sees that any conditionality that there may be in the covenant of grace refers to actions which God will himself fulfill within his elect.[48] In his *Hebrews*, Owen further elaborates this by distinguishing between conditions *of* the covenant (that is those things which must be fulfilled in order to be set within the covenant) and conditions *in* the covenant, referring to those things which are required by those within the covenant and which are supplied by God's gracious activity within the believer. Thus, language of conditionality must be used with precision when referring to the covenant of grace, and in a manner which preserves the anti-Pelagian, unilateral action of God in salvation.[49]

What is significant in this discussion is the lack of interest which Owen demonstrates in talking about the decrees of predestination, especially given the structural and logical obsession with the idea that certain scholars have imputed to the Reformed Orthodox.[50] Owen's doctrine of God and his understanding of human depravity both make election a necessity if salvation is ever to be a reality for any individual; yet the structural significance of the decrees is subsumed under their revelation in the covenant of grace; and one searches in vain in Owen for elaborate discussions of such topics as the points at issue between supra- and infra-lapsarians. In fact, when it comes to salvation Owen is much more concerned with Christology than with the decrees, probably because the former is where he sees most of the significant polemical pressure coming, even in the matter of predestination more

---

46 See *Works*, 16, 258–63.

47 *Works*, 11, 207–08, 210–11.

48 *Works*, 11, 218.

49 *Works*, 23, 137.

50 See Bizer, *Frühorthodoxie und Rationalismus*; Hall, 'Calvin against the Calvinists;' J Dantine, 'Les Tabelles sur la Doctrine de la Prédestination par Theodore de Bèze' , in *Revue de Theologie et de Philosophie* 16 (1966), 365–77. Cf. Muller, 'Calvin and the Calvinists' .

strictly considered. And this leads us inevitably from the soteriological covenant of grace to its Christological foundation in the covenant of redemption.

The Traditionary Doctrinal Matrix of the Covenant of Redemption

The covenant of redemption is the foundation of the economy of salvation and of the Incarnation and it is this, therefore, that should be the starting-point of any discussion of the person of Jesus Christ in Owen's theology. Now, given the novelty of the conceptual distinction and terminology of the covenant of redemption to later Reformed theology, it is without doubt one of the most obvious doctrinal loci where the nature of Reformed Orthodoxy, and that of its development over the course of a century, can be most clearly illustrated. This is because the terminological innovation which it involves is itself the result of extensive reflection on a series of related points which are of singular importance to understanding the broader Reformed theological field: linguistic discussion of the term 'covenant' ; the development of a doctrinal locus for which a superficial glance at scripture would suggest scant exegetical support; the honing of a conceptual vocabulary out of prior doctrinal discussion; and the precise expression of a concept which undergirds the Trinitarian dimension of Reformed soteriology. Further, its arrival as a specific part of the Reformed conceptual vocabulary in the mid-seventeenth-century renders it a relatively late, essentially post-confessional development and thus of particular importance in seeing how doctrinal development and confessional orthodoxy were connected.[51]

It is, of course, a truism that concepts almost invariably predate the specific terms with which they are later described; and so the question needs to be asked: whence did the covenant of redemption originate? In fact, it was a critical innovation by the Reformed within the Chalcedonian Christological tradition which provided the context for this development. Take, for example, Owen's declaration in his relatively late 1679 treatise, *Christologia: Or, A Declaration of the Glorious Mystery of the Person of Christ*:

> The perfect complete work of Christ, in every act of his mediatory office, in all that he did as the King, Priest, and Prophet of the church, in all that he did and suffered, in all that he continueth to do for us, in or by virtue of whether nature soever it be done or wrought, is not to be considered the act of this or that nature in him alone, but it is the act and work of the whole person, of him that is both God and man in one person.[52]

This argument, that Christ is Mediator according to his person, and thus according to both natures, is continuous with that argued, for example, by Calvin in the *Institutes* II.xiv.iii, but marks a basic point of discontinuity with the medieval theological

---

51   The concept has proved somewhat controversial over the years, with perhaps its most famous critic being Karl Barth, who dismissed it as 'mythology' and as basically inimical to the doctrine of the Trinity in the way it appears to set up the First and Second Persons as two separate legally contracting parties: see CD 4/1, 65.

52   *Works*, 1, 234.

tradition which regarded Christ as Mediator according to the human nature only.[53] Medieval theologians had a serious problem with the notion of a divine person, enjoying equality with the Father, mediating between God and humanity. As they conceived of mediation as involving a mid-point between two poles, it made no sense to speak of God as the midpoint between God and humanity. Thus, they located his mediation exclusively in the human nature which, while not divine, was yet exalted by grace above other human natures. The Reformed, however, focused on the integrity of the person of the Mediator, and refused to talk abstractly about mediation according to metaphysical nature rather than historical person. In large part this was the result of a far less speculative and more historically-grounded approach to theology. Now, to modern ears this is an perhaps apparently abstruse point, but it is one of great Christological significance and one which did not pass unnoticed by the Catholic polemicists and apologists who emerged in the latter part of the sixteenth and the early seventeenth centuries. For example, the issue forms a significant point of discussion in the response of William Ames to Jesuit polemicist, Joseph Bellarmine, where Ames has to respond to Bellarmine's arguing of precisely the medieval point about the nonsensical nature of God being mediator with God.[54] Ames himself is careful to start his discussion by drawing a distinction between *medius*, a term denoting a substantial quality, and *mediator*, a term referring to an office, thus making an important distinction for the ensuing Christological construction.[55] Nevertheless, such a distinction points to the deeper issue of the foundations of such in the Trinitarian relations which underpin discussions of both divine substance and office.

The origins of the concept thus lie in the initial Reformation theology of Calvin and his contemporaries, and clear hints of it can be found in the Trinitarian articulation of the foundations of Christ's threefold office.[56] Nevertheless, the earliest apparent use of the term occurs in David Dickson's address on the dangers of Arminianism delivered to the 1638 General Assembly of the Church of Scotland, an event marked, no doubt, by preoccupation with all things covenantal, given the burning issue in the political sphere of the National Covenant. Dickson's treatment at this point indicates the basic doctrinal concerns which shaped the later development of the doctrine: the covenant of redemption between the Father and Christ as Mediator is logically prior to, and the foundation of, the covenant of grace; the number of the elect is fixed in this covenant; the precise nature and value of the Mediator's work and suffering is

---

53 For example, Aquinas, *Summa Theologiae* 3a.25 and 26. For the Reformed position, see, for example, William Perkins, *A Golden Chaine* in *Works* (London, 1603), 20; *Synopsis purioris theologiae*, XXVI. For discussion of this point, see Richard A Muller, *Christ and the Decree: Christology and Predestination in Reformed Theology from Calvin to Perkins* (Grand Rapids: Baker, 1988), 29–31. The position is also clearly articulated in the Reformed confessional material: for example, Heidelberg Catechism, questions 12–19; WCF 8.2.

54 William Ames, *Bellarminus Enervatus* (Oxford, 1629), 129–30.

55 *Bellarminus Enervatus*, 126–27.

56 For an early Trinitarian adumbration of the notion, see *Synopsis purioris theologiae*, XXVI.xvi; see also Muller, *Christ and the Decree*, 166–71. Hints of the notion, at least in an embryonic form, can also be found in Arminius: see his *Private Disputation* 33.

defined by the covenant; and the success of the Mediator's mission is guaranteed.[57] Thus, in 1638 we find a clear declaration of the concept in explicitly covenantal language; yet, for some reason, it is not until the mid-1640s that the terminology of covenant of redemption/*pactum salutis* starts to gain common currency both in Britain and on the continent. It is only then that we start to find it figuring prominently in the dogmatic structure of Reformed federal theology, as evidenced, for example, by the work of Edward Fisher and Peter Bulkeley in English, and that of Johannes Cocceius on the continent.[58] This partly accounts for the lack of explicit reference to the idea in the Westminster Confession of Faith (1647), and for the lack of consensus on the issue within the bounds of confessional orthodoxy in the years after the Westminster Assembly.[59] In this context, it is worth noting, however, that the Savoy Declaration, generally regarded as significantly modifying the Westminster Confession of Faith only at points of polity and state relations, does alter Chapter 8 of the Confession to make explicit reference to a covenant between Father and Son. This addition is surely the result both of the later date of composition and of the key role played by John Owen in the Savoy Conference.[60]

These early references are fairly basic: in *The Marrow of Modern Divinity*, Fisher makes a brief but significant reference to Christ's mediation being rooted in a covenant between Father and Son.[61] Bulkeley's statement of the concept is very

---

57   Alexander Peterkin (ed.) *Records of the Kirk of Scotland, containing the Acts and Proceedings of the General Assemblies from the year 1638 downwards*, (Edinburgh: Peter Brown, 1843), 159. On Dickson's significance in the development of the concept, see Carol A Williams, '"The Decree of Redemption is in Effect a Covenant: David Dickson and the Covenant of Redemption', PhD dissertation (Calvin Theological Seminary, 2005).

58   Edward Fisher, *The Marrow of Modern Divinity* (London, 1645); Peter Bulkeley, *The Gospel-Covenant; or The Covenant of Grace Opened* (London, 1646); for Cocceius's development of the concept of *pactum salutis*, see Willem J Van Asselt, *The Federal Theology of Johannes Cocceius* (Leiden: Brill, 2001),227–47.

59   The closest the WCF came to stating the doctrine was in Chapter 8, but the language of covenant is absent from the detailing of the Father–Son relationship. Early on, however, others had no difficulty in finding the doctrine there: for example, David Dickson gives his most famous articulation of the idea in *The Summe of Saving Knowledge, With the Practical Use Thereof* (Edinburgh, 1671), Head II. This work enjoyed the status of a standard summary of the Confession's teaching and has often been printed with the Westminster Standards, thus enjoying quasi-confessional status. That the Reformed tradition continued to embrace those who used the concept and those who did not within the boundaries of acceptable confessional orthodoxy is evident: for example, the doctrine is clearly stated by Edward Leigh, *A System or Body of Divinity* (London, 1662), Book V, Chapter 2; while Thomas Watson, in his sermonic commentary on the Shorter Catechism, is happy to ground Christ's mediation simply in the covenant of grace: *A Body of Practical Divinity* (London, 1692), 93–96.

60   WCF 8.1 reads 'It pleased God, in His eternal purpose, to choose and ordain the Lord Jesus, His only begotten Son, to be Mediator between God and man;' the Savoy Declaration reads 'It pleased God, in his eternal purpose, to chuse and ordain the Lord Jesus his onely begotten Son, according to a Covenant made between them both, to be the Mediator between God and Man.' See *A Declaration of the Faith and Order Owned and practised in the Congregational Churches in England* (London, 1658), 8.1.

61   *Marrow*, 36–37.

similar, though he carefully delineates the respective commitments of Father and Son in the arrangement in a manner more elaborate than Fisher: the Father appoints the Son as Mediator to bring fallen humans back into covenant with him; He commands him to bring knowledge of the truth to men and women, and to offer himself as a sacrifice; and he makes the Son a fivefold promise – of an abundance of the Holy Spirit, of full assistance in his work, and of ultimate success in bringing the elect to faith, of rule and dominion, and of final glory. The Son, for his part, promises to accept the office, to depend upon the Father, to submit to the Father's will, and to expect the final glory for himself and the elect to come from the Father.[62]

The Use of the Term Covenant for Intratrinitarian Relations

At this point, it is worth addressing the issue of why the arrangement between Father and Son came to be denominated a covenant, given the fact that obvious exegetical support for the use of the term in this context would appear to be slim, if not non-existent. In the first folio of his Hebrews exposition (1668) Owen himself offers an elaborate defence of the use of the term in this context, but it will be useful at this point to note that his discussion is not untypical; and that the point is established in Reformed Orthodoxy by careful linguistic reflection upon the biblical text, not simply some kind of apriorism or dogmatic straitjacketing.

For example, useful insight into the development of covenant language vis-à-vis the Father–Son relation in the economy of salvation can be found in the work of Patrick Gillespie, whose analysis of covenant terminology we noted above. His *The Ark of the Covenant Opened* (London, 1677) is probably the most elaborate work in the English language on the covenant of redemption; and, as it contained a preface by John Owen, it can be reasonably assumed to be broadly representative of the latter's thinking in this area. Further, while the work is a posthumous publication of 1677, it reflects in its arguments the broad linguistic and conceptual consensus of the relevant scholarship of the earlier seventeenth century and thus provides a good basis for seeing how the application of the term *covenant* to the Father–Son relationship regarding Christ's mediation was not at all surprising or objectionable by the canons of the day.

Gillespie's treatise on the covenant of redemption needs to be understood against the background of his earlier work, *The Ark of the Testament Opened* (1661) where the meaning of *berith* and its cognates, as well as the concept of *covenant* in general is discussed.[63] With the argument of this earlier work in mind, we can now turn to the later work, *The Ark of the Covenant Opened*, and see how Gillespie articulates the intrinitarian relationship regarding salvation in terms of such language. In this context, Gillespie is, of course, perfectly aware that the term 'covenant of redemption' has no precise equivalent in scripture, but that what he is doing is using a term to refer to what is arguably a scriptural concept. Indeed, his central biblical justification for arguing that the covenant of redemption exists as a separate

---

62   *The Gospel-Covenant*, 29–31.
63   See the discussion of this work above.

covenant, to be distinguished from the covenant of grace, is rooted in biblical texts which speak of a covenant between God and his Elect One which make no reference to the latter's Seed. Using Gillespie's established taxonomy of covenants, the need for understanding two separate covenants, of redemption and of grace, can be seen to relate to his distinction between personal and real covenants: the former refers to an arrangement between two parties which is focused on their mutual obligations and benefits; of which type is the covenant of redemption; the latter to an arrangement which has an impact upon the progeny of the parties; of which type is the covenant of grace.[64] Further, he argues that scripture clearly teaches that there is a reciprocal relationship between Father and Son relative to the economy of salvation which comports with the broad legal definition of covenant as requiring two or more parties, voluntarily bound together by mutual obligations and promises. There is no need for scripture to use the word 'covenant' in the relevant passages, because the concept is clearly there. Sources for this argument, in addition to scripture, include the patristic author, John Chrysostom , and the Lutheran, John Gerhard.[65] Gillespie, however, also employs linguistic arguments to make his point. There is not space to examine them all here, so one will have to suffice, but it is a typical example of Gillespie's exegetical procedure. A good example is provided by his treatment of Ps. 2:7, a verse which David Dickson, Gillespie's covenanter colleague, takes as self-evidently teaching a covenant of redemption.[66] While Dickson, writing a homiletic commentary, spends no time in offering a defence of such a reading, Gillespie demonstrates that such a view, while perhaps not self-evident, can be grounded in careful linguistic analysis and exegesis. While the Authorised Version translates the verse as 'I will declare the decree,' Gillespie argues that the Hebrew word חק can be translated as 'covenant.' This suggestion is not found in either the Westminster Annotations of 1645, nor in the English edition of the Dutch Annotations of 1657, but does receive some support from the third edition of the Westminster Annotations of 1657.[67] Gillespie himself cites as one of his principle authorities for this reading Bishop Hammond, who treats the verse in some detail, arguing that the Hebrew here points to a covenant between God and Christ. Indeed, Hammond also engages in interaction with the Arabic, Ethiopic, Syriac, Septuagint and Vulgate in his analysis of the verse, and this reference on its own would have indicated that Gillespie would have been well aware of the various linguistic complexities in the task of translation.[68] In addition to Hammond, Gillespie himself cites an etymological thesaurus dealing with the root of the word, Conrad Kircher's *Concordantiae Veteris Testamenti graecae, ebraeis vocibus respondentes polychresoi* (Frankfurt, 1607), Buxtorf's *Lexicon Chaldaicum, talmudicum et rabbinicum* (Basel, 1639), and the Septuagint. Three arguments are of particular interest: first, he notes that the Chaldee

64   *The Ark of the Testament*, 69–70.

65   *The Ark of the Covenant*, 6–10; cf. *The Ark of the Testament*, 50.

66   *A Brief Explication of the First Fifty Psalms* (London, 1655), 10–12.

67   See *Annotations upon all the books of the Old and New Testament* (London, 1657).

68   Henry Hammond, *A Paraphrase and Annotations upon the Books of the Psalms* (London, 1683) Book I, 8.

Paraphrase renders the term as 'pactum' while the Septuagint translates the word as *prostagma*, which he understands as 'order' or 'agreement,' a translation which he states is consistent with the Targum. Second, he notes that Buxtorf remarks that in the Talmud the word in question is frequently used for the quality, condition, or nature of a thing; thus, given that the decree is spoken of in the Psalm as an address to a son, a point which Gillespie reads Christologically, it is quite legitimate to read the term as referring to the covenant of redemption. Third, he notes the interchangeability of the closely related Hebrew terms *ḥūqqâ* and *ḥōq*, as used in Je. 31:35–36, with *berith* in 33:20, where the latter is routinely translated as *covenant*.[69] Given the careful marshalling of such a range of linguistic arguments to establish his reading of Ps. 2:7 as a reference to the covenant of redemption, it is quite clear that to characterize Gillespie's exegesis as dogmatically driven or as proof-texting would be to do him a profound injustice. What we have here is the careful interaction of the best linguistic and textual analysis available with the kind of theological issues we noted earlier which arise out of the doctrinal tradition. The result is neither crass proof-texting nor a situation where dogmatics overrides exegesis; it is, rather, a classic example of the Reformed Orthodox move from exegesis to doctrinal synthesis within the context of the analogy of faith and the need to co-ordinate a Trinitarian understanding of God with the historical action of Jesus Christ in salvation.

When we turn to Owen's discussion of the terminology, we find similar care to that in Gillespie. In a series of twenty-one basic points about covenants and about the relationship between the Father and the Son, Owen deals with linguistic, legal and theological issues. First, he address the etymology of the Hebrew word *berith* and the Greek *syntheke*, drawing attention to the variety of ways in which these terms and their cognates are used both in scripture and in ancient classical literature (as an agreement, as the giving of a precept, as an absolute promise).[70] Then he moves on to discuss in more detail the varieties of nuance which can exist within an arrangement denoted by the term covenant. For example, he indicates that covenants require some form of verbal agreement, and that covenants should be voluntary agreements of two or more parties which refer to things within the power of the various parties to deliver.[71] At the end of pages of biblical exposition, demonstrating that these various factors applied to the relationship between Father and Son vis-à-vis salvation, Owen concludes that the matter can quite happily be described as a covenant. As with Gillespie, though, it should be noted that this is the conclusion of the various linguistic and conceptual arguments, not the Procustean bed on to which the various biblical texts are forced to fit. Owen is not so naïve as to believe the doctrine in terms of its linguistic formulation simply falls off the pages of scripture into the lap of the reader; but he does think that careful analysis of the biblical text, linguistically and conceptually, legitimizes use of the term.

---

69 *The Ark of the Covenant*, 11.

70 *Works*, 19, 78–81.

71 *Works*, 19, 82–83.

Owen's Development of the Concept

The watershed nature of the 1640s as regards the development of the covenant of redemption is exemplified by the work of John Owen, whose 1643 treatise, *A Display of Arminianism*, takes to task both Arminian and Socinian theologians with respect to their doctrines of God, creation, fall and redemption. Owen was writing as a young theologian at the start of his career, and the work is therefore (as one might expect) somewhat overwrought and full of passages which conflate Arminian and Socinian positions for the sake of a good polemic. Indeed, the book is dedicated to the Parliamentary Committee of Religion, and this astute attempt at flattery and ingratiation clearly worked as the Committee subsequently conferred upon him the living of Fordham in Essex. Interestingly enough, while Owen shows a clear understanding of Reformed Christology in his articulation of the saving work of Christ, he does not explicitly ground this in an eternal covenant between Father and Son. Thus, in discussing the mediation of Christ, Owen frames his argument in response to two issues: the objects of the merit of Christ, that is those for whom he died; and the efficacy and end of his death, that is what exactly his death did in fact achieve. In 1638, Dickson had anchored both points in the covenant of redemption; in 1643, however, Owen does not explicitly articulate such a covenant but seems rather to subsume them under the covenant of grace.[72]

Subsequently in *The Death of Death* (1647), Owen narrows his focus to the particularity and efficacy of Christ's death, set within the wider context of his mediation, and here writes at some length about the arrangement between Father, Son and, significantly, Holy Spirit, using the language of covenant. In the space of four years, therefore, the concept and the terminology has become a crucial part of Owen's discussion of Christ as Mediator; and so it was for the wider Reformed world. Owen clearly feels no need to offer any justification of his basis for adopting the language: the concept was in place in the tradition long before the terminology; the kind of linguistic argument so ably summarized some years later by Gillespie is presumably presupposed by the tradition in general, and Owen in particular, at this point.

Where Owen does make a significant contribution is in his attention to the role of the Holy Spirit with reference to covenant, a point which represents a distinctly Trinitarian advance on the works of Fisher and Bulkeley who, with their exclusive attention to the Father–Son relationship were arguably vulnerable to the accusation of developing a sub-Trinitarian foundation for the economy of salvation. Owen avoids this by describing the various roles played in the covenant of redemption by Father, Son, and Holy Spirit; and in so doing, he is being consistent with his basic premise that every external act of God is in its deepest sense an act of the whole Trinity. Thus, the Father sends his Son out of love to the world to die for sinners, and, in the actual accomplishment of that end, lays the punishment due to our sins upon him;[73] the Son voluntarily assumes the role of Mediator assigned to him by the Father, becomes incarnate, and then offers himself as a sacrifice on behalf of the

---

72   *Works*, 10, 87–99.
73   *Works*, 10, 163–74.

elect;[74] finally, the Holy Spirit is engaged in the work of incarnation and of Christ's earthly ministry, his oblation, and in his resurrection.[75]

Given Barth's criticism of the covenant of redemption as a piece of theological mythology, and the other criticism which come from various quarters and which argue that Reformed Orthodoxy represents a radical intrusion of abstraction and metaphysics into theology at the expense of history, it is important to understand a number of points relative to the covenant of redemption. First, the Christological focus of the covenant indicates that it is rather the foundation of salvation history, its necessary Trinitarian presupposition, if you like, which then makes the historical ministry of Christ, the work of the Holy Spirit in applying the same, and thus the salvation of the elect, an historical reality. It is the nexus between eternity and time with respect to salvation. Second, as we shall see particularly in discussing the Christological role of the Holy Spirit, the Reformed Orthodox construction of Christ's mediation as involving both humiliation and exaltation, and as involving his role as prophet, priest, and king, places historical movement right at the heart of the constructive principles shaping the way Reformed Orthodoxy explicates its Christology. What we see, both in Owen's articulation of a covenant of redemption in eternity, and in the subsequent execution of the terms of that covenant in history, is an example of how pre-modern theology sought to connect classic, orthodox Trinitarian and Christological theology with the historical accounts of salvation as given in the Gospels. Far from a radical divorce between time and eternity, to the great loss of the former, we see the exact opposite talking place.[76]

The Covenant of Redemption and the Priesthood of Christ

While Owen elaborates the details of Christ's mediatorial office by using the standard Reformed taxonomy of prophet, priest and king, the major focus of his attention is Christ as priest. This is undoubtedly in large part because he sees the priesthood of Christ as the point where orthodoxy is most under pressure in his day: as the title

---

74 *Works*, 10, 174–77.

75 *Works*, 10, 178–79.

76 It is perhaps ironic that one of the principle pieces of evidence used by advocates of the 'Calvin against the Calvinist' thesis are Beza's *Tabula Praedestinationis* and Perkin's adaptation of this in *A Golden Chaine*. These are cited as examples of how predestination comes to dominate Reformed theology and reflect its nature as a predestinarian deductive system. However, as Barth so clearly understood, the tables were intended to be read from the bottom up rather than the top down, and so are anything but deductive; further, and more important for this section, Perkins's addition of a central column to Beza's much sparser original, a column which outlines the work of Christ and connecting the history of Christ to the order of salvation, clearly indicates the concern of the Reformed Orthodox to do justice to Christology and historical narrative flow in their formulation of salvation. What they refuse to do is to abandon either ontology or economy for the sake of the other. For Barth's views, see *CD* 2.2, 78; contrast this with the misreading of the Perkins' table offered by James B Torrance, 'Strengths and Weaknesses of the Westminster Theology' in Alasdair I C Heron, *The Westminster Confession in the Church Today* (Edinburgh: St Andrew Press, 1982), 40–54.

of his first, lost work suggests, the priesthood of Christ is under attack from three powerful enemies: from Catholicism, whose doctrine of the mass derogates from the finality of the cross; from Arminianism, whose understanding of atonement and free will undermines the efficacy of Christ's atonement; and Socinianism, whose reconstruction of Christ's work in the light of the denial of the Incarnation turned the Messiah into little more than an inspiring teacher.

In the context of Owen's positive soteriology, Owen's Christology needs to be understood in light of the parallel between Adam and Christ as elaborated in Rom. 5 which is foundational to Reformed understanding of federal headship and of the covenant of works. Indeed, the covenant of redemption serves to make explicit Christ's role as the Second Adam, as the one who acts on behalf of those given to him in the covenant of grace to remedy the disastrous results of the breaking of the original covenant. Within this context, however, Owen regards the priesthood of Christ, particularly with reference to his death, as embodying three different aspects which he makes explicit in his 1655 work against the Socinians, *Vindiciae Evangelicae*: payment of a price; a sacrifice; and a punishment.

Regarding Christ's death as payment of a price, Owen roots his argument entirely in linguistic analysis. He examines the Greek of 1 Cor. 6:20, 1 Pe. 1:18–19, and Mt. 20:28, which he sees as complemented by 1 Tim. 2:6 and as applying redemption language to the work of Christ. This he then supports further by examining the use of cognate terms in the Old Testament, comparing, for example, Ex. 21:30 in the Hebrew with the Septuagint reading; he also engages in a survey of redemption language in the Old Testament, as well as a brief analysis of the use of redemption language in classical Greek sources. The net result is that the notion of Christ's death as a redeeming payment is explicitly grounded on careful exegesis which represents the linguistic state-of-the-art in Owen's day.[77]

As for Christ's death as a sacrifice, the key scriptural book in this regard is that of Hebrews. Indeed, in *Vindiciae Evangelicae*, Owen uses Hebrews as his basic entry point both for understanding the Old Testament sacrificial priesthood and its relationship to Christ. Highlighting both the repetitive ritual nature of the Old Testament sacrifices and thus their inadequacy to deal once and for all with the problem of sin; in this regard, he is clear that Christ's sacrifice is materially discontinuous with those of the Levitical priesthood, yet is clearly foreshadowed in them as antitype to type.[78] In terms of positive sacrifice, however, Owen argues that Christ offers his own human nature, body and soul; he is both priest and sacrifice; and the whole action is, in typical Reformed fashion, to be ascribed to the person of the Mediator even as distinctions are made regarding the separate roles of the two natures within that action; the whole is to be seen as an offering to the Father, through the Spirit, thus laying out the Trinitarian dimensions of the sacrifice.[79]

---

77   *Works*, 12, 419–21.

78   *Works*, 12, 421–29, 431.

79   *Works*, 12, 429–33. In this context, exegesis of Hebrews is central to Owen's argument, and the embryonic arguments of *Vindiciae Evangelicae* will be expanded in *Hebrews*: Heb. 10:5 (*Works* 23, 460–61); Heb. 9:14 (*Works* 23, 304–18).

In terms of Christ's death as punishment, Owen argues in 1655 that punishment is a function of divine justice. Owen himself hangs his primary biblical argument for Christ's death as a punishment on Is. 53. Interestingly enough, given Reformed Orthodoxy's reputation for mindless dogmatism, he roots his argument for this identification first in the work of Chaldee paraphrast and the rabbis, who identify the Suffering Servant with the Messiah and yet are unable to provide a better candidate for Messiahship than Jesus of Nazareth; from this, he turns to New Testament allusions to the passage; and finally, he argues that the prophecy is immediate and not typical in any way. Again, Owen's doctrinal claims are rooted in wide-ranging scholarship, both directly biblical and in the exegetical traditions on a particular passage.[80]

The primary polemical background to Owen's discussion of Christ's death as punishment is provided by Socinianism. We know from *A Dissertation on Divine Justice* that the issue of divine justice, to which the question of punishment was intimately connected, dominated his theological reflections in the early 1650s, in the light of the perceived rise of the Socinian threat in England via the writings of John Biddle.[81] Socinian theology, often seen as an early form of rationalism, was not simply an antimetaphysical, epistemological critique of orthodoxy, as we noted in Chapter 2; it was also a rejection of the moral categories of orthodoxy in terms of divine retributive justice and vicarious sacrifice. Thus, Owen makes sure at the outset of his discussion of the topic in *Vindiciae Evangelicae* that various potential misconstructions of Christ's punishment are ruled out: Christ was not punished for his own correction; nor for his own protection; nor to provide an example; nor to bear witness.[82]

With these more-or-less exemplary options excluded, Owen argues for a view of Christ's death as punishment which has a twofold reference: God the Father as punishing; and God the Son as being punished. Exegesis and theology here go hand-in-hand. We noted in Chapter 2 how Owen's understanding of justice changed in the early 1650s; his mature view meant that, given the antecedently free choice of God to save, Christ's priesthood thus became necessary as the means by which this salvation could be accomplished in a manner which manifested and preserved the Creator's rights over his creation.

There are numerous points of interest which arise from this. First, Owen is very clear that the nature and value of Christ's death as a sacrifice is not the direct result of his constitution simply as a person who is both divine and human. In debate with Richard Baxter, Owen emphasizes that Christ's death is a sacrifice with salvific value only because it is offered in the context of the covenantal arrangement

---

80   *Works*, 12, 440–41.

81   *Works*, 12, 433. See the discussion in Chapter 2. For an influential example of English concern over the matter, which narrates a history whereby Socinianism culminates in the mainstream Laydian Anglicanism of the 1630s and 40s, see Francis Cheynell, *The Rise, Growth, and Danger of Socinianisme* (London, 1643).

82   *Works*, 442–43; cf. Biddle, *Twofold Catechism*, 67–71

between Father and Son. [83] This highlights the importance for Owen of avoiding abstract speculation in his Christology and of stressing the role which the salvific economy plays in determining who Christ is: his person is constituted in terms of the work he is to perform.[84] Nevertheless, there are points where Owen himself seems to be in conflict with this basic premise: thus, on several occasions, he argues the hypothetical sufficiency of Christ's death, rooted on one occasion explicitly in his divine-human constitution, as one of the bases for making a universal offer of the gospel in preaching. These references are, however, in comparatively early works (*A Display of Arminianism* and *The Death of Death*) and Owen rarely deploys such an argument after the controversy with Baxter which, presumably, led to a sharpening of the conceptual framework provided by, and the doctrinal implications of, the covenant of redemption.[85]

Second, while Owen is committed to the basic Trinitarian point that all acts of God *ad extra* are the work of God considered as a whole, he also believes that each person within the Trinity takes a specific role in relation to all such. Thus, in the covenant of redemption, the Father's specific roles are to send the Son into the world as Mediator and then to place upon him the punishment due to humanity's sin.[86] In this way, Owen connects the covenant of redemption both to the covenant of works, which determines the punishment to be suffered by sinful humanity, and the covenant of grace, which specifies to whom the benefits of Christ's mediation are to accrue. Thus, Owen makes it clear that the Father ensures that Christ's punishment is the same (a *solutio eiusdem*) as that which is deserved by sinners.[87]

As the Father is the one who appoints and sends the Son, so the Son voluntarily accepts the appointment and undergoes life on earth, obeying the law and enduring death on the cross at Calvary before rising again and then ascending to intercede at

---

83   'The value of any satisfaction in this business ariseth not from the innate worth of the things whereby it is made, but purely from God's free constitution of them to such an end ... . Nothing can possibly tend to the procurement and compassing of any end, by the way of payment, with the Lord, but what is built upon some free compact, promise, or obligation of his own.' *Works* 10, 441; cf. *Works* 10, 458; *Works* 19, 89. The notion of covenantally determined merit, which we noted in discussion of the covenant of works, is thus evident in Owen's Christological discussion, a result of the parallel between the covenant of works and the economy of salvation.

84   *Works*, 10, 157–60; 19, 118. It is arguable that the basic pattern for generating Reformed Christology was provided by a modification of the Anselmic argument within a critical Scotist framework: see Muller's comments on Calvin, *Christ and the Decree*, 27–29.

85   *Works*, 10, 89; cf. *Works* 10, 383. A later example of such an argument occurs in *Hebrews*, where, in commenting on Heb. 9:12, Owen refers to the infinite value of Christ's death, rooted in his constitution as both God and human, but does qualify the comment to indicate that this made his death sufficient to ransom *the church*. He thus injects a note of particularity: see *Works*, 23, 282.

86   *Works*, 10, 163–74.

87   'It [Christ's satisfaction] was a full, valuable compensation, made to the justice of God, for all the sins of all those for whom he made satisfaction, by undergoing the same punishment which, by reason of the obligation that was upon them, they themselves were bound to undergo.' *Works* 10, 269. For further discussion of Owen's argument for *solutio eiusdem*, see Chapter 4; also Trueman, *The Claims of Truth*, 211–17.

the right hand of the Father.[88] Two things in particular are important to note here. First, the whole life of Christ, from Incarnation to ascension, is thus part of his mediatorship, a point which will have crucial implications for Owen's understanding of justification in the context of seventeenth-century debates about imputation.[89] Second, the oblation of Christ (his life and death) and his intercession are two sides of the same coin and possess a basic unity which defines Owen's understanding of the particularity and the efficacy of Christ's atonement. In this, Owen stands within the mainstream of Reformed Orthodoxy.[90]

Limited atonement, the notion that the saving intention of Christ's death was limited to the elect alone, is a doctrine which has generated more than its fair share of controversy over the years.[91] As noted in Chapter 1, it was a focal point of dissent between the Orthodox and the Amyraldians of the School of Saumur in the seventeenth century; and, in more recent days, it has proved a (somewhat arbitrary) testing ground for those who wish to establish to what extent later Reformed theology was faithful to the legacy of John Calvin. The development of the doctrine has also been variously blamed on the emergence of predestination as a *Centraldogma* and on the impact of an alleged Aristotelian 'one-end teleology,' (the latter of which raises the obvious question of whether such a thing as a 'two-end teleology' was a remotely coherent notion in the seventeenth century.[92] The various problems with the 'Calvin against the Calvinists' thesis have already been examined in Chapter 1 and in an increasing body of historiographical literature.

Before examining Owen's own arguments at this point, it is worth noting that, prior to the 1640s, it would appear (at least in public) that there was a pretty broad tolerance of a variety of views on the topic within English Reformed thinking, with figures such as John Davenant being very comfortable with using language of universal intent with regard to Christ's atonement and yet not being subject to any major objections in this matter from those of a more precise orthodoxy. In the 1640s, however, it would seem that the sectarian freedom/chaos provided by the trauma of war somewhat shattered the public consensus on the issue and allowed for vigorous public debate on the matter of the atonement's particularity in a way not seen before.

The basic elements of Owen's position on the extent of the atonement are laid out in the 1642 work, *A Display of Arminianism*. Here the constructive focal point is not so much predestination (though election clearly plays a role in determining the nature of Christ's death as the atonement connects to the covenant of grace) and certainly not some putative Aristotelian teleology, but the unity of blood sacrifice and heavenly intercession in the work of Christ. Christ's whole life is rooted in his role as mediator: his sacrifice provides the basis for the heavenly intercession; the

---

88   *Works*, 10, 174–77; 19, 94–97.

89   *Works*, 10, 179–81; for this issue relative to justification, see Chapter 4.

90   Cf. Perkins, *Works*, 302–03.

91   See Torrance, 'The Incarnation and "Limited Atonement" '; R T Kendall, *Calvin and English Calvinism*; Clifford, *Atonement and Justification*.

92   For an examination of this eccentric thesis, see Trueman, *The Claims of Truth*, 233–40.

heavenly intercession is where the sacrifice finds its completion; and the two cannot and must not be separated.[93] To prove this, Owen cites, among other things, texts which refer Christ's death to his church, texts which speak of Christ as sponsor or representative substitute (a notion which Owen sees as demanding particularity), and texts which point to the unity of death and resurrection in the salvific economy. The whole is a classic example of textual analysis and doctrinal synthesis, albeit marked by the over-confidence one might expect in the first published work of a young theologian.[94]

While this basic point is thus established in Owen's earliest published writings, he does go on to elaborate this notion of the unity of Christ's priestly action at length, particularly in *The Death of Death* and the exposition of Hebrews. In both of these works the covenant of redemption emerges as an explicit doctrinal concept, a point which does not indicate basic discontinuity with his earliest work but which does allow for more precise theological reflection upon the matter in hand. Thus, from 1647 onwards, we find Owen explicitly using the intratrinitarian federal transaction to underscore the fact that Christ's priesthood, both death and intercession, only derive significance from the Father–Son agreement, and thus have unity of scope and purpose.[95]

While the covenant of redemption, as it connects to the covenant of grace, provides one element of establishing the particularity and unity of Christ's priesthood, the key argument regarding the unity of the priestly action is provided by biblical exegesis of passages which set up a typical relationship between the Old Testament priesthood and the work of Christ. This has been entirely overlooked by critics of limited atonement, perhaps because it is not pronounced in *The Death of Death*; yet, whether or not one agrees with the exegetical conclusions, it is undeniably an important part of Owen's mature argument as laid out supremely in *Hebrews*.[96]

Incarnation, Mediation and the Christological Role of the Spirit

Owen's elaboration of the Trinitarian structure of the covenant of redemption continued throughout his career, and receives perhaps its most sophisticated expression in his *Pneumatologia*, where he employs some of the most sophisticated concepts in patristic Christology particularly to expand upon the role of the Holy

---

93   'His intercession in heaven is nothing but a continued oblation of himself.' *Works*, 10, 90; 'We must not so disjoin the offices of Christ's mediatorship, that one of them may be versated about some towards whom he exerciseth not the other; much less ought we to separate the several acts of the same office. *Works*, 10, 91.

94   *Works*, 10, 91–92.

95   *Works*, 10, 185; *Works*, 19, 195–96.

96   It is undoubtedly part of the problem of some Owen research that the iconic/infamous stature of *The Death of Death* as the definitive exposition of particular redemption has obscured the importance of Owen's other writings as they touch on areas relevant to the topic. Yet this work of 1647 was that of a comparatively young theologian with another 36 years of active theological activity in front of him, and needs to be understood as such when assessing the full measure of his thoughts on the topic.

Spirit relative to the Incarnation. Chalcedonian orthodoxy had solved the immediate problems raised by Nestorianism but, as with so many theological formulations, the new formula itself generated new questions and problems which required further resolution. For example, if the Incarnation was only one person, then how was this single person constituted? On the grounds that divine personhood could not be rejected for obvious reasons, and a synthesis of divine and human personhood would lead to an unacceptable *tertium quid*, the answer that Leontius of Byzantium, a sixth-century theologian, provided was that Christ's human nature did not possess any personhood of its own. This sounds awkward but, as with so many Trinitarian and Christological formulations, the maxim of Sherlock Holmes would seem to apply: when one excludes the impossible, then whatever is left, however improbable, must be the truth. The human nature of Christ was thus anhypostatic, a position which enjoyed wide currency in subsequent medieval theology, although not accepted by Duns Scotus. By Owen's time, it was commonplace in Reformed theology.[97]

The concept is picked up by Owen who, in line with orthodoxy, stresses the anhypostatic nature of Christ's human nature outside of its union with the Logos. Where Owen elaborates the tradition is the way that he uses this to open a space in his theology of the Incarnation for offering a finely-tooled understanding of the role of the Spirit. The only direct act of the Logos upon the human nature, Owen argues, was the assumption of the latter into the hypostatic union; all other acts were voluntary and mediated by the Holy Spirit. In making this point, Owen establishes the explicitly Trinitarian nature of the historical, saving work of the incarnate Christ.[98]

It is important to note at this point that Owen is not arguing that the human nature ever enjoyed actual existence outside of its union with the Logos. The anhypostatic humanity is a logical construct; from the very moment of its existence, it existed in personal union with the divine and therefore had personhood. This is significant because this underlines the need to be careful about talking in abstract terms about the human nature of Christ: it is always the human nature of the person of the Mediator, and all acts performed by it are thus acts of the Mediator, not of the nature. This points to two of the basic concerns of the Reformed Orthodox: first, the desire to emphasize the historical person of Christ in a manner which does justice to the narrative of salvation as laid out in the Bible, supremely in the Gospels, and which deploys metaphysical discussion as a means of grounding that narrative; and, second (and intimately connected to the first), the appointment of Christ as Mediator according to both natures, a point which tracks back to the covenant of redemption, and which reminds us once again that this covenant is far from being a point of metaphysical abstraction.

---

97   For example, *Synopsis purioris theologiae* XXV.xxiv; Perkins, *Works* 18.

98   '[T]he only necessary consequent of this assumption of the human nature, or the incarnation of the Son of God, is the personal union of Christ, or the inseparable subsistence of the assumed nature in the person of the Son … . [A]ll other actings of God in the person of the Son towards the human nature were voluntary and did not necessarily ensue on the union mentioned.' *Works* 3, 160–61. '[N]otwithstanding the union of the human nature of Christ with the divine person of the Son, yet the communications of God unto it, beyond subsistence, were voluntary.' *Works* 3, 180.

Owen's use of anhypostatic human nature in the Incarnation not only allows him to avoid Nestorianism and Appolinarianism in his Christology, but also to clarify the incarnational role of the Spirit. In typical Reformed fashion, Owen regards all God's acts *ad extra* as acts of all three persons, but that the direct agent in such is the Spirit. In addition, he also holds as basic the axiom that the finite cannot comprehend the infinite, a point with acute Christological implications since it points immediately to the problem of the communication of attributes within the Incarnation. Lutheran theologians regarded such communication as occurring *directly between the natures*, a position which allowed for cogent defence of the real presence of Christ's humanity in the eucharistic elements and helped to give a coherent theological foundation for Luther's radical emphasis upon God as being revealed as gracious solely in the flesh of Christ. Reformed theology, by contrast, argued for an indirect communication of properties which occurs *in the person*. Owen provides a framework for understanding this point in a manner which avoids both the problems of the Lutheran position and Nestorianism by stressing the anhypostasis and arguing that the communication of properties has a threefold reference. First, as noted, the divine gives the human hypostatic existence in the context of the union. Second, the divine filled the human with all necessary graces via the action of the Holy Spirit; and third, the divine invests all actions of the human nature with worth and dignity.[99]

The other result of this construction is that Owen is able to expound the role of the Spirit in a way that does justice to the historical flow of the biblical narrative. Because the role of the Logos is restricted in direct relation to the human nature to that of providing hypostasis, thus the growth of Christ and the movement of his ministry, from humiliation to exaltation, becomes the economic framework for understanding the role of the Spirit at well. This is far from the metaphysical abstraction often imputed to Reformed Orthodoxy; rather it represents a working-out of the Trinitarian implications of Reformation insights and ideas.

In the Christological economy, the Spirit is the agent of conception in the womb of the Virgin Mary.[100] This is a theological commonplace, being directly taught in the New Testament account. Owen's second point regarding the role of the Spirit in the Incarnation is, however, somewhat more subtle. This is that of filling the human nature of Christ with all necessary graces, a point which is developed in Owen's later works. In *The Death of Death*, Owen defines the Spirit's role simply in terms of the virginal conception, Christ's oblation, and his resurrection; thus, in his initial discussion of the covenant of redemption, he makes little reference to any theologically elaborate relationship between Christ and the Holy Spirit;[101] but in the 1670s he expands upon this position considerably in *Pneumatologia* (1674). Here, in addition to the virginal conception, he also argues that the Spirit sanctified Christ at the moment of conception. What is interesting here is that Owen's argument is that human nature, albeit pure and undefiled as in Christ, is as yet on its own incapable of living supernaturally to God, an argument reminiscent of Thomistic understanding of human nature, and one which connects both to medieval notions of the *donum*

---

99 *Works*, 1, 233–34.
100 *Works*, 3, 162–67.
101 *Works*, 10, 178–79.

superadditum and, by way of structural analogy, to the divine condescension in the original covenant of works.[102]

This notion of the necessary exaltation of the human nature of Christ by the divine, above and beyond its basic sinlessness, is standard Reformed fare. For example, Ussher's discussion of the Incarnation makes the same point, with specific reference to the Adam–Christ parallel:

> Adam was not able to make himselfe holy; but what holinesse he had, he received from him who created him according to his owne Image: so that whatsoever obedience Adam had performed, God should have eaten of the fruit of the vineyard which himselfe had planted; and of his owne would all that have been, which could be given unto him. But Christ did himselfe sanctifie that human nature which he assumed ... and so out of his own peculiar store did he bring forth those precious treasures of holy obedience, which for the satisfaction of our debt he was pleased to tender unto his Father.[103]

Thus, the need for something beyond a strict natural relationship between Creator and creature (which we observed in Chapter 2 in the structure of the covenant of works) is acknowledged, and, via the Adam–Christ parallel of Romans 5, impacts upon the Reformed understanding of the relationship between the two natures in the Mediator. The difference here between Ussher and Owen is not one of theological substance; it is rather that Owen elaborates upon the relationship by rooting the exaltation specifically in the direct action of the Spirit, a point made earlier by, among other, William Perkins in *A Golden Chaine*.[104]

Two things follow from this endowment of grace by the Spirit. First, the endowment does not disrupt or undermine the reality of Christ's humanity. Christ as human thinks and acts as a human, with his rational soul as the principle of operation. Thus, he grew and developed as other men and women, and the Holy Spirit endowed him with incremental grace and gifts as he matured. Owen thereby avoids any hint of Docetism and also does justice to the historical dynamic of the gospel narratives, which clearly portray a Christ who grows up and develops over time. In addition, in order to underline this point, Owen makes it very clear that Christ, according to his human nature was capable of having new objects proposed to him and of learning new things by observation and so on. The real humanity of Christ, identical to ours in all things but sin, is thus safeguarded by the action of the Holy Spirit.[105] Further, Owen's careful delimitation of the Logos's role simply to that of giving hypostasis to the anhypostatic human nature is crucial: were there a direct communication of attributes between the natures and that simply by virtue of incarnation alone, then such a defence of Christ's true humanity and the dynamic of the gospel narrative would be impossible without resort to an heretical view of kenosis.[106] This is

---

102 *Works*, 3, 168–69.

103 *Immanuel, or, The Mystery of the Incarnation of the Son of God* (London, 1653), 9. Cf. Leigh, *A Systeme*, 559.

104 Perkins, *Works*, 18; cf. *Synopsis purioris theologiae*, XXV.xxv.

105 *Works*, 3, 170.

106 On the epistemological consequences of the Incarnation, and the differences between Lutheran and Reformed traditions on this point, see Richard A Muller, *Post Reformation*

important because it clearly flies in the face of claims that Reformed Orthodoxy abandoned the exegetical orientation of the Reformation and reverted to the alleged metaphysical preoccupations of medieval theology. In fact, what we see here is typical of Reformed Orthodoxy's desire to connect metaphysical and historical considerations in such a way that the former provides a coherent ontological basis for the latter, while the latter itself requires a significant recasting of the former. The whole notion of Christ as Mediator according to both natures is a classic example of this, in the way it breaks with medieval precedent because of the demands of the history of salvation; and this particular point is a subset of that very issue. Most significantly, both points are ultimately grounded in the covenant of redemption in eternity, showing clearly that this covenant does not represent a piece of theological abstaction but rather the necessary eternal presupposition which grounds and gives meaning to the whole history of salvation, both in terms of Christ's mediation and the salvation of those individuals embraced within the covenant of grace.

That this is indeed the case is clear from the other roles which Owen ascribes to the Spirit in the life of Christ. The Holy Spirit anointed Christ with the gifts necessary for his execution of his mediatorial office under each of its three heads. Yet Owen makes it very clear that this occurred particularly at the point of Christ's baptism, which he supports on three grounds: first, with reference to Mt. 3:16–17 and Jn. 6:27; second, by pointing to the fact that his point marked the start of Christ's public ministry, albeit, as Owen acknowledges, he had on occasion indicated his special status and mission prior to this; and third by pointing to the language of fullness which gospel writers use of him after baptism. Again, what is striking is the sensitivity to the theological implications of the movement of the historical narrative.[107]

Other points where Owen elaborates the role of the Spirit include the miracles which Christ wrought, his guiding, directing, comforting, and supporting of the Messiah. On this latter point, Owen shows some discomfort with Mark's use of *drive out* at 1:12, preferring Luke's *led* in 4:1 as implying less external compulsion and more the action of reason in Christ's action;[108] yet he is clear that the Spirit does play a role in supporting the human nature in the person of the Mediator, a point which shows him clearly wrestling to connect post-Chalcedonian Christological Orthodoxy with the demands which the gospel texts place upon the exegete to do justice to the real effort which they ascribe to Christ's resistance of temptation, suffering and so on. By positing the anhypostasis and stressing the voluntary nature of the communication of attributes via the action of the Holy Spirit, Owen uses classical theological categories to achieve Reformation ends. Again, this is a strange

---

Reformed Dogmatics, 4 vols (Grand Rapids: Baker, 2003) I, 248–55; Willem J Van Asselt, 'The Fundamental Meaning of Theology: Archetypal and Ectypal Theology in Seventeenth-Century Reformed Thought,' *Westminster Theological* Journal 64 (2002), 319–35, especially 331–32.

107   *Works*, 3, 171–74.
108   *Works*, 3, 174.

emphasis if Reformed Orthodoxy is interested in metaphysical abstraction rather than the theological implications of biblical exegesis.[109]

Following the economic order of Christ's life, the next role Owen ascribes to the Spirit in terms of Christology is that of the part he plays in the atonement itself. In this context, the key text for Owen's view of the role of the Spirit is Heb. 9:14. In dealing with this text, Owen is aware of the textual debate surrounding the reading, whether it is to be taken as 'by the eternal Spirit,' referring to the Spirit of Christ himself (as in the Vulgate) or 'by the Holy Spirit' (as in the Syriac).[110] The doctrinal difference is that the former can be taken to mean the divine nature of Christ acting in the person of the Mediator, the latter to the actions of the Holy Spirit on Christ in supporting and helping him in his mission. Owen himself refuses to choose absolutely between the two, and regards the passage as embodying both elements. While he does concede that the reading 'eternal Spirit' is more likely, being attested more frequently in the earlier manuscripts, with the subsequent support of the Syriac and the Greek scholiasts; and the context of the passage is urging the superior efficacy of Christ's sacrifice over those of the Law, and thus the focus is most naturally to be understood as being on the superiority of Christ's person.[111] This would appear to be the conclusion of mainstream contemporary Reformed exegesis. Indeed, one of the other great Puritan commentaries on Hebrews, that of William Gouge, with which Owen was familiar, is emphatic in rejecting any reference to the Holy Spirit in this passage, and he is more typical than Owen on this point.[112]

Given this, it is hard not to read Owen here as knowing that the passage does not speak of the Holy Spirit, but as being yet unwilling to abandon it as part and parcel of the textual basis for his understanding of the role of the Spirit. He is certainly trying to find something in the passage which the main current of Reformed exegesis appears to reject. Gouge and company see the reference as speaking of the way in which Christ as Mediator offered up his human nature as a sacrifice which, by virtue of its union with the divine, thus had infinite value as a satisfaction.[113] Owen himself asserts this as taught by the passage; and the role of the anhypostasis is clearly implicit in this argument, given the role of the Logos in giving the human nature personhood, and in providing a context for the sacrifice and value of the death of the human nature through hypostatic union.[114] But he also adds that, because the human nature was both endowed with graces and was also a willing participant in the sacrifice, both of which things connect to the work of the Spirit in the person of the Mediator, then it is legitimate to read the passage as also implying that Christ

---

109 *Works*, 3, 175.

110 *Works*, 23, 303; cf. *Works*, 3, 176.

111 *Works*, 23, 305–06.

112 William Gouge, *A Learned and Very Useful Commentary on the Whole Epistle to the Hebrewes* (London, 1655), 356–57. This is also the position of the *Westminster Annotations* (1645); *Dutch Annotations* (1657); and Diodati, *Annotations* (1664). None of these sources entertain the possibility that the reference is to the Holy Spirit. Thus, Ussher, when he opts for the reference being to the divine nature, he stands within the mainstream exegetical tradition on this point: see *Immanuel*, 9.

113 See references in the previous note.

114 *Works*, 23, 304–05.

offered himself by the Holy Spirit.[115] In the earlier *Vindiciae Evangelicae*, he showed no such caution, identifying the fire on the Old Testament altar as a type of the Holy Spirit, and thus Heb. 9:14 as presenting the antitype with reference to the fulfillment in Christ.[116] Perhaps the years injected exegetical caution into Owen's thought since the earlier typological solution is decidedly muted in the later work.[117] It is of little doctrinal import, however, as Owen's basic dogmatic points concerning the role of the Spirit in Christ's gifts of grace, his real struggle in the prayer in the garden, his voluntary submission to suffering and death out of love for humanity and zeal for his Father's glory, all depend upon the Christological work of the Spirit as a dogmatic point and do not depend upon any single text for their basis.[118]

After the sacrifice on Calvary, Owen ascribes three more specific roles to the Holy Spirit in the Christological economy. First, while Christ's human soul was separated from his body in death, the hypostatic union of the two natures continued in the grave, thus preserved by the Holy Spirit.[119] Second, the Spirit is an agent in the resurrection. Here, Owen is aware that scripture ascribes the resurrection to each of the persons of the Trinity: the Father on account of his authority (for example Acts 2:24); Christ also claims authority over his own life and death (for example Jn 10:17–18); but the reuniting of soul and body was the peculiar action of the Holy Spirit, again consistent with the dogmatic axiom that all divine communicative actions vis-à-vis the human nature beyond that of giving hypostasis, are voluntary.[120] Third, the Spirit which had endowed the human nature of Christ with graces to make it holy now acts to make it glorious.[121] Thus, in positing a role for the Spirit in the glorified humanity of Christ, Owen provides a final touch to the profoundly Trinitarian way in which he understands Christology. The Spirit, like Christ, of course, has a significance beyond the history of salvation, however, in the actual economy of salvation as it relates to individuals; and it is to this we turn next in our examination of Owen's understanding of that quintessentially Protestant doctrine, justification by grace through faith alone.

Conclusion

It is clear from the arguments presented in this chapter that Owen's understanding of God's dealings with humanity finds its supreme articulation through the notion of covenant. A careful examination of Owen's method, typical of Reformed Orthodoxy in general, indicates that this is no naïve intrusion of commercial categories into the interpretation of scripture, but a conceptual vocabulary developed in careful relation both to exegesis, linguistics, conceptual reflection, and Trinitarianism. At

---

115 'Through the actings of these graces of the Holy Spirit in the human nature, his offering of himself was a free, voluntary oblation and sacrifice.' *Works*, 23, 305.

116 *Works*, 12, 432.

117 There is the briefest of passing allusions to it: *Works*, 23, 305.

118 *Works*, 3, 177–78.

119 *Works*, 3, 180–81.

120 *Works*, 3, 181–83.

121 *Works*, 3, 183.

one level, covenant is a typical seventeenth-century way of expressing relationships of various kinds between two or more parties: it is thus useful in explaining the relationship between God and humanity in the Garden of Eden, both as it helps explain the federal headship of Adam and the nature of human merit in relation to an infinite God who, in himself, is no one's debtor. Yet it also becomes significant in terms of God himself: it helps articulate the parallel headship of Christ to Adam in the covenant of grace; and it serves to explicate the precise nature of the voluntary economic relations that exist between the Persons of the Trinity as they connect to the great work of salvation. In this respect, Owen is a man of the late 1640s, able to utilize the language of covenant to describe the arrangement between Father and Son. Yet in discussing the details of how this covenant connects to history, we see once again that Owen, and the Reformed Orthodoxy for which he stands, represent a serious attempt to take the Catholic teaching on God as Trinity and on the person of Christ, and medieval discussions of issues such as merit and mediation, and connect them both to Protestant insights into the nature of creation and salvation and, where necessary, to correct and improve upon previous formulations; and this whole task is undertaken in a way which takes seriously conceptual, exegetical and linguistic developments. The Protestantism for which Owen stands is not a form of iconoclasm, whether a biblicist, anti-traditional, or obscurantist kind; rather it is a *critical traditionary* exercise which seeks to bring the best of the past into the present, offering critique, correction, and improvement where it is deemed necessary.

Chapter 4

The Article by Which the Church Stands or Falls

Introduction

The doctrine of justification, famously dubbed by Luther as 'the article by which the church stands or falls', was no less a controversial doctrine in Owen's time than it had been at the inception of the Reformation.[1] As with the other areas we have so far examined in this study, it is of course necessary at the outset to acknowledge the fact that Owen's context for his discussion of justification is a complex one. For a start, the basic significance of the doctrine as one of the key theological distinctives which marked Protestantism off from Roman Catholicism, meant that discussion of justification was always going to be profoundly political, both ecclesiastically and in the more general social sense. There were, by Owen's time, well-established polemical lines of debate between Protestants and Catholics into which his own exposition of the doctrine needs to be fitted. Second, the wider Western trajectories of doctrinal discussion within which the Reformed Orthodox stood also need to be taken into account: for all of the radical differences between Protestant and Catholic theologians on this issue, particularly as these positions received confessional codification at the Council of Trent and then in subsequent Protestant creeds, both Catholics and Protestants conducted their discussions in terms which one might broadly characterize as Augustinian, being rooted in the anti-Pelagian writings of the Bishop of Hippo and in the understandings of righteousness, divine and human, and other corollary doctrines which were developed in its aftermath. Once again, we need to remember Owen was not just a Reformed, or even Protestant, theologian; we also need to keep in mind that he was an *Augustinian* theologian.[2] Third, Owen

---

1   Owen quotes Luther (without giving a specific textual reference) as saying 'Amisso articulo justificationis, simul amissa est tota doctrina Christiana' ('When the article of justification is lost, the whole of Christian teaching is lost at the same time'), *Works* 5, 67. Standard histories of the doctrine are: Albrecht Ritschl, *The Christian Doctrine of Justification and Reconciliation*, trans. H R Mackintosh and A B Macaulay (Edinburgh: T&T Clark, 1900); Alister E McGrath, *Iustitia Dei: A History of the Christian Doctrine of Justification*, 3rd ed. (Cambridge: Cambridge University Press, 2005).

2   I am aware of the problematic nature of this term; I use it to refer to a theologian who stands within the broad, anti-Pelagian tradition of Western theology, and who has a high regard for the authority of Augustine's writings. The problem with the term is not, of course, simply that which typically affects any broad tradition or collection of traditions which take their name from an individual and thus raise complex question about fidelity, continuity and so on with the conceptual content of the work of the original writer. For example, theologian

wrote on justification in the context of an England where specific local difficulties had imposed peculiar requirements on theologians dealing specifically with this doctrine: antinomianism and neonomianism both arose in specific social contexts and were symbiotic in an antagonistic way; Owen needed to bear the Scylla of one and the Charybdis of the other in mind as he penned his great treatise on the topic.[3]

Developments in Protestant Notions of Justification Prior to Owen

When Luther first launched his assault on Tetzel's hawking of indulgences, and, in the heat of subsequent polemic, came to give clear shape to his understanding of justification by faith, it was not immediately obvious either to him or indeed to many of his opponents, that what he was saying was heretical by the dogmatic standards of the Catholic Church simply because the Church had no clear definition of the doctrine at this point. The Council of Trent subsequently plugged this gap by establishing clear boundaries of dogmatic reflection on the topic and thus setting the basic agenda for the debate between Roman and Protestant communions, Lutheran and Reformed.

Prior to Trent, the earliest period of Reformed confessionalisation was to a large degree the work of the Swiss Reformation which typically exhibited less concern with the centrality of justification than did Luther and his colleagues. Thus, for example, there is no elaborate discussion of justification in Zwingli's *Theses* (1523), but simply a clear declaration that sins are only forgiven because of Christ, a point which in the context is aimed at the abusive nature of the Roman penitential system.[4] In similar vein, the *Berne Theses* (1528) also make only brief reference to Christ as the only wisdom, righteousness, redemption, and ransom in what is little more than a paraphrase of 1 Cor. 1:30.[5] As Protestantism developed, discussion became more elaborate and it becomes clear from later documents that, while Reformed and Lutheran may have disagreed over the structural importance of justification, the

---

Daphne Hampson has raised the significant question of whether the underlying notions of humanity and personhood in Catholicism and Protestantism are not fundamentally different, the former being primarily substantial, the latter more relational. From this, she has argued that Protestantism deviates significantly from Augustine in a manner which has decisive impact on the notion of justification: see her *Christ Contradictions: The Structure of Lutheran and Catholic Thought* (Cambridge: Cambridge University Press, 2001).

3   Two recent studies on the subject of the context of antinomianism which are worth consulting are David R Como, *Blown by the Spirit: Puritanism and the Emergence of an Antinomian Underground in Pre-Civil-War England* (Stanford: Stanford University Press, 2004); and Theodore Dwight Bozeman, *The Precisianist Strain: Disciplinary Religion and Antinomian Backlash in Puritanism to 1638* (Chapel Hill: University of North Carolina Press, 2003).

4   As a source for Reformed confessions, the best collection available is that in E F K Müller, *Die Bekenntnisschriften der reformierten Kirche* (Leipzig: Deichert, 1903), hereafter *DBDRK*, a far more comprehensive collection than that available in Philip Schaff, *The Creeds of Christendom*, 3 vols (Grand Rapids: Baker, 1983). The relevant section of Zwingli's *Theses* is found in *DBDRK*, 5 (Theses 50–56).

5   *DBDRK*, 30 (Thesis III).

basic content of the doctrine (by grace, Christ's righteousness being imputed to the believer, faith being the instrument) was a Protestant given. Thus Article 11 of the *Forty-Two Articles* (1552) states that justification is by faith alone, and explicitly connects this to the teaching in the *Homily on Justification* which, according to Article 34 has the status of authoritative church teaching. While the 1562 *Thirty-Nine Articles* expanded Article 11 somewhat, this was only to underline the essential Protestantism of the original.[6] Detailed elaboration of the Christological foundation of this is found in 34–38 of *The Irish Articles* of 1615.[7] On the continent, a similar consensus is evident:

Given the confessional consensus on justification as involving remission of sins and imputation of Christ's righteousness, it will be useful to make two further comments. The first is that this consensus did not represent a divorce of theological conceptualization from careful linguistic and exegetical study of the Bible. If any were to assume such, it would indicate a serious misunderstanding both of the close general connection between exegesis and theological formulation which existed in seventeenth- century Reformed dogmatics, and a failure to acknowledge that the Reformed Orthodox were well aware of the difference between a conceptual term used to refer to a specific technical theological doctrine and the variety of ways in which the word might be used in scripture. As with covenant, so with justification: Reformed Orthodox discussion exhibits considerable consensus on the broad meaning of the doctrinal term and sensitivity to the various meanings and nuances of the language of justification, righteousness and their cognates in scripture.

This is evident from some of the basic treatments of the doctrine produced in the early seventeenth century. For example, William Pemble, in his *Vindiciae Fidei*, starts his discussion by outlining the different uses of the relevant word groups.[8] Thus, he distinguishes legal righteousness (of obedience, of punishment) from evangelical righteousness (Christological); and justification by infusion from justification by *apologie* or declaration. In this latter category, he notes the different nuances in scripture: sometimes it is used of outward conformity to the law, either in general or in some specific point wherein a person is accused of transgression; and sometimes it refers to those who are guilty of some transgression but for whose transgression satisfaction has been offered, either by another, by the transgressor, or by some combination of the two. This latter is, of course, how Protestantism in general understood the righteousness of Christ to function relative to the believing sinner.[9]

While the imputation of Christ's righteousness as the formal cause of justification before God was thus basically a given within Protestantism as a whole by the middle of the seventeenth-century, debate on what precisely this meant was far from over. Central to these discussions were differing opinions about the definition of Christ's righteousness, and which aspects of this righteousness were specifically imputed

---

6   *DBDRK*, 40, 34. Further Anglican formulation of justification is found in the Lambeth Articles (1595): *DBDRK*, 525–26.

7   *DBDRK*, 530–31.

8   *Vindiciae Fidei: Or, A Treatise of Justification by Faith* (Oxford, 1629).

9   *Vindiciae Fidei*, 1–7.

to the believer. That this was an issue which actually divided the orthodox was most dramatically demonstrated within the Reformed camp by the debates at the Westminster Assembly, where no less important individuals than the first prolocutor, William Twisse, and the renowned linguist and theologian, Thomas Gataker, both argued that it was only Christ's passive righteousness, not his active righteousness, which was imputed to the believer.[10]

At first glance, the debate seems somewhat obscure to readers today, but it was of some significance at the time, developing in the seventeenth century as a response to various particular contemporary issues, a point which explains the silence of earlier theologians and confessional documents on the matter. On one level, the argument connected to Christological questions relative to the office of Christ as sponsor of the covenant of grace: did his salvific work start at conception or when he was handed over to the authorities in the Garden of Gethsemane? Differences on this were reflected in the construction of the twofold state of Christ, with Arminians tending to locate the state of humiliation proper as beginning with the latter. For example, in his *Private Disputation XXVIII*, Arminius follows the emphases in the Apostles' Creed and locates the humiliation as starting with his suffering under Pontius Pilate and ends with his descent into Hell.[11] The overall dogmatic impact of this was twofold: the work of Christ which was then imputed to the believer in justification did not directly involve his positive fulfillment of the law prior to Gethsemane but was focused much more sharply upon his death and resurrection.

The formalizing of the distinction between Christ's active and passive righteousness in the later sixteenth century is clear in the work of Daniel Tilenus and Johannes Piscator, the Herborn theologian. Indeed, two works of Piscator on justification were published in England in the decades before the Westminster Assembly. The first, *A learned and profitable treatise of mans justification* (London, 1599), a translation of a 1594 treatise written at the request of his friend, the soon-to-be infamous Conrad Vorstius, was a response to the Jesuit, Bellarmine, on the issue of whether justification involved imparting or imputing of righteousness. Not surprisingly, Piscator argued for the latter; but, perhaps more significantly, he consistently identified justification as merely remission of sins, and focused his argument on the death of Christ as the basis for this remission, with the life being notable in its absence from inclusion in the work of satisfaction.[12] The second work is a Latin treatise, presented as a three-way discussion between Piscator, Lodovicus Lucius of Basle, and Thomas Gataker.[13] In this work, Piscator's argument is that

---

10 Mitchell and Struthers, lxvi.

11 *The Works of James Arminius*, trans. James Nichols, 3 vols (Grand Rapids: Baker, 1991), 2: 386–88.

12 For example, *A learned and profitable treatise*, 2, 5–6, 13, 105–06. This identifation of justification as simple remission marks a move away from Arminius, who still maintained that justification involved both remission and an accounting as righteous: see *Private Disputation* XLVIII (*Works* 3: 405–07). Turretin devotes an entire question to refuting the idea that justification is merely remission: *Institutes* 16.4.

13 *D Ioannis Piscatoris Herbonensis et M Lodovici Lucii Basiliensis, Scripta quaedam adversaria; De Causa meritoria nostri coram Deo Justificationis: una cum Thomae Gatakeri Londinatis Animadversionibus in utraque* (London, 1641).

Christ's active obedience is that which qualifies him to act as mediator, but is not in itself a part of the mediatorial work, something reserved for the passive obedience.[14] This argument appears to lie at the heart of Gataker's own position, whereby Christ *as creature* is obliged to the law because of his own status as creature and is therefore no part of what one might term the work of supererogation which constitutes the vicarious work of salvation which he performs for others.[15] We should be wary, however, of too closely identifying the position of Gataker with that of Piscator: the argument of law obligation is a commonplace in Western theology, and finds its most notable and influential expression in Anselm's work, *Cur Deus Homo*; further, given that Gataker is adamant that remission of sins is not identical with, and is indeed, really separable from, justification, his position clearly needs to be distinguished from that of Piscator on this issue.[16]

The question of active/passive righteousness and imputation was raised at the Westminster Assembly before the arrival of the Scottish delegation, at a point in the proceedings when the debate was really focused on the revision of the Thirty-Nine Articles. In a series of speeches on Article 11, 'Of the Justification of Man before God', Daniel Featley offered the most elaborate and significant arguments for the twofold righteousness of Christ in justification.[17] Ultimately, Featley won the day, with the majority of divines approving the term 'whole obedience and satisfaction' in the revised article, though the adjective 'whole' is absent from the later Westminster Confession 11:3.[18] Given the content of Questions 70–73 of the Larger Catechism, I am inclined not to read huge significance into this omission: possibly it was a move designed to preserve the consensual nature of the confessional documents, perhaps a mild concession to the party of Twisse and Gataker.[19] Recent research on the original minutes of the Assembly indicates that this is a mystery which is likely to remain

---

14   'Activam vero obedientiam praestitit Christus ut esset idoneus as passivam pro nobis praestandam, et ad nos per illam redimendos.' *Scripta quaedam adversaria*, Part One, 5.

15   *Scripta quaedam adversaria*, Part One, 68; Part Three, 10–11.

16   Contrast the claims of Piscator, *Scripta quaedam adversaria*, Part One, 33–34, with Gataker, Part 1, 9–10, 21; cf. Gataker, *An Antidote against Errour concerning Justification* (London, 1679), 11–14, where Gataker offers linguistic and logical arguments for seeing the two as separate.

17   Daniel Featley, *The Dippers Dipt*, 5th ed (London, 1647), 192–211. Featley represents the mainstream English Reformed view in this argument; for example, while William Perkins does not address the issue directly and precisely in the same terms as Gataker and Featley, it is clear that he regards the imputation of Christ's righteousness as involving that of both his death and his obedience to the law: see his comments in *A Golden Chaine*, *Works* (1603), 87, and in *A Reformed Catholike*, *Works* (1603), 681; James Ussher, *Eighteen Sermons Preached in Oxford 1640* (London, 1660), 370–92. Cf. *Synopsis purioris theologiae* 33.8; Turretin, *Institutes* 14.13.

18   *The Westminster Standards: An Original Facsimile* (Audubon: Old Paths Publications, 1997) contains a facsimile of both the revised Articles and the final Confession.

19   It is interesting to note that, when the question was put in the Assembly, Featley himself brought to the Divines' attention an old letter of James I which urged the delegates to a synod in France not to divide over the issue, as being one of recent vintage and of little importance. The letter, with translation, is reprinted in Featley, *Dippers Dipt*, 212–24.

a moot point, given the lack of a solid enough evidential base for any definite and precise conclusions to be drawn.[20]

The question arises, of course, as to why a figure like Gataker and, even more so, the highly orthodox Twisse, should be prepared to argue the case at the Westminster Assembly for a position which was arguably a more typical position for Remonstrants to hold. There is no decisive answer to this: we could simply take Gataker's linguistic, exegetical and Christological arguments at face value and conclude that he simply found these more compelling than any of the alternatives. Such would be a perfectly legitimate conclusion. It is worth noting, however, that, in the context of the 1640s, the issue of justification was something of a hot potato, not simply as a glass-bead game for ivory-tower theologians but also as something of profound political and social significance. Richard Baxter, for example, in his 1649 treatise, *Aphorismes of Justification* (London), expounds three positions: active and passive obedience both imputed;[21] passive obedience only imputed;[22] and a third position whereby the traditional active and passive distinctions are effectively made redundant by recourse to the Grotian distinction of *solutio eiusdem/tantidem*. This distinction was borrowed from Roman law and deployed by Grotius in his 1617 treatise, *A Defence of the Catholic Faith concerning the Satisfaction of Christ against Faustus Socinus*.[23] In the face of Socinian objections that, if God punishes sin on the cross, then salvation subsequent to that becomes not so much a matter of forgiveness as a matter of right and justice, Grotius argues that debts can be paid in one of two ways: by an identical satisfaction (*solutio eiusdem*) or by an equivalent satisfaction (*solutio tantidem*). If Christ's death is identical, then the Socinian point is valid; but if equivalent, then a further act of God intervenes between atonement and salvation, and it is in this act that mercy can be seen.[24]

Baxter confesses he spent ten years believing in the second option, mainly because of what he saw as the multiple weaknesses of the first, but has now come to believe in the third, Grotian, position.[25] It is clear from the way he speaks that the real fear he has is that the first option gives too much ground for antinomianism, something which Baxter, traumatized by the chaos he witnessed as an army chaplain,

---

20   See Chad B Van Dixhoorn, "Reforming the Reformation: Theological Debate at the Westminster Assembly 1643–1652", (PhD dissertation, University of Cambridge, 2004) 7 vols, vol 1, 324–330. Van Dixhoorn summarises what is known of the debate and offers a series of possible explanations for the change from the revised Article 11 of the 39 Articles to the final draft of Chapter 11 of the *Westminster Confession*. I find myself in sympathy with his view that the revision of the Westminster Confession of Faith (WCF) at Savoy, when imputation of active and passive obedience is made explicit, indicates a probably consensual motive for the Westminster Assembly's earlier action.

21   *Aphorismes*, 44–52. Earlier in the treatise, he warns the reader of his rejection of the traditional distinction: see 23.

22   *Aphorismes*, 52–54.

23   The text can be found in *Opera Omnia Theologica* (Amsterdam, 1679), III.

24   Grotius, *Opera* III, 319–20. Cf. Trueman, *The Claims of Truth*, 210–11.

25   *Aphorismes*, 54.

will spend his life writing against.[26] This fear of antinomianism cannot be discounted as a factor in the debates at the Westminster Assembly, and the writings of Gataker, particularly his refutation of John Saltmarsh, would appear to support this, as does Daniel Featley's identification of antinomianism as one rather unwelcome source of support for the imputation of Christ's active obedience.[27] But the antinomian background has systematic significance for Baxter as well: he also underscores the connection that exists between justification and atonement, because both are functions of Christ's office as mediator, specifically, his office as high priest; and the Grotian distinction in this regard allows Baxter to avoid what he sees as the implication of eternal justification which the *solutio eiusdem* concept implies: if the actual sins of a particular sinner are really imputed to Christ and punished on the cross, then that sinner is, from that moment onwards, really justified, regardless of when they come to exercise faith. In other words, for Baxter the problem with Reformed Orthodox views of imputation is not simply that what is imputed to *the believer* subverts the need for good works; it is also that what is imputed to *Christ* subverts the need for good works as well.

Owen on Imputation of Active and Passive Righteousness

When Owen comes to write on justification in 1677, then the debate about justification, specifically with reference to imputation and Christology, was considerably more elaborate that it had been in the sixteenth century. In fact, Owen's commitment to imputation of both is evident from the *Savoy Declaration* of 1658 which was essentially a modification of the Westminster Confession. Most of the modifications involve the teaching on church polity, but the article on justification is expanded from the Westminster Confession of Faith to include specific reference to the imputation of both the active and passive righteousness of Christ. Owen, along

---

26   On Baxter's theology in the context of antinomianism, the older study of Packer is still useful: J I Packer, *The Redemption and Restoration of Man in the Thought of Richard Baxter* (Regent: Vancouver, 2003), a virtual reprint of his previously unpublished 1954 Oxford DPhil dissertation. The more recent work of Timothy Cooper is of particular help in this context: *Fear and Polemic in Seventeenth Century England: Richard Baxter and Antinomianism* (London: Ashgate, 2001). On the theology, H. Boersma, *A Hot Peppercorn: Richard Baxter's Doctrine of Justification in its Seventeenth Century Context of Controversy* (Zoetermeer: Boekencentrum, 1993) should also be consulted, although the Amyraladian sympathies of the author tend, from my perspective, to influence the analysis, particularly in terms of how antinomianism is understood.

27   *Antinomianism Discovered and Confuted: and Free-Grace as it is held forth in Gods Word* (London 1652), 32–33. Here Gataker expresses concern that John Saltmarsh's soteriology is rooted in an emphasis upon the objectivity of Christ's work which really undoes all moral imperatives in the Christian life to the point of absurdity, as when Saltmarsh even speaks of Christ *repenting* on behalf of his people. In his third speech to the Assembly on Article 11, Featley identifies four groups as standing outside of the Assembly's consensus on the matter: Antinomians; Papists; Arminians; and Socinians. Of these four, the Antinomians support the doctrine but conclude therefrom that the moral law is consequently irrelevant to believers: see *Dippers Dipt*, 199–200.

with Thomas Goodwin, was one of the principal architects of the document, and thus the document can be assumed to reflect his theology and his view of the inadequacy or ambiguity of the original Westminster Confession of Faith formulation.[28]

Owen's major discussion of justification is *The Doctrine of Justification by Faith, through the Imputation of the Righteousness of Christ; Explained, Confirmed, and Vindicated* (London, 1677), although some of the issues had been touched on numerous occasions in previous works, most notably those in the exchange with Baxter surrounding the latter's *Aphorisms of Justification*. In *The Doctrine of Justification*, Owen makes the claim in the preliminary chapter that he does not intend to deal with the passive/active distinction at any length.[29] Nevertheless, he then proceeds in the treatise itself to tackle the issue head on, as it lies very much at the heart of the debates in which he was engaged.

As one would expect, particularly in light of the *Savoy Declaration*, Owen maintains the standard orthodox position of the imputation of both Christ's active and his passive obedience; and he articulates this position through polemical examination of the arguments against this point. As far as his opponents go, he divides them into three groups regarding the role of Christ's active obedience in the work of justification: those who see it as impossible; those who see it as useless; and those who see it as pernicious.[30] In the first group, he cites Socinus, *De Jesu Christo Servatore* 3.5, as arguing that Christ's obedience was necessary for his own salvation, and that even his death was an offering on behalf of himself, which God then rewarded with adoption.[31] This is clearly consistent with Socinian soteriology, rejecting as it does the vicarious nature of Christ's work and insisting instead upon its paradigmatic significance. Thus, Smalcius's *Racovian Catechism*, Chapter 8, 'Of Christ's Death' , makes it clear that the death is purely an example and an encouragement to believers, and that any notion of vicarious sacrifice or satisfaction is 'fallacious, erroneous, and very pernicious' a point which has obvious significance for the nature of justification.[32]

It is worth remembering, however, that, although Owen chooses to focus on the Socinians in refuting this position, it is not entirely different to that articulated by Piscator and Gataker who regarded Christ's positive obedience to the law as being

---

28   *Savoy* XI.i reads as follows: 'Those whom God effectually calleth, he also freely justifieth, not by infusing righteousness into them, but by pardoning their sins, and by accounting and accepting their persons as righteous, nor for any thing wrought in them, or done by them, but for Christ's sake alone; nor by imputing Faith itself, the act of believing, or any other Evangelical obedience to them, as their righteousness, but by imputing Christs active obedience unto the whole Law, and passive obedience in his death for their whole and sole righteousness, they receiving and resting on him and his righteousness by Faith; which Faith they have not of themselves, it is the gift of God.' *A Declaration of the Faith and Order Owned and practiced in the Congregational Churches in England* (London, 1658), 20–21.

29   *Works*, 5, 63.

30   *Works*, 5, 252.

31   *Works*, 5, 253.

32   *The Racovian Catechism* (Amsterdam, 1652), 122–139, especially 126; cf. the comments of Francis Cheynell, *The Rise, Growth, and Danger of Socinianisme* (London, 1643), 24.

part of his obligation as rational creature, although the teleological significance is clearly very different. Indeed, the connection between Socinianism and those who were 'soft' on the imputation of Christ's active obedience was already well-established in the controversial rhetoric of the time, and not entirely without some historical foundation. For example, Piscator's *Profitable Treatise* was, the author tells us, written at the request of his friend, Conrad Vorstius who wished him to refute Bellarmine on justification. The preface is dated 18 December 1593, some time before Vorstius became Public Enemy No. 1 in the Reformed world; but the connection was surely not insignificant, either theologically or in terms of public association.[33] Further, Anthony Wotton, a leading English proponent of something akin to Piscator's position, was subject to a decades-long campaign accusing him of being a Socinian, a campaign mounted by the vigorously orthodox George Walker. Walker himself was to be a delegate at the Westminster Assembly, and was to target Gataker also as a Socinian.[34] We should note, however, that the notion that Christ's obedience to the law was an essential component of fitting him to offer his death as a satisfaction on behalf of others had a long pedigree in Western theology and lay very much at the heart of Anselm's rationale for incarnation in *Cur Deus Homo*.

In opposition to this rejection of the imputation of both active and passive righteousness, Owen argues from the integrity of the person and work of the mediator to the necessity for seeing both active and passive righteousness imputed to the believer. Central to this is the typical Orthodox primary emphasis upon the *person* of the mediator, not the *natures* of the mediator:

> If the obedience that Christ yielded unto the law were for himself, whereas it was the act of his person, *his whole person*, and the divine nature therein, were 'made under the law;' which cannot be. For although it is acknowledged that, in the ordination of God, his exinanition was to precede his glorious, majestical exaltation, as the Scripture witnesseth, Phil. 2:19; Lk 24:26; Rom. 14:9; yet absolutely his glory was an immediate consequent of the hypostatical union, Heb. 1:6; Mt. 2:11.[35]

---

33   *A profitable treatise*, Preface.

34   Walker pursued Wotton with an obsessive commitment which can only lead later observers of his campaign to speculate about what personal issues lay beneath the surface. He even kept up the campaign long after Wotton's death in 1626. Walker's account of the dispute, which began in 1611, can be found in his *A True Relation of the chiefe passages betweene Mr Anthony Wotton, and Mr George Walker* (London, 1642). Wotton's position can be found in the work which his son published posthumously, *Mr Anthony Wotton's Defence Against Mr George Walker's Charge, Accusing him of Socinian Heresie and Blasphemie* (Cambridge, 1641), itself a response to Walker's *Socinianisme in the Fundamentall point of Justification discovered and confuted* (1641). Wotton's work contained a preface and postscript by Gataker. Gataker himself had to go into print to defend himself against the charge of Socinianism made against him by Walker: *An Answer to Mr George Walkers Vindication or rather Fresh Accusation* (London, 1642). See also P Lake and D Como, '"Orthodoxy" and its discontents: dispute settlement and the production of "consensus" in the London (puritan) "underground,"' *Journal of British Studies* 39 (2000), 34–70.

35   *Works* 12, 256. Cf. the similar argument of George Downame: 'But these men shold have remembred, that the person, who ... did obey the Law, was and is not onely man but God also, and therefore, as his bloud was Gods bloud, so his obedience was the obedience of God,

Of course, such an argument is scarcely likely to persuade any Socinian because they would reject the major presupposition, the Chalcedonian definition of Christ's person. Nevertheless, within a Reformed Orthodox framework, the argument is clearly a coherent one, pointing back to the establishment of Christ as mediator under the terms of the covenant of redemption, and assuming mediation according to both nature and the anhypostatic nature of Christ's humanity. The union of natures in the Incarnation is what qualifies Christ as capable of acting as mediator, and this is because that union is determined by the voluntary covenant of redemption, the doctrinal context for understanding the incarnate Mediator.[36] Owen accepts the medieval Scotist terminology of *viator* and *possessor* as applied to Christ, to distinguish his earthly sojourn from his later glory, but sees the historical movement contained therein as reflecting the voluntarily established terms of the covenant, and not as indicating any initial deficiency in his qualifications as mediator.[37]

The importance of federalism is also clear in several of Owen's other arguments on this issue. For Owen, it is crucial that Christ's appointment as mediator in the covenant of redemption means that all his works are those of voluntary condescension in the ordained economy of salvation, not necessary to his being, and as such their significance and value is determined by the covenant which is the defining ground of the work of incarnation.[38] In addition, the position of Christ as federal sponsor means that he always acts in a public, not a private or personal capacity, and that strict comparison with any other individual is not legitimate. His whole life, having its causal ground in the covenant of redemption, is that of the sponsor of the covenant of grace, and thus in its entirety it has a significance which embraces all of the objects of the covenant of grace. The theology of federal headship, rooted in the covenant of redemption between Father and Son, thus repeatedly connects to the debate on

---

and consequently was performed not of duty, nor for himselfe. For if of duty, then God had been a debtor to the Law: Neither needed the humane nature, being by personall union united to the divine, to obey, or to merit for it selfe; seeing from the first moment of the conception therof, it was personally united to the Deity of the Sonne of God, in whose person it subsisting was, from the beginning of the being therof, most happy, and enjoying the beatificall vision, being at that time, as the Schoolemen speake both *viator et comprehensor*. Neither did the humane nature, which doth not subsist by it selfe, work any thing by it selfe in the work of our redemption, but God manifested in the flesh, did in and by it both obey and suffer for us.' *A Treatise of Justification* (London, 1634), 29. Cf. the argument of Featley to the Westminster Assembly, *Dippers Dipt*, 196; also Ussher, *Immanuel, or, The Mystery of the Incarnation of the Son of God* (London, 1653), 11.

36   'The Lord Christ was every way meet for the whole work of mediation, by the ineffable union of the human nature with the divine, which exalted it in dignity, honour, and worth, above any thing or all things that ensued thereon ... Again, that which is an effect of the person of the Mediator, as constituted such, is not a qualification necessary unto its constitution; that is, what he did as mediator did not concur in the making of him meet so to be.' *Works* 5, 258. '[T]he compact between the Father and the Son as unto his undertaking for us ... undeniably proves all that he did in the pursuit of them to be done for us, and not for himself.' *Works*, 5, 258–59.

37   *Works*, 5, 259.

38   *Works*, 5, 257–58.

justification and allows for conceptual precision in clarifying the status and role of Christ as mediator.[39]

In this context, Owen engages both in his treatise on justification and in his commentary on Hebrews in an extended refutation of the notion that Christ's sponsorship, as mentioned in Heb. 7:22, refers to his sponsorship on behalf of God, whereby the covenant is shown to human beings to be sound. This was the exegesis favoured by Socinians such as Schlichtingius, Remonstrants, such as Grotius, and the influential seventeenth-century English commentator, Bishop Hammond, all of whose works are explicitly mentioned by Owen in this context.[40] Owen, standing within an established and respectable exegetical tradition at this point, argues rather that the sponsorship is on behalf of men and women and directed to God, not on behalf of God and directed to men and women.[41] What this does, of course, is secure the priesthood, and thus the sacrifice, of Christ as something which is offered to God, and which thus refuses to reduce the significance of the incarnation simply to revealing something of God. Again, the roots of Owen's argument in this context lie theologically with his understanding of the covenant of redemption, but, as noted, his exegesis is not exceptional.[42] Further, his understanding of the etymology of the Greek word itself leads him to argue that sponsorship presupposes inadequacy or defect on behalf of the party being represented by the sponsor; and this cannot apply to God but only to the sons and daughters of Adam. Here, his thinking connects with Roman law: Owen translates the Greek as *surety*, as do the Geneva Bible and

---

39 *Works*, 5, 260–61; also *Works* 10, 174–177; *Works* 12, 502–03; cf. David Dickson, *The summe of saving knowledge* (Edinburgh, 1671), Head II; also Patrick Gillespie, *The Ark of the Covenant Opened* (London, 1677). In this context, it is interesting to note that the Savoy Declaration modifies Chapter 8 of the WCF by explicitly using covenantal language to describe the appointment of Christ as mediator by the Father. As the specific conceptual terminology of the covenant of redemption did not start to become commonplace in Reformed theology until the late 1640s, it is not significant that it is absent from the WCF.

40 *Works*, 5, 182–83; 22, 499–500. Hammond's comment reads as follows: 'Christ was Sponsor and Surety [of that covenant] for God, that it should be made good to us on Gods part (on condition we performed that which was required of us) viz. the Covenant confirmed to us by Christ in the Gospel, a better Covenant then the Covenant of the Law, wherein Moses undertook for God to us.' *Annotations upon all the Books of the New Testament* (London, 1659), 741.

41 *Works*, 5, 184–96; 22, 501–12.

42 See especially *Works* 5, 191; 22, 505. Cf. William Gouge, *A Learned and Very Useful Commentary on the Whole Epistle to the Hebrewes* (London, 1655), 193–94; David Dickson, *An Exposition of all St Pauls Epistles*, 196; Edward Leigh, *A Systeme or Body of Divinity* (London, 1657), 575; See also the definition in Thomas Wilson, *A Christian Dictionary* (London, 1647), n.p.: 'Surety 1. One that undertaketh for the debt of another man. Prov. 6.1 ... 2. Christ, who undertooke to answer the debt of our sins to Gods justice, by his obedience to death. Heb. 7.22.' While this particular point is not a matter of comment in either the *Dutch Annotations* or the various editions of the *Westminster Annotations*, Giovanni Diodati does mention it, and offers something of a mediating position, whereby Christ is surety for the elect in satisfying God's wrath, and for God by assuring believers of the Father's favour through the Spirit: *Pious and Learned Annotations upon the Whole Bible* (London, 1648), 375 (New Testament).

the Authorised Version, and states that this is the equivalent of *fideiussor*.[43] This is a term drawn from Roman law to refer to a guarantor of a debt or obligation who acts voluntarily and on behalf of the one in debt.[44] In all of this, particularly in his use of the language of *sponsor* (the term used in the Vulgate) and *fideiussor*, he stands within typical Reformed Orthodox treatments of Christology in the context of the covenant of redemption.[45]

The final argument Owen offers in this refutation of the Socinian claims concerning the impossibility of imputation of active obedience, relates to the meaning of the term *under law*, which he reads his opponents as meaning 'obliged to obey God by virtue of the relationship that necessarily exists between the Creator and all rational creatures' Owen accepts that this is indeed the case, but then pushes the argument forward into the eschatological realm: Christ's human nature, as a creature, will be obliged to God as creator even in the eschaton, a point he supports with reference to the communication of properties which will never involve the direct communication of self-existent deity to Christ's humanity; but, argues Owen, to claim that this involves the heavenly Christ being *under law* in the Pauline sense of *obliged to fulfill it on his own account* is clearly absurd in such a context. Further, the notion of the law as specially imposed by God with a view to reward also points to the absurdity of seeing Christ as *under law* for his own sake: again, the hypostatic union itself was quite sufficient to make Christ's human nature worthy of eternal life for itself. Here we see the obvious doctrinal intersection of the covenant of works and that of redemption in the context of Christology and mediation.[46]

Indeed, as Owen elaborates upon the saving efficacy of Christ's mediation, he is very clear that the terms of Christ's penal work on the cross are set by the Creator–creature framework as covenantally established in Genesis 1–3. Working against the background of Reformed exegesis of Romans 5, with its parallel of Adam and Christ, Owen argues in *Of the Death of Christ*, his 1650 response to Baxter's *Aphorisms*, that the penalty which Christ underwent as federal sponsor on behalf of the elect was death; and in so doing, he connects Gal. 3:13, Rom. 8:3, and Gn. 2:17.[47] Thus, as representative human being, Christ must both fulfill the law positively on behalf of humanity because of Adam's abject failure so to do, and he must undergo punishment of death because of Adam's breaking of the original covenant. It is not Christ's ontology as the Divine–human person which requires this, but his covenantal status as representative which demands it.

The presence of these three types of argument (from hypostatic union; from condescension; and from federal headship) at least in a very brief form in earlier works by Downame and Featley suggests that, by the time he writes in the 1670s, Owen is working within an established framework of standard Orthodox responses

---

43   *Works*, 5, 184, 187.

44   For example, Justinian, *Institutes* III.xx.

45   See the entries under *fideiussio* and *sponsio* in Richard A Muller, *A Dictionary of Latin and Greek Theological Terms* (Grand Rapids: Baker, 1985).

46   *Works*, 5, 261–62.

47   *Works*, 10, 448.

to criticisms of the mainstream position.[48] As is typical of Owen, however, this lack of originality in the basic trajectories of argument does not prevent him from engaging in significant theological elaboration, of a kind which lays bare the sophisticated underlying structure of the Reformed Orthodox theology to which he is committed, particularly as it finds its ground in the doctrine of the Trinity, specifically the covenant of redemption and its determinative impact upon both the history and the order of salvation. Having highlighted this, it is now necessary to turn to one of the implications which his opponents saw in the connection he drew between atonement and justification: the problems of eternal justification, with its connotations of antinomianism.[49]

Owen and Eternal Justification

The primary criticism of Owen on atonement and justification came from Richard Baxter, for whom the issues of antinomianism and its perceived conceptual foundation, eternal justification, were more than just theological games. His experience in the Civil War as an army chaplain left a lasting impression on him: the impact and influence of radical sectarianism and its frequent connection to what Baxter regarded as moral anarchy left Baxter with a lasting fear of anything which might disrupt the smooth-running of the godly commonwealth, be it antinomianism or pedantic doctrinal militancy.[50]

It should be noted at the outset that the Protestant doctrine of justification by imputation was always going to be vulnerable to criticisms of tending towards eternal justification. Late medieval theologians had used the distinction between God's absolute power and his ordained power, along with that between congruent and condign merit, to break the necessary connection between the logical priority of actual righteousness in a real sense, and God's declaration that a particular

---

48 Featley, *Dippers Dipt*, 196–197; Downame, *Treatise*, 29.

49 It is worth mentioning that one final argument used by Owen's contemporaries to deny the imputation of Christ's double righteousness to the believer is a more straightforwardly exegetical one, and this again serves to bring out the importance of federalism to Owen's own theological position. Gataker is a good example of this: in his *Antidote*, he argues that scripture never associates the life of Christ with the works of redemption, remission, and justification; rather, the textual evidence points squarely towards the suffering and death of Christ as being the grounds for this: see *An Antidote against Errour*, 5, 28–31. Featley himself responded to such arguments as proposed by Tilenus and Piscator in his second speech on Article 11 to the Westminster Assembly: *Dippers Dipt*, 196–97. By Owen's day, then, the standard response to this was to argue that references in the New Testament to the blood of Christ and so on are to be taken synecdochically, and that they simply subsume both active and passive obedience under the one term; it is thus hardly surprising that we should find Owen making this conventional case: *Works* 5, 271.

50 See Carl R Trueman, 'Richard Baxter on Christian Unity: A Chapter in the Enlightening of English Reformed Orthodoxy', (*WTJ*) 61 (1999), 53–71; on the question of Baxter and the church in general, of particular note is the work of Paul H-C Lim, *In Pursuit of Purity, Unity, and Liberty: Richard Baxter's Puritan Ecclesiology in Its Seventeenth-Century Context* (Leiden: Brill, 2004).

person was justified. Thus, in placing the declaration in God's will, not the intrinsic qualities of the one justified, it is arguable that the necessary connection not only between ontological factors and justification but also between chronological factors and justification had been decisively abolished. Given that Protestantism actually intensified this medieval emphasis, it is not surprising that some Reformed theologians, including Owen, should find themselves under suspicion of holding to eternal justification.

The name perhaps most associated with sophisticated expressions of the doctrine of eternal justification in Owen's day was that of Tobias Crisp. Indeed, the republication of his works in 1690 was to bring the elderly Baxter out of retirement on the grounds that he needed to refute the dangerous tenets of 'Crispianism'.[51] In the 1640s, however, the posthumous publication of his sermons occasioned vigorous opposition not simply from the likes of Baxter, but also from orthodox figures such as Samuel Rutherford, who, in the wake of the debates at the Westminster Assembly, saw Crisp's work as part and parcel of a dangerously antinomian trajectory in English Puritan thought which was also connected to the sinister calls for that most un-Presbyterian tenet, liberty of conscience in religious matters.[52] Others, such as Stephen Geree and John Benrigge were also quick to respond, concerned that Crisp's teaching on eternal justification subverted the need for the moral imperatives of Christian sanctification.[53]

In fact, an examination of Crisp's writings reveal that his position on the timing of justification was somewhat more sophisticated than the bald characterization implied by the term 'eternal justification' First, it is important (particularly for our subsequent discussion of Owen and Baxter) to note the covenantal/Christological context of Crisp's understanding of justification. For Crisp, the covenant of grace is, in a threefold sense, to be identified with Christ: fundamentally, in the sense that he is the one who establishes the covenant with God the Father (Crisp here anticipating the development of the covenant of redemption; materially, as he both represents God to the people and the people to God; and equivalently, in the sense that once the believer has Christ as an earnest of salvation, then he or she has the equivalent of the whole covenant, even though there will be progress in the Christian life.[54] This latter point is particularly significant as it points towards the problems inherent in dismissing Crisp as antinomian *tout court*: if there is progress in the Christian life, then there is need for nuance in understanding how time and eternity are connected. It does, however, point to the strong Christological federal representation which underlies Crisp's scheme and which thus parallels that of Owen. As the covenant is objectively fulfilled in Christ, what significance can history have?

---

51   In 1690, his son republished his works and this so disturbed the elderly and ailing Richard Baxter that he reentered the polemical lists to fight once more the battle over justification and good works on the 1640s and 1650s.

52   Samuel Rutherford, *A Survey of the Spirituall Antichrist* (London, 1648).

53   Stephen Geree, *The Doctrine of the Antinomians by Evidence of Gods Truth plainely Confuted* (London, 1644); John Benrigge, *Christ Above All Exalted as in Justification so in Sanctification* (London, 1645).

54   Tobias Crisp, *Christ Alone Exalted* (London, 1643), 171–77.

Crisp is very clear that justification does precede faith. In this context, faith serves to manifest that which is already true, that is, one believes that one is already justified and this act of belief makes manifest that which was before hidden. This is rooted in the objectivity of Christ's work in the covenant of grace.[55] Yet, even as he is emphatic in teaching that reconciliation was effected in Christ and thus completed on Calvary, Crisp sets God's eternal justifying love, the atonement, and the life of individual elect, in the context of a basic distinction between God in eternity, conceived of in Boethian terms of simultaneous access to all points in time, and the sequential nature of time as experienced by creatures. Thus, from all eternity God knows who are his, and he knows that Christ has made satisfaction for them; yet, given the fact that human beings experience life sequentially, it can be really said that, considered in themselves, men and women do actions that are at enmity with God.[56] The solution, therefore, lies in the logical problems generated by language which reflects human experience of time rather than the divine relationship to time in eternity. It is arguable that the solution is unsatisfactory, but it highlights the complexity of argument with which the Reformed Orthodox addressed such issues and once again indicates the need to avoid simplistic categorical arguments which seek to reduce Reformed Orthodoxy to systems of logical deduction from single axioms. Further, anticipating a point which connects directly to the problem which Baxter sees in Owen's theology of justification because of the latter's understanding of atonement, Crisp makes it clear that his view assumes the identity of Christ's punishment with that which elect sinners deserve.[57]

It is this point on which Baxter focuses in the appendix to *Aphorismes of Justification*: presupposing the force of the Socinian critique of Reformed atonement theory, and the usefulness of the Grotian response, Baxter claims that if Christ has paid the actual price for our sins, as Owen argues in his 1647 work, *The Death of Death*, then this payment is not refusable by God; nor is it possible that there be a chronological delay between payment and dissolution of the personal debt, since it is either paid or not paid; thus, the elect are justified in Christ, and faith must fulfill a mere epistemological function whereby the members of the elect come to acknowledge that which they are already, namely, justified. In other words, justification by faith is justification in the forum of the conscience, not in the forum of God himself.[58]

Baxter is particularly upset with the implications of a passage in Owen's work which he sees as clearly reducing faith to acknowledgment of prior justification and thus of laying the groundwork for a radical antinomianism.[59] While he gives no

---

55   Crisp, *Christ Alone Exalted* 168, 198–99.

56   Crisp, *Christ Alone Exalted* 393–97; cf. 328–30.

57   Crisp, *Christ Alone Exalted*, 398–401.

58   Baxter, *Aphorismes of Justification*, Appendix, 146–59. Owen responded to *Aphorismes of Justification* in *Of the Death of Christ* (London, 1650), though Baxter, never one to allow others to have the last word, kept up the polemic in *Richard Baxter's Confession of his Faith* (London, 1655). Owen, himself no slouch in the matter of controversy, then responded to this work in the appendix to his long treatise on Socinianism, *Vindiciae Evangelicae* (London, 1655), entitled *Of the Death of Christ, and of Justification*.

59   *Aphorismes of Justification*, Appendix, 155–57.

precise reference, the passage in Owen to which he appears to be objecting occurs in Book III of *The Death of Death*. Here, Owen declares that Christ, by his death, did, '*ipso facto*, deliver us from the curse, by being made a curse for us'. He then proceeds to explain why this did not mean that all the elect were not immediately justified from that moment, by drawing an analogy with a prisoner detained in a foreign country: though he has a right to liberty from the moment the ransom is paid, yet he does not enjoy possession of that liberty until such time as the news of his delivery is brought to him.[60] The analogy is weak and unfortunate because it really does play to the notion that faith is a merely epistemological tool whereby those of the elect come to realization that they are what they always, in fact, have been; and the only movement from wrath to grace in history is in the forum of the individual conscience. This point is not lost on Baxter, who hits Owen hard at this point.[61]

Of course, Owen's analogy, and indeed, the language which he uses, do tend when taken in isolation to lend themselves to the kind of reading (and criticism) offered by Baxter; and it would seem that, under such pungent polemical pressure, Owen is forced to elaborate his position in the two later treatises which give a much clearer grounding and articulation of his point that the rather unfortunate prisoner passage of 1647. At the heart of his mature argument is the covenantal structure of salvation. In this context, he argues, it is crucial to understand that God's desire to save is prior to the establishment of the covenant of redemption between Father and Son, and thus to any consideration of Christ's satisfaction. Thus, he precludes at the outset any crude notion that Christ's death in any way changes the Father's mind or somehow buys his favour in a crude, commercial sense.[62] The power of this argument is reinforced when Owen draws attention to the fact that Christ's death, considered in abstraction from its covenantal context, has no meaning or significance as a payment because, considered as such, it is no payment.[63] If, however, the death is considered as a covenantal action, then it does have meaning as a payment; but the force of this is to focus attention on the will of God as the determining factor in the economy of salvation. The positive relationship of Owen's theology to the more

---

60   *Works*, 10, 268.

61   '1. Whether a man may fitly be said actually, and *ipso facto*, to be delivered and discharged, who is not at all delivered, but onely hath right to deliverance, I doubt. 2. Knowledge and possession of a deliverance, are farre different things: A man may have possession and no knowledge in some cases; or if he have both, yet the procuring of knowledge is a small matter, in comparison of possession. 3. Our knowledge therefore doth not give us possession; so that the similitude failes; for it is the Creditors knowledge and satisfaction that is requisite to deliverance. And our creditour was not in a farre and strange courtrey, but knew immediately and could either have made us quickly know, or turned us free before we had knowne the cause. 4. Nor can it easily be understood, how God can so long deny us the possession of Heaven, if wee had such absolute actuall Right (as he speaketh) so long ago.' *Aphorismes of Justification*, Appendix, 156–57.

62   *Works*, 10, 455–56. This point is simply a clarification of Owen's position as laid out at length in Book I of *The Death of Death*:

63   'The suffering of Christ may be considered…[a]bsolutely, as in itself, abstracting from the consideration of any covenant or compact thereabout; and so it cannot be said to be a refusable payment; not because not refusable, but because no payment.' *Works* 10, 458.

voluntarist/Scotist trajectories of late medieval thought is here evident and allows him to argue that the economy of salvation, of which Christ's sacrifice is a part, is to be understood as an act of God's sovereign will and not to be subjected to the narrow canons of particular human logic.[64]

It might be argued, of course, that Owen's shift on divine justice in the early 1650s would render this argument somewhat weaker, given that he adopts a position whereby atonement is necessary if God is to forgive sin.[65] Yet this is not the case: the question of necessity of atonement vis-à-vis God's attributes and his intention to save, is a determining factor in the nature of the atonement, covenantally considered, but in itself exerts no decisive influence on the overall structure and disbursement of covenant blessings. As the death of Christ purchases all benefits for the elect, including faith (which is, in a sense, a condition of the covenant of grace), so even after 1653 Owen sees that the atonement needs to be understood within the broad contours of the covenant and of the order of salvation; and he regards faith as given at a point in time determined by the will of the Father, with the voluntarist accent still strongly evident. This tracks to the second covenantal strand of Owen's thinking on justification which defuses the issue of eternal justification: if the covenant of redemption establishes the nature of Christ's death as satisfaction, then the covenant of grace, made by God the Father with Christ on behalf of the elect, embodies within itself not only the election of individuals to salvation, but also the times, circumstances, and means by which the elect will come to enjoy salvation and all its benefits.[66]

In fact, Owen regards Baxter's claims that his (Owen's) theology requires that the elect be justified from the moment of Christ's death as resting upon a misconstruction of the union of the elect with Christ.[67] What Owen does claim is that the union of Christ with the elect in his atonement is not a real union in the sense of some form of actual, direct participation but that it must be understood in terms of federal representation, again with the whole context of covenant and covenantal terms being crucial. The imputation of sin to Christ is thus not strictly parallel to the imputation of Christ's righteousness to sinners because it is not simply Incarnation, absolutely considered, which is the foundation of the salvific scheme, but the covenant which lies behind the Incarnation and which gives the Incarnation meaning for salvation. Thus, imputation of sin to Christ and imputation of righteousness to the elect both need to be set against the background of covenant terms; and the covenant terms

---

64   In discussing the distinction between the death of Christ considered abstractly and covenantally, Owen concludes: 'This distinction is not accommodate to this difficulty [of the non-refusability of payment]; the sole reason thereof being what was held out before, of the interest of God's sovereign right to the bestowing of purposed, purchased, promised blessings, as to times and seasons, according to the free counsel of his own will.' *Works* 10, 458.

65   See *A Dissertation on Divine Justice* (London, 1653) in *Works* 10; also Chapter 2 above.

66   'This is that I say, *Christ hath purchased all good things for us*; these things are actually to be conferred upon us in the *time* and *order* by God's sovereign will determined and disposed. This order, as revealed in the gospel, is, that we believe and be justified, etc.' *Works* 12, 608. Cf. *Works* 5, 216–18.

67   *Works*, 12, 606.

are such that union with Christ by faith is necessary in order for the imputation of righteousness to take place.[68] This takes place in time, at the point of conversion; and it is only then that the believer can be said to be justified.[69]

Faith and Works

Despite Baxter's concern that Owen's writings were, at the very least, antinomian in tendency, it is very clear that he actually placed a very high priority on the role of good works in the believer's life. Thus, in both the systematic treatment of the Holy Spirit, and in the more pastorally focused writings on mortification of sin, he maintained very clearly the need for the Christian to exhibit the fruits of sanctification in works.[70] This is rooted in his understanding of conversion, which involves not only a moral change in the individual, in terms of a persuasion of the mind by the word of God towards the right path; but also what Owen describes as a *physical* work which involves the actual infusion of a gracious principle of spiritual life into the believer. This principle is inseparable from the external persuasions of the word but takes fully into account the nature of human depravity and the sovereignty of God in salvation. As all grace is to be connected to the work of God, so this principle of spiritual life is one of the benefits of the work of Christ. In other words, regeneration respects fallen human beings both as rational, thinking creatures and as those whose sin is not simply a matter of ignorance but of a fundamentally depraved nature.[71]

Given this emphasis both on gracious transformation and on imputation, it is worth bringing this study to a conclusion by looking at two aspects of Owen's thinking which connect to these: his understanding of the relationship between Paul and James; and his understanding of justification as an eschatological reality.

As to Paul and James, by Owen's time this path had been well-trodden by Protestants, from Luther, who relegated the book of James to the status of being sub-canonical, through the early wrestlings of men like William Tyndale down to the work of Perkins and company, where the issue of distinctions in the biblical usage of 'justification' and its cognates had become a standard part of the overall discussion of

---

68 'God hath appointed that there shall be an *immediate foundation* of the imputation of the satisfaction and righteousness of Christ unto us; whereon we may be said to have done and suffered in him what he did and suffered in our stead, by that grant, donation, and imputation of it unto us; or that we may be interested in it, that it may be made ours: which is all we contend for. And this is our *actual coalescency into one mystical person* with him by faith.' *Works*, 5, 217–18; cf. *Works*, 5, 353–54; also *Works*, 12, 606–07.

69 See *Works*, 3, 297–337. The influence of the narrative of Augustine's *Confessions* on Owen is evident in that he uses this as a basic paradigm from Christian conversion in the subsequent chapter, *Works* 3, 337–66.

70 'Sanctification … is the immediate work of God by his Spirit upon our whole nature, proceeding from the peace made for us by Jesus Christ, whereby, being changed into his likeness, we are kept entirely in peace with God, and are preserved unblamable, or in a state of gracious acceptation with him, according to the terms of the covenant, unto the end.' *Works*, 3, 369. For Owen on mortification of sin, see *Works* 6.

71 *Works*, 3, 307–10.

salvation, justification, faith, and works.[72] Given this well-established background, Owen's own treatment is conventional. He starts with the clear supposition that the status of both Paul's letters and James as canonical means that there can be no ultimate contradiction between them. Thus, the underlying commitment to scripture as the supreme noetic foundation for theology provides one of the basic interpretative principles for approaching the apparent problem. Owen then combines this with a methodological commitment to grant basic priority to those passages or books which speak of a subject directly over those which address the issue tangentially, in passing, or in relation to some other primary concern. This allows him, obviously, to grant priority to Paul over James when it comes to understanding the nature of justification.[73] In doing so, however, he cites the consensus of early church Fathers and especially Chrysostom as his historic authorities for this position, in answer to unidentified critics who claim the obscurity of Paul precipitated the writing of James as clarification. Thus the point is not simply stated; it is made with judicious use of patristic testimony and respect to church tradition, albeit subordinated to argument from the nature of scripture itself.[74]

When he comes to more detailed argument, Owen offers four reasons why there is no contradiction between Paul and James. First, they differ in scope and purpose: Paul is talking specifically about how a guilty sin comes through the blood of Christ to have sins forgiven; James is combating a form of antinomianism which rejected the need for good works in the life of the believer. Second, they are talking of two different types of faith: Paul speaks of true, saving faith which is alive and unites to Christ; James speaks of mere intellectual assent which has no life-giving aspect to it. Third, they speak of different justifications: Paul is describing justification as a change of status before God; James is describing a justification which is the outward manifestation before the world of that change of status.[75] This parallels closely the kind of double justification idea found in such theologians as Bucer and Tyndale.[76]

The fourth point is more interesting: here, Owen argues that both Paul and James are referring to the same works, as such works are necessary for the believer, even if not for justification in the Pauline sense. Much of Owen's argument about the role of works in justification here hinges on his exegesis of Jas 2:21, 'Was not Abraham our father justified by works, when he offered Isaac his son upon the altar?' Owen understands this verse as set against the background of Gn. 15:6 and thus as pointing not to justification before God but to the public declaration of that justification in outward action, a point which he further supports with reference to Gn. 22:12. In addition, he notes Jas 2:22, and argues that this verse teaches first, that faith is always active in manifesting itself in works and, second, that the Greek verb *teleioumai*

---

72 On Tyndale and early discussions of justification in the English Reformation, see Carl R Trueman, *Luther's Legacy: Salvation and English Reformers, 1525–1556* (Oxford: Clarendon Press, 1994); also William Perkins, *Works*, 681–82. Cf. WCF 11.2 (with Jas. 2: 17, 22, 26 and Gal. 5:6 as supporting texts); also Turretin, *Institutes* 16.8.5–22.

73 *Works*, 5, 284–85.

74 *Works*, 5, 386–87.

75 *Works*, 5, 387–94.

76 On Bucer and the similarities between his thought and understandings of justification in the English Reformation, see Trueman, *Luther's Legacy*, 102–04, 141–42.

never denotes in scripture the formal perfecting of anything but the external complement or perfection or manifestation of it.[77] Thus, there is no contradiction between Paul and James, only a distinction in exactly which aspects of justification they are addressing.

This basic distinction also underlies Owen's understanding of final, or eschatological justification. There were Protestants, for example, William Tyndale, who appear to have articulated at points a proleptic understanding of justification whereby final judgment before God at the end of time would be based, at least in part, on the individual's own intrinsic righteousness.[78] For Owen, however, eschatology could not be allowed to trump the uniqueness, the reality, and the sufficiency of justification in time; thus, he calls the declaration on the Day of Judgment 'sentential justification' in order to safeguard against any misconstruction or undermining of present justification. Final justification is simply an act of public declaration and vindication of what has been true since the individual's justification by faith.[79]

In this context, Owen does make a statement which, at first glance, might seem odd. In speaking of the evangelical righteousness which is required of the one justified by faith, Owen says the following:

> [U]pon it we shall be *declared righteous* at the last day, and without it none shall so be. And if any shall think meet from hence to conclude unto an *evangelical justification*, or call God's acceptance of our righteousness by that name, I shall by no means contend with them. And wherever this inquiry is made, – not how a *sinner guilty of death*, and obnoxious unto the curse shall be pardoned, acquitted, and justified, which is by the righteousness of Christ alone imputed unto him – but how a man that *professeth evangelical faith*, or faith in Christ, shall be tried, judged, and whereon, as such, he shall be justified, we grant that it is, and must be, by his own personal, sincere obedience.[80]

What Owen seems to be doing at this point is twofold: underlining the necessity of the Christian performing good works; and the reality of some kind of discrimination on the Day of Judgment between believers according to the works done. In the context of the chapter as a whole, it is clear that he cannot be saying that the final judgment is on the basis of the individual's works, nor that there is a twofold justification before God on the basis of a faith–works synthesis nor that justification in time is simply some kind of proleptic intrusion through faith of a final judgment on the basis of works. The Protestant position on faith alone and imputation is maintained by Owen even at the point of Final Judgment where careful attention to the precise scriptural use of expressions about judgment relative to works is absolutely critical if the true Protestant position is to be maintained in the face of antinomian, neonomian and Roman Catholic challenges.[81]

---

77 *Works*, 5, 399.
78 See Trueman, *Luther's Legacy*, 92–94.
79 *Works*, 5, 152; cf. *Works* 5, 160.
80 *Works*, 5, 159–60.
81 For example, 'It is nowhere said that we shall be judged at the last day "ex operibus;" but only that God will render unto men "secundum opera." But God doth not justify any in this life "secundum opera:" being justified freely by his grace and not according to the works of

Conclusion

John Owen's treatment of justification is a classic example of Reformed Orthodoxy at its best: rooted in the ongoing anti-Pelagian trajectory of Western theology and operating within the established Protestant consensus, Owen yet demonstrates the ways in which that consensus was itself under strain, exegetically, theologically, and socially, in the seventeenth century, and how it was necessary for doctrinal formulation of the doctrine to undergo careful elaboration in order to respond to such. In particular, his defence of the imputation of Christ's active and passive righteousness, and his vigorous rejection of Baxter's accusations that his theology was antinomian and demanded a doctrine of eternal justification both points toward the covenantal/Christological heart of his theology and the way in which this integrated the eternal and temporal economies, and the objective work of Christ for the believer with the subjective work of Christ within the believer. As such, Owen's thought is an example of how federal theology could be deployed to set the broad concerns of the Protestant confessional consensus on issues such as justification a much firmer conceptual foundation than was the case in the early Reformation; and also how Reformed Orthodoxy's theological structure was by necessity highly elaborate and irreducible to sound bites about dogmatising – though this is not the result of a pathological need for logic-chopping and hair-splitting but of the pastoral need to articulate, expound, and defend the faith in a highly sophisticated polemical environment; rather, Owen's treatment exhibits the typical Reformed attention to the exegesis, doctrinal synthesis, and church consensus and is one more piece of evidence as to how and why the Reformed faith became more elaborate in its argumentation during the course of the seventeenth century, a development which has little to do with needle-headed numptiness and everything to do with the ecclesiastical and pastoral task at hand.

---

righteousness which we have done. And we are everywhere said to be justified in this life "ex fide," "per fidem," but nowehere "propter fidem;" or, that God justifieth us "secundum fidem," by faith, but not *for our faith*, nor according unto our faith. And we are not to depart from the expressions of the Scripture, where such a difference is constantly observed.' *Works*, 5, 161.

Conclusion

In 1674, Rev William Sherlock, Rector of St George's Church, Botolph Lane in London, published a work entitled *A Discourse concerning Jesus Christ, and Our Union and Communion with Him*. The work created a storm of controversy for its suspected heterodoxy, indeed, alleged incipient Socinianism and provoked a number of sharp responses.[1] One of the strangest aspects of Sherlock's work, however, was not so much its dubious theology as the fact that the author chose to pick a fight with John Owen over something the latter had written some seventeen years earlier: his treatise *On Communion with God in Three Persons* (London, 1657) wherein he had argued that the Trinity stood at the heart of Christian soteriology and thus must stand at the heart of Christian worship as well. By 1674, of course, Owen was politically marginalized; the ecclesiology which he had advocated was broken and being written out of the history books like an embarrassing mistake; and the theological tradition of which he was a part was about to be overwhelmed by precisely the kind of enlightened reasonableness of which Sherlock's work was an eloquent herald. In retrospect, and perhaps even at the time, Sherlock's move looks to have all the gratuitousness of kicking a man when he is well and truly down.

Whatever Sherlock's reasons for writing against Owen may have been, it is clear that he did have a certain degree of understanding of Owen's theology even as he rejected it. Thus, he attacked Owen's notion of the necessity of divine, vindicatory justice if sin is to be forgiven.[2] He also had a few choice things to say about justification by imputation.[3] At the same time, he failed to grasp some of the subtleties of Owen's thought: thus, he incorrectly saw Owen as teaching a kind of supralapsarianism;[4] and he also implied that Owen held to a radically Christomonistic understanding of revelation.[5]

Sherlock's most significant misunderstanding of Owen's theology, however, related not so much to the specifics of any given doctrine but to his claim that Owen's theology was novel and innovative. Sherlock was not the first and certainly not the last to dismiss Owen's theology on the basis of a simplistic category designed to foreclose any careful analysis and discussion; the effect of such is simply the reduction of a finely-tooled and elaborate theology to the level of a sound bite which can be ridiculed and then safely ignored. Moreover, there is, of course, an obvious irony in the fact that it is Sherlock, a very moderate Anglican, who makes

---

1   For example, Samuel Rolle, *Prodromus, or the Character of Mr Sherlock's Book* (London, 1674); Edward Polhill, *An Answer to the Discourse of Mr William Sherlock touching the Knowledge of Christ and our Union and Communion with Him* (London, 1675); Vincent Alsop, *Antisozzo sive Sherlocismus enervatus* (London, 1676).

2   Sherlock, *A Discourse* 45–46.

3   Sherlock, *A Discourse* 53–55.

4   Sherlock, *A Discourse* 57–59.

5   Sherlock, *A Discourse* 61.

this accusation; yet more significant is the fact that the accusation is profoundly wrong-headed. As we have seen in the preceding chapters, Owen's theology was anything but original in its basic content, and he would have blanched at the very suggestion. Owen's concern throughout his career was to articulate and defend the faith which he regarded as once and for all delivered to the saints; and that involved not only a commitment to the scripture principle but a careful listening to, critical interaction with, and judicious appropriation of the church's theological, exegetical, and polemical traditions.

In this context, it is a further irony that Sherlock chose to target Owen's work on communion with God as providing the evidence for his accusation of novelty. While one could make a case for saying that the book was innovative in the way that it really did try to take seriously the importance of the Trinity for personal piety and devotion (and that, one might add, might be a necessary innovation, filling in an embarrassing gap in the church's tradition), the doctrine of God which Owen applied in the work was profoundly and intentionally unoriginal in origin and content – even, as we have seen, in the view of divine justice which it expressed. To target this book as novel was, therefore, at best a cheap shot, at worst a sign of Sherlock's own ignorance of the catholic tradition of the Western church. After all, this book by Owen, perhaps more than any other single treatise, brings together so many of his theological concerns in a synthesis that is at once both catholic in scope, anti-Pelagian, Protestant, Reformed, and Puritan. Indeed, if the burden of this monograph has been to demonstrate that the analytic categories of earlier scholarship are not in themselves subtle enough to yield a truly satisfying historical explanation of Puritan theology in general, and Owen's theology in particular, then there can be no better demonstration of this than his work on communion with God where all these strands come together.

First, as to Owen's catholicity, we have only to look at the significance of the Trinity in his theology as a whole for this to become plain. Throughout his works – whether those dealing with God, redemption, or justification – the doctrine of the Trinity is always foundational; and this points towards two basic dimensions to his theology. First, at a doctrinal level, he is clear that Christianity deals with a very particular God who is both the Three and the One. Time and again, he insists that all external works of God are to be understood as works of the one God, and that all such are also to be ascribed in particular and distinct ways to each of the three persons of the Trinity. Whether it is creation, Christology, pneumatology, or issues such as justification, Owen conceives of them each as having their foundation in the identification of God as Triune. In his work on communion, all he does is bring out the practical significance of this for personal devotion, both as theoretically understood and as practiced. Second, Owen's clear grasp of the significance of Trinitarianism naturally leads him both to a great respect for the Catholic creeds of the church and to the patristic authors whose works led to the creedal formulations and then explicated and defended such. Any who regard the likes of Owen as crude fundamentalists, ignorant of church tradition and theological history have simply not read him with any care or sensitivity. The lavish references to patristic authors in almost every chapter of every major book he ever wrote put the lie to such caricatures in devastating, one might even say embarrassing, fashion.

Yet the catholicity and continuity with the great theological traditions of the church, goes further than straightforward creedal Trinitarianism. Owen's theology is also anti-Pelagian, once again both at the level of theology and of practice. Theologically, his love of Augustine, both the doctrinal author of the anti-Pelagian treatises and the warm experientialist of the *Confessions*, is evident, the former in his polemics against the Arminians, the Jesuits and the Socinians, the latter in his sermons on the mortification of sin. If Calvin could try to claim for Protestantism that 'Augustine is completely ours', then Owen could do the same. When it came to the grace of God, Owen's theology and his piety drew deeply from the purest wells of the catholic tradition. Yet, once again, in his articulation of an anti-Pelagian understanding of God's grace, his sources were not restricted to the early church Fathers, 'before the papal rot set in' as one might say. Rather, his writings evidence significant borrowing from medieval sources as well, particularly Thomas Aquinas, on matters relating to the metaphysical articulation of the relationship between God and his creation. As Augustine demonstrated the moral dependency of humanity upon God, so Aquinas demonstrated the ontological dependency of the same. In this context, it is worth noting once again that what Sherlock saw as Owen's innovative understanding of God's justice had, in fact, clear patristic and medieval precedents (of which Owen was aware) and was constructed by Owen in a manner which self-consciously drew on earlier and contemporary paradigms. The accusation of novelty, therefore, demonstrates only the bad-tempered ignorance of the accuser and the superiority of Owen's own grasp of historical theology.

Of course, to emphasize the catholicity and continuity of Owen with patristic and medieval paradigms should not blind us to the fact that he was a Protestant theologian whose immediate theological milieu was that of the Reformation. This is clear in numerous ways. Methodologically, it is evident in his commitment to scripture alone as the norming norm of doctrinal formulation; doctrinally, it is obvious in his firm defence of the notion of justification by grace alone through faith alone; and ecclesiastically, it is obvious from his consistent opposition to Rome, indeed, to any form of Protestantism which smacked of prelacy or ceremonialism. At a more subtle level, it manifests itself in the ease with which Owen operates in Hebrew and Greek and the exegetical care he demonstrates in works such as his massive commentary on Hebrews, arguably the most significant precritical commentary on the book ever produced. As Protestantism in the sixteenth century identified scripture, as given in the original languages, as *the* word of God, so Protestantism in the seventeenth century drew out the pedagogical implications of this and pioneered the greatest flourishing of linguistic scholarship Europe had ever seen. *Pace* the tiresome myths about their proof-texting and the woodenly dogmatic apriorism of their exegesis, the Protestant Orthodox showed a deep and consistent concern for textual, linguistic, and exegetical studies. Owen was no exception, and his use of original languages, textual variants, lexical aids, translations, as well as the exegetical history of given texts, all demonstrate that he possessed the typical Protestant concern for rightly dividing the word of truth in the most sophisticated way possible.

This concern for exegesis manifested itself in Owen's concern for the narrative dynamic of the Bible as well. This is most evident in Owen's insistence, in line with the Reformers and in contradistinction to the dominant theological tradition

of the Middle Ages, that mediation was the act of a person, not a nature, and that
Christ was thus mediator according to both natures and not simply according to his
humanity. This concern for the personal integrity of Jesus Christ is indeed a great
example of how doctrinal and exegetical concerns led Owen and the Reformed to
dramatic reformulation of Christology, yet a reformulation which was conducted
not in a principially iconoclastic manner with regard to the tradition but in a manner
which sought to correct the tradition in ways demanded by the biblical text. As a
Reformation Protestant, Owen did not reject tradition per se; he rejected tradition as
possessing ultimate or independent authority, but yet assumed it and indeed used it
as a critical dialogue partner.

Yet Owen was not simply a Protestant. He was also Reformed. His commitment
to the basic Reformed axiom (the so-called *extra calvinisticum*), that the finite cannot
comprehend the infinite, is evident in his epistemology, where the archetype/ectype
distinction clearly guards the Creator/creature distinction both ontologically and
epistemologically. As much as anything, this puts to death any notion that Owen
and his Reformed Orthodox contemporaries were *rationalist* in any Cartesian or
Enlightenment sense. He was as acutely aware of the fragility of finite human language
when speaking of the infinite divine, and of the need for divine condescension in
revelation, as any of the theologians, patristic, medieval or Reformation, who had
gone before. In addition, his application of the *extra calvinisticum* to his Christology
allows him not only to address questions of Christ's life which underscore the
dynamic nature of his education and ministry; it also opens up space for a truly
Trinitarian understanding of that ministry. In Owen, in other words, it is arguable
that his Christology is innovative; but it is innovative through its careful and original
interconnection of elements of classic catholic theology.

The same is true of his understanding of salvation, even as it comes to focus on
justification. Owen used the federal structure of salvation, so typical of Reformed
theology by his time, to set the more general Protestant doctrine of justification on a
clear conceptual foundation. In this, of course, we saw how Owen's discussion of the
covenant of works was quintessentially Reformed and yet was also part of an ongoing
debate about the nature of human beings as created and then as fallen which went
back through the Middle Ages to patristic times. Thus, there are interesting structural
parallels between Owen's covenant theology and earlier medieval discussions
about the *donum superadditum*, congruent merit, and creation *in puris naturalibus*,
discussions which themselves addressed issues raised by patristic controversies.
In these areas, Owen is Reformed precisely because his thinking stands both in
discontinuity and continuity with aspects of the ongoing Western tradition. Indeed,
his work represents a signal contribution to that tradition.

Of course, for all of this, Owen's work also exhibits the stresses to which
Reformed Orthodox theology in his time was increasingly subject. Arminianism
and Socinianism had raised in an acute form the problem faced by a Protestantism
which articulated a clear scripture principle and yet increasingly struggled to offer
a unified interpretation of that same scripture; these groups also raised significant
philosophical questions, both moral and metaphysical, about the relationship of
God to his creation and, more generally, about the role of human reason relative to
revelation; particularly in the area of Trinitarian theology, Owen's writings show

clearly the signs of strain induced by the pressures of biblicism and the general crisis afflicting the established language of substance, essence, and personhood, so crucial to the theological tradition. And these areas were not the only problems: while space has not permitted discussion in this monograph, the rise of textual criticism, as evidenced by the production of polyglot Bibles and the debates over the antiquity of the Masoretic vowel points, also played havoc with the Protestantism of Owen's day. That these textual developments were the direct result of Protestantism's own emphasis upon the Bible in the original languages as the very word of God, was ultimately one of history's ironies and not any source of comfort. Moreover, in all of these areas, the Catholics, as always, stood in the wings, ready to press home any advantage offered by the increasingly fragmented culture of a Protestantism riddled with internecine conflict and struggling to articulate a coherent notion of authority. Ironically, *pace* the arguments of much of the older scholarship on Reformed Orthodoxy, Owen and his Reformed Orthodox contemporaries failed not because they were incipient rationalists or because they conceded too much of the old orthodoxy to what would later become the Enlightenment; they failed because they held their ground too long and too hard in the face of overwhelming cultural forces which swept them away regardless.

Owen's theology was part of the losing side in the culture war in seventeenth-century Britain. It represented the last, finely-tooled and sophisticated hurrah of a thoughtful, learned, articulate theological tradition which was about to collapse in the face of the very stresses and strains noted above. Yet this should not blind us to the brilliance of his project, nor to the profoundly learned way in which it was executed. Compared to say, Calvin or Bullinger, Owen exhibited just as great a knowledge of the patristic tradition, a better understanding of medieval theology and philosophy, a more sophisticated grasp of theological metaphysics, more facility with the original languages, and an exegetical sensitivity which was second to none in his day. His work may have come too late to enjoy lasting influence; but it failed because the cultural rip tide was too great, too powerful for him ever to have succeeded. It was not because he deviated from the pre-modern tradition of catholic theology too much; it was (ironically) because he deviated too little.

We should, however, end on a positive note. There is one category that I mentioned above to which I have not yet returned. Owen was, of course, a Puritan theologian. I have not said much in this study about Owen as Puritan because, as I indicated in Chapter 1, the term is at least as problematic as it is helpful; and Owen can be better accessed when set in a wider context than the narrow Anglican world which the term Puritan connotes. I noted in Chapter 1 that studies of Reformed Orthodoxy have been marred not only by anachronistic doctrinal agendas, but also distorted by simplistic and, on occasion, simply false analytical categories. The difference between a heuristic and a Procrustean category is often very slight; and the more simplistic the categories used, the more likely it is that the conclusion will be distorted. Thus, any student of Owen's thought needs to take account of the complexity of his context. Thus, as we have seen, it is critical to set his writings against the background of patristics, medieval scholasticism, Reformation theology, and Renaissance philosophy and culture. Indeed, he was at least as much a true son of the Renaissance as of the Reformation. Yet he was a *Puritan*. The points that distinguished him from, say, his brilliant tutor and friend, Thomas Barlow, were not points of theology; rather they were points of ecclesiology and issues of conformity. While not unrelated to theology, these were yet issues which were not necessarily required by Owen's commitment to Reformed Orthodoxy. Owen had strong views on Independency and on worship; and thus it is fitting to close by referring to the work which so upset the indignant Rev Sherlock. In his work on communion with the divine, Owen connects his theology, in its catholic, Protestant, and Reformed dimensions, to that most critical of Puritan concerns: the worship of God. And in so doing, Owen demonstrates that most delightful aspect of precritical theology: its essentially ecclesiastical and practical purpose. None of his theology was intended for its own sake, as some kind of glass-bead game to be played by an elite few in isolation from the world around. On the contrary: it was theology done within the church for the benefit of the church. As speculative and as metaphysical as many of the issues we have addressed in this book have been, for Owen none of it was purely abstract. Whether polemic, commentary, or doctrinal exposition, his work always connects to the life of the church and the health of Christians, individual and corporate. The divorce of theology as an academic discipline from the ecclesiastical context, so basic to the modern discipline, would have been inconceivable to Owen and is another point of basic continuity between his work and that of his predecessors. As the great patristic writers were capable of flights of intellectual brilliance in developing a theology which was basically concerned for the health of Christ's flock; as the great medievals put their massive intellects to the service of the church and wrote both massive theological systems and profound and moving hymns and prayers; as Luther and Calvin always saw their theology as having a primarily ecclesiastical function and as terminating in the preaching of the word and the administration of the sacraments; so Owen draws on that most Christian of doctrines, that of the Trinity, refracts it through a Reformed soteriology, and applies it to that most basic and universal aspect of the Christian faith, the devotional life. Many may disagree with the details of theology; but surely none can disagree that his theological aspirations should be those of every Christian theologian; and, given all that has been said in the previous chapters, no one should dispute his right to be taken seriously as one of early modern England's most articulate and thoughtful theological voices.

Index